INHERITING GADAMER

INHERITING GADAMER

New Directions in Philosophical Hermeneutics

Edited by Georgia Warnke

EDINBURGH
University Press

© editorial matter and organisation Georgia Warnke, 2016
© the chapters their several authors, 2016

Edinburgh University Press Ltd
The Tun – Holyrood Road
12(2f) Jackson's Entry
Edinburgh EH8 8PJ

www.euppublishing.com

Typeset in 10.5/13 Sabon by
Servis Filmsetting Ltd, Stockport, Cheshire

A CIP record for this book is available from the British Library

ISBN 978 0 7486 9897 4 (hardback)
ISBN 978 0 7486 9898 1 (webready PDF)
ISBN 978 1 4744 0488 4 (epub)

The right of Georgia Warnke to be identified as the editor of this work has been asserted in accordance with the Copyright, Designs and Patents Act 1988, and the Copyright and Related Rights Regulations 2003 (SI No. 2498).

Contents

Introduction   1
Georgia Warnke

Part I Critique and Causality

1. Critical Fusions: Towards A Genuine 'Hermeneutics of Suspicion'   21
   Lorenzo C. Simpson

2. What is Interpretive Explanation in Sociohistorical Analysis?   41
   Isaac Ariail Reed

3. The Anarchy of Hermeneutics: Interpretation as a Vital Practice   67
   Santiago Zabala

Part II Hermeneutics and Openness

4. Elements of Style: Openness and Dispositions   81
   Whitney Mannies

5. Openness to Critical Reflection: Gandhi beyond Gadamer   102
   Steven Paul Cauchon

6. Philosophical Hermeneutics and the Politics of Memory   121
   Georgia Warnke

Part III Place, Play and the Body

7. Place and Hermeneutics: Towards a Topology of Understanding   143
   Jeff Malpas

8. Verbal and Nonverbal Forms of Play: Words and Bodies in the Process of Understanding 161
   Monica Vilhauer

Part IV Science, Medicine and Biotechnology

9. On the Integration of Scientific Knowledge into Self-Understanding 183
   Peter Fristedt

10. A Dialogic Approach to Narrative Medicine 203
    Leah McClimans

11. If Enhancement is the Answer, What is the Question? 218
    Lauren Swayne Barthold

Contributors 237
Index 240

Introduction

GEORGIA WARNKE

In the course of trying to rehabilitate the concept of tradition in *Truth and Method*, Hans-Georg Gadamer notes that traditions do not continue out of "inertia" but must rather be "affirmed, embraced, cultivated."[1] He also makes it clear that affirming, embracing and cultivating do not preclude, but rather require, rethinking and re-evaluation. In this regard, he thinks that both the Enlightenment and Romanticism erred in opposing tradition and reason. Whereas the Enlightenment falsely presumed it could rid knowledge of all presumptions not grounded in rational foundations, Romanticism viewed tradition as a natural substrate that could not be questioned. For Gadamer, however, "the romantic faith in the 'growth of tradition' before which all reason must remain silent, is fundamentally like the Enlightenment, and just as prejudiced."[2] This volume of essays takes up the tradition of Gadamer's own philosophical hermeneutics, affirming, embracing and cultivating it in the critically engaged way that Gadamer emphasizes.

The volume includes contributions from different generations of theorists and scholars, from those just beginning their careers to senior figures. And it represents different fields of expertise: philosophy, sociology, and political theory as well as different subfields within these, such as aesthetics, critical theory and the philosophy of science. The volume is thus meant to provide at least a glimmer of the multiple ways Gadamer's work is being examined and appropriated as well as the new directions it is taking in relation to new arenas and to fresh developments in existing arenas. In order to set the stage for these new and re-mapped directions, I would like to begin by recalling some of original discussions of Gadamer's work. I start with discussions of the proper place of understanding in the social sciences.

GADAMER AND THE PHILOSOPHY OF THE HUMAN SCIENCES

When *Truth and Method* was published in 1960 it immediately entered into ongoing discussions of understanding's place in the social sciences. Theorists such as Theodore Abel had reopened this discussion in criticizing what they took to be a theory of *Verstehen* promulgated by Wilhelm Dilthey and Max Weber in the late nineteenth century and first part of the twentieth century.[3] In his famous 1942 essay, "The Operation Called *Verstehen*," Abel insisted that the proper methods of the social sciences were exactly those of the natural sciences and he argued that *Verstehen* was a failed attempt at a short cut. While explanation in the natural sciences required rigorous testing procedures and reproducible results, Abel said *Verstehen*'s proponents thought that because humans studied humans in the social sciences those sciences could be much more direct. One could internalize the stimulus for an action by imagining the emotions a situation would arouse in the actor based on one's personal experience. One could then internalize the actor's response to the stimulus and ascribe a motive to him or her by, again, using one's imagination and experience. Finally, using one's personal experience once more, one could construct a behavior maxim to connect stimulus and response. For example, if marriage rates decrease in a certain rural area that is experiencing crop failures, one explains this phenomenon by first attributing to farmers the feelings of anxiety one would oneself feel at the prospect of a drop in one's income. One then imagines the response one would have namely: a reluctance to take on new commitments. Finally, one explains the decrease in marriage rates by formulating that behavior maxim that those who are anxious avoid entering into new entanglements.

Abel suggested that the problems here are obvious. *Verstehen* depends upon one's personal experience, which is necessarily limited, and, moreover, *Verstehen* cannot serve as a method of verification. Abel conceded that the imagination and internalization that *Verstehen* involves can help with formulating hypotheses such as the hypothesis that a fear of commitment under financially insecure circumstances explains a reluctance to marry. Nevertheless, he said, "We do not accept the fact that farmers postpone intended marriages when faced with crop failure because we can 'understand' it." He went on: "It is acceptable to us because we have found through reliable statistical operations that the correlation between the rate of marriage and the rate of crop production is extremely high."[4]

Part of the immediate impact of *Truth and Method* stemmed from the response it suggested to this sort of view. For without mentioning Abel or other positivists, Gadamer suggested that the assumption with which they began missed the point. In taking understanding to offer a false shortcut to genuine science, Abel assumed that its aim is to explain human behavior, to find the causes of particular actions. Yet Gadamer maintained that understanding enters the picture at an earlier point than the one Abel selected; it is directed not at explaining why a piece of human behavior happens, but at figuring out what that behavior is and the same holds for attempts to understand practices, events, institutions, texts and the like. In simply assuming that farmers are men and that marriage involves commitments to provide for a wife and possibly children, Abel thus precisely skips over understanding's domain. Understanding is not meant to help us explain the decrease in marriage rates; rather, its concern is what the institution of marriage is, what a text says and, indeed, what any text or text-analogue such as an action, event or practice means. Moreover, Gadamer said, understanding the latter necessarily precedes the former. Unless we understand what a text or text-analogue says, or is, we will be at a loss in locating the factors that generate or cause it. More specifically, unless we understand that for a certain group of people at a certain time the meaning of marriage presupposes the capacity to be financially independent and involves the idea that it is a man's job to provide for a wife and family, then we cannot begin to locate the causes of its decrease under crop failures.

If understanding's concern is the meaning of particular texts, actions, institutions and the like, however, how does it go about its work? Gadamer is as adamant as Abel that if understanding what something is or what someone is saying is a question of using one's own experience to feel the feelings one's subject or interlocutor feels, then understanding has no place in either the humanities or the social sciences. Like Abel, he thinks this approach blocks understanding insofar as it undermines the possibility of one's ever getting outside of oneself. Indeed, if we understand only what we can internalize or empathize with we can never learn more than we already know. Hence, internalization is problematic from the point of view of knowledge. Gadamer also thinks that attempts at internalization are patronizing and therefore problematic from the point of view of morality. In claiming to internalize or empathize with the concerns of others I presume that his or her concerns and intentions are identical to my own and I thereby erase his or her autonomy.[5] I appropriate him or her as already exactly like myself. At its core, however, the attempt to conceive of understanding as internalization is quixotic, Gadamer points out, for it overlooks the specificity of the researcher's or inquirer's own historical situation. To suppose that we *can* internalize the actions and reactions of others, that we can re-experience what they experience, is to suppose either that history does not occur so that any event is available for re-occurrence or that we can jump out of our own skin to experience events as someone else.

Rather than internalization, then, Gadamer allies understanding with precisely the participation in history that makes recourse to internalization problematic. This participation has two implications, he suggests. First, it means that we do not come to the task of interpretation *de novo* but already oriented with pre-understandings we inherit in belonging to particular cultural, historical and interpretive traditions. These pre-understandings, or what Gadamer calls prejudices, reflect the experiences and shared understandings of previous generations and comprise the background consensus they hand down to us for making sense out of our world and out of the texts, activities, actions, institutions and practices that compose it. Understanding is possible, then, because we always already understand; we can make sense out of the contents of our world because we grow up in interpretive traditions that have already understood them and that hand down these understandings as resources for us. Second, however, we always understand differently. Despite the interpretive resources our predecessors hand down to us, we can never understand the way our predecessors did because we are privy to the consequences of the actions and events in which they participated, future connections and relationships into which the texts they read become involved and the subsequent histories of their institutions and practices. When we inherit the understandings and assumptions of our predecessors, we inherit the after-history, or what Gadamer calls the effective history, of those understandings and assumptions, just as those who come after us inherit the effective history of ours. "The special feature of historical experience," Gadamer writes, "is that we stand in the midst of an event without knowing what is happening to us before we grasp what has happened in looking backwards. Accordingly, history must be written anew by every new present."[6] Or as he writes in *Truth and Method*, "It is enough to say that we understand in a different way, if we understand at all."[7]

GADAMER, LITERARY CRITICISM AND LEGAL HERMENEUTICS

This statement put Gadamer in direct conflict with literary critics as part of another of the first discussions in which *Truth and Method* was involved. Critics such as E. D. Hirsch and the team of Steven Knapp and Walter Benn Michaels focused on what they saw as Gadamer's rejection of intentionalism, the idea that the meaning of a text is what its author intended it to mean. In the English-speaking world, anti-intentionalism was associated with the work of W. K. Wimsatt, Jr.'s and Monroe C. Beardsley's famous, 1946 article, "The Intentional Fallacy". In his 1967 book, *Validity in Interpretation*, Hirsch was particularly scathing in his criticism of what he saw as Gadamer's version of this argument.[8] According to Hirsch, Gadamer's purpose was to separate textual meaning from the author's meaning and therefore to deny "the author's prerogative to be the determinator of textual meaning." What determined textual meaning is, instead, only language itself, necessitating the conclusion that whatever language says to us is its meaning. "It means whatever we take it to mean."[9] It follows, Hirsch claimed, that Gadamer was both a radical historicist and a nihilist.

In the 1980s Knapp and Benn Michaels criticized Hirsch's own intentionalism for leaving too wide a gap between meaning and intention: the author's intention is not the determinator of meaning; it just is the meaning. Nevertheless, they were equally dismissive of Gadamer's approach and for reasons identical to Hirsch's. The circumstance they thought hermeneutics took up is the case in which linguistic conventions allow for more than one meaning. In this case, a text or utterance can mean both what its author or speaker intends and something more, what the reader or hearer prefers it to mean. Yet, Knapp and Benn Michaels argued, if we are to delimit the possible meaning of linguistic intentions, we must go with the author: "there is no necessary relation between the meaning the author intends and any one of the meanings the author's words can have in the language – except the one the author intends."[10]

Knapp and Benn Michaels extended this account of literary interpretation to legal interpretation in the form of discussions of original intent. If we ask what the Fourteenth Amendment's guarantee of equal protection means, in their view we can be asking only what the authors of the guarantee intended by the words. If they did not intend the words to prohibit segregated schools then they do not. At the same time, Knapp and Benn Michaels offered a way out of the discrimination for which this conclusion seems to allow. While the authors of the amendment did not intend it to prohibit segregated schools, subsequent findings indicate that they were wrong about the way these schools enforce inequality. Hence we can preserve an intentional account of meaning while dissenting from its consequences by appealing to our greater knowledge about the effects of segregation on equality. In other words, Knapp and Benn Michaels insisted, "The court would have arrived at different beliefs about the relation between inequality and segregation, but its having such beliefs would in no way alter its account of the law's meaning."[11]

The debate over legal intentionalism has been taken up by Stanley Fish and John Searle among others. It is by no means clear, however, that the version of Gadamer's anti-intentionalism that Hirsch, Knapp and Benn Michaels criticize bears a close resemblance to the claims he makes. Gadamer begins not with the question of meaning but rather with the question of understanding meaning. To the extent that the latter participates in history, our understanding of practices, actions and the like necessarily goes beyond particular actors' intentions. One driver intends to turn left as the light turns yellow and another driver, headed in the opposite direction, intends to go through the light. A thud ensues and although this is an outcome neither driver intended we understand the event as a car crash. Because our actions intersect with the actions of others, they often fail to comply with our intentions. Indeed, even where we do what we intend to do, our actions intersect with those of others and become parts of sequences of action and events over which we have no intentional control. We intend to increase crop production and do, but also contribute to the Dust Bowl. We may succeed in our intention to kill Archduke Franz Ferdinand of Austria but do we intend to start the First World War? In these cases, understanding the meaning of what happened requires going beyond any actor's particular intentions.

The same holds for an author's or legislator's intentions. Neither Hirsch nor Knapp and Benn Michaels tell us which of the author's or legislator's intentions (or the intentions of which legislator or group of legislators) we should link to the meaning of the text. The literary scholars that Wimsatt and Beardsley criticized looked to an author's biography to locate the intentions appropriate to a text. In part because this strategy requires a means of verifying that the scholar has linked the right intention gleaned from the author's biography to the right text, later intentionalists insist on gleaning the author's intentions from the text itself. But then Gadamer's claim is that we have to understand the meaning of the text. Our focus is on the text and what we take to be the author's intentions we surmise from our understanding of the text. Indeed, if an author tells us he or she intended a meaning that we cannot find in the text, we doubt whether the author is telling us the truth about his or her intentions. When T. S. Eliot calls "The Waste Land" a piece of "rhythmical grousing," as Terry Eagleton puts it, the only problem with this description, as Eagleton continues, "is that it is palpably untrue."[12] The same holds for a legislator's or legislature's intention. If we cannot see in a statute what the legislator or legislature says it intended, we have an issue rather than an answer to the statute's meaning. Our judgment of the validity about the claims about intention depends upon our understanding of the meaning of the text of the work or the law.

Furthermore, that understanding is bound up with history. Because an individual's actions intertwine with the actions of others, we cannot assume that the action that actually happens mirrors the individual's intentions. Likewise, because a text enters into relations with other texts as well as with new events and institutions, we cannot assume that the meaning we understand reflects its author's intentions. After all, Shakespeare did not intend to write clichés. Yet in reading his work we read the influence he has had on the English language and on a Western frame of reference. We can make the same point about the law. Knapp and Benn Michaels assume that the concept of equal protection remains the same both before and after its application to the case of segregated schools. Yet the concept surely changes in concert with an expanded notion of the fields of social interaction it governs. Because of our participation in a history that includes and fosters Shakespeare's influence, we cannot detach the meaning we read in *Hamlet* from the presuppositions we have of its importance. Likewise because *Brown vs. Board of Education* abolished state-supported segregation, our conception of equality no longer allows for "separate but equal." At work here is what Gadamer sees as the applicative moment in interpretation in which understanding what a law or text says means understanding the way it addresses us and our situation just as we and our situation contribute to the meaning the text or law comes to have.

HERMENEUTICS AND CRITICAL THEORY

By helping to disentangle understanding from both explanation and internalization, *Truth and Method* helped to re-establish the place of understanding in the social sciences. Nevertheless, critics such as Jürgen Habermas thought Gadamer went too far in suggesting that it was the whole of those sciences. In particular, Habermas argued that hermeneutics is unable to distinguish between those orienting prejudices that enable understanding and those that distort it. In his view, Gadamer focuses too entirely on the interpretive resources that our history offers us and too little on the exclusions, marginalizations, coercions and the like that are also part of its legacy. What about the racist and sexist assumptions that are handed down to us? What about inherited resources that are shot through with distortions arising from the repression of certain voices and the coercive effects of certain social and political arrangements? Habermas claimed that exposing these sorts of distortions requires methodologically grounded approaches and, indeed, a rethinking of the relation between understanding and explanation.

Freudian psychoanalysis serves him as an example of the sort of analysis in which he is interested.[13] Here the task of the psychoanalyst is to clarify the meaning of expressions that cannot be understood at face value because they do not fit within an ongoing communicative situation. Instead, the psychoanalyst must make use of a theory about neurosis or pathology, one that in the Freudian case traces the expressions back to childhood situations. The child suffers a profound trauma with which he or she can cope only by repressing the experience. What emerges in its place is a symptom. Though transference, the psychoanalyst allows the patient to enact the symptomatic behavior and is able to decode it by translating back into the original traumatic situation. The point, for Habermas, is that if we are to understand the patient's expression we must understand it as a symptom and that in order to do that we must have a causal theory of what gives rise to it. The same holds for social systems at large. If we are to decode ideological distortions in the assumptions we inherit, we must make use of a causal theory that traces them back to their social structural causes.

Gadamer's reply to Habermas questioned both the suitability and the capacity of the critical theorist to stand outside his or her society in the way a trained psychoanalyst might stand outside the patient's situation. Why, he asked, assume psychoanalytic theory or any causal theory could be immune to the historical hermeneutic situation and hence free of inherited assumptions? Will these not always be part of the theorist's conception of what counts as a pathological expression on the part of either an individual or society? At the same time, Gadamer conceded the importance of critically examining one's prejudices, an examination he insisted occurred in putting one's prejudices in play. If we listen to another person, investigate a practice or action or read a text, we do so because we assume we might learn something. Gadamer calls this assumption the fore-conception of completeness. We presuppose the validity of what another person or text says or what a practice or action implies about a subject matter and set its presumed validity against our own previous understanding. What follows, according to Gadamer, is a dialogue in which by taking seriously the claims of the other, we become aware of certain of our assumptions and consider the consequences of those claims for them. If necessary, we modify our own views and/or urge a modification of those of the other so that they can become contributions to a larger and shared consensus.

To be sure, this answer was scarcely suited to appeasing Habermas, since it reinforced precisely his worry: that we will take the claims of the tradition too seriously and accept what we would do better to criticize. Yet if critical theorists thought Gadamer went too far in leaving explanation entirely outside the social sciences in favor of hermeneutic understanding, in the realm of post-intentionalist literary criticism, many thought he had not gone far enough in untying textual meaning from an author. Indeed, from the perspective of Jacques Derrida's deconstruction, Gadamer retains too close a hold on the idea that the text has a stable meaning. For Derrida, there is no definitive text, only a multiplicity produced by an arbitrary system of self-deferring signs. What is important, in his view, is not determining what a text or another person means but acknowledging that this question is undecidable.[14] Gadamer thus begins with two assumptions that Derrida denies: that understanding and, moreover, mutual understanding is possible and that the possibility of understanding depends on openness or a good will toward the text. In the famous "encounter" between Gadamer and Derrida in 1981 Derrida arguably tried to make just this point about undecidability by talking past Gadamer, equating his openness to the text and goodwill toward it with Kant's conception of the goodwill and disrupting the normal academic practice of talk and response.

Sandwiched between initial criticisms of his work for destabilizing the determinate meaning associated with an author's intentions and Derrida's intimations that hermeneutics over-emphasizes understanding and openness at the expense of rupture and destabilization, Gadamer is, for many literary critics, both too radical and not radical enough. In contrast, as Richard Bernstein pointed out, in the course of the so-called Habermas–Gadamer debate both philosophers moved closer to one another.[15] In his conception of communicative reason, Habermas developed a version of Gadamer's suggestion that reason develops in dialogue with others. Similarly, although Gadamer continued to deny that instances of distorted intelligibility were the standard case in understanding and although he also continued to stress the importance of openness, he conceded the importance of what Paul Ricoeur calls the "hermeneutics of suspicion."[16]

PART I: CRITIQUE AND CAUSALITY

The first part of *Inheriting Gadamer* explores the possibility of moving hermeneutics further in this or another sort of critical direction. In the first essay, "Critical Fusions: Towards a Genuine 'Hermeneutics of Suspicion,'" Lorenzo Simpson takes a number of steps. First, he begins not with texts or interpreter's attempt to understand his or her own tradition but rather with cross-cultural understanding. In this case, he thinks we are obliged to find touchstones within our own experiences that can address the same or similar topics as those the activities and practices we are trying to understand. He concedes the ethnocentric character of this approach but insists that the hermeneutically self-aware ethnocentrism holds its understanding open to revision. Also open to revision is the "we." Simpson sees cultural identity as a "cluster" concept, features of which can be subjected to critical reflection without a complete loss of the identity. As a second step on the way to a critical hermeneutics, Simpson points out that every culture thinks that its practices offer the best way for it to flourish. He calls this thought a culturally rooted but criticizable validity claim and argues that we can attribute to all cultures a "second-order rationality" that reflects the interest in reforming practices the rationality of which has been criticized. Finally, in a third step, we can invoke a conversational practice that Simpson calls "counterfactual dialogical critique", in which members of a culture are encouraged to consider alternatives to certain of their practices – here he looks at clitoridectomies – that the members might prefer, given who they are.

The second article in this first section of the present volume, Isaac Ariail Reed's "What is Interpretive Explanation in Sociohistorical Analysis?" is interested in a critical sociology that rethinks the divide between explanation and understanding that also comprised the thrust of Habermas's original critique of Gadamer. Reed criticizes contemporary hermeneutics for giving up on causal explanation and insists on two kinds of causes: forcing causes and forming causes. Forcing causes, to use Aristotle's schema, are final and efficient causes, now seen as motives and mechanisms, while forming causes refer to material causes, now seen as technology and the built environment, and formal causes now seen as the meaningful or intelligible background or context for action. The latter two forms of causes are the proper domain of hermeneutics; they work, Reed argues, by way of arrangements of signs, borders, boundaries, and other aspects of the grounds for action.

Reed illustrates the value of his distinction between forcing and forming causes by looking at some of the historiography of the French Revolution, distinguishing between, on the one hand, analyses using forming causes and explaining the French Revolution through "culture" and, on the other hand, analyses using forcing causes to look at it in terms of the fiscal crisis of the French state. Reed ends by proposing a third option: a cultural forcing cause argument. The idea is to connect the concern with interpretation to both the explanatory interest in causal history of, and the normative interest in, possible futures.

Another take on the critical potential of hermeneutics appears in Santiago Zabala's contribution to this volume, "The Anarchy of Hermeneutics: Interpretation as a Vital Practice." Following Reiner Schürmann, Zabala defines anarchy not as the lack of rules but as the lack of a unique and universal rule. Given the insistence of Gadamer's hermeneutics that understanding is understanding differently, Zabala maintains that anarchy lies at its heart. At the same time he thinks Gadamer's political conservatism prohibited him from drawing out the anarchic character of hermeneutics and he therefore turns to three other figures: Martin Luther, Sigmund Freud and Thomas Kuhn who, he thinks, do illuminate this core. Luther translated the Bible, thereby releasing it from the grip of the Catholic Church and leaving it open to individual interpretation. In some degree of contrast to Habermas, Zabala also sees Freud as essentially hermeneutic and, indeed, as releasing the human mind from the positivist scientific culture of the early twentieth century. Finally Zabala looks at Kuhn's work, which explicitly bills itself as hermeneutic. In confronting a developmental conception of scientific progress with a notion of revolutions in incompatible paradigms, Kuhn sees scientific change as a "social struggle between contending interpretations of scientific communities." According to Zabala, all three approaches indicate the extent to which interpretation is a vital practice, one that, he thinks Gianni Vattimo has taken beyond Gadamer. Seeing the anarchic impulse of hermeneutics as a wedge against oppression and control, Vattimo diverts hermeneutics from a Gadamerian emphasis on dialogue to a new emphasis on anarchic excess.

PART II: HERMENEUTICS AND OPENNESS

Part II of *Inheriting Gadamer* takes up the question of openness to the claims of others on which Gadamer insists in reaction to the Habermasian challenge and in his encounter with Derrida. For Gadamer, conversation with others and openness to the claims they make are the means by which we question our prejudices. He writes, "To allow the Other to be valid against oneself . . . is not only to recognize in principle the limitation of one's own framework, but is also to allow one to go beyond one's own possibilities, precisely in a dialogical, communicative, hermeneutic process."[17] This sort of communication does not involve dogmatic arguing or the attempt to find only errors in the opinions and views of others so that we can strengthen our own view. The point is rather to strengthen the views of others to search for the ways in which they may be legitimate and in the process to put our own assumptions and claims in play. We open ourselves to the challenges brought by the views of others so that we can illuminate the presuppositions behind our own opinions and even discover that what we thought we knew is not as certain as we previously believed.

In the first article of Part II of the present volume, "Elements of Style: Openness and Dispositions," Whitney Mannies wonders whether Gadamer is succeeding in plumbing the full depths of openness. She notes the political polarization and marginalization to which a lack of openness can lead when political factions talk and listen only to themselves or when members of social groups fail to listen to non-members. Yet how do we foster openness? Focusing on texts, Mannies argues that more is required than the attention to the content of their claims that Gadamer stresses. Rather we must attend to the style and form through which texts ask us to develop the particular dispositions that will allow them to appear in their best light.

Mannies looks at three sorts of dispositions, emotional, social and reflective. Montesquieu's *Persian Letters*, for example, uses an epistolary form in order to encourage intimacy with the letter writers and free us from nostalgia for benevolent absolutism. In contrast, Spinoza's *Theological–Political Treatise* employs a detached and dispassionate style to subdue the sorts of emotions he thinks wed individuals to superstitious ideas. With regard to social dispositions, Mannies notes research showing that people are more open when they feel secure in a valued social identity. Hume's *Essay Concerning Human Understanding* is thus written in a spirit of camaraderie in order to open his readers to the radical content of his claims. Finally, Foucault, she argues, encourages reflective dispositions by employing a labyrinthine style to effect disorientation and loss of self that he sees as emancipatory and unmasking.

Steven Cauchon's article "Openness to Critical Reflection: Gandhi beyond Gadamer" is also interested in ways of encouraging openness and, like Mannies, Cauchon thinks Gadamer falls short of providing these. In his view, the problem here is that, although Gadamer claims his account of philosophical hermeneutics is descriptive rather than prescriptive, our dialogues and particularly our political dialogues rarely comply with his account. To be sure, Gadamer sometimes uses prescriptive language as when he refers to a hermeneutically trained consciousness. Nevertheless, Cauchon thinks that if we want to look to a theorist who can help us to develop openness and to develop openness in our interlocutors, we need to look beyond Gadamer to Gandhi. Specifically, Cauchon is interested in Gandhi's conceptions of *satya-*

graha, nonviolent political action, and *ahimsa,* nonviolence. *Ahimsa* is not simply an idea that forbids its adherent from injuring any living being, but is also a discipline that involves self-suffering in the service of humility. For Gandhi, emotions and affects are not impediments to, but crucial parts of, reason and understanding. The humility affected by suffering reduces the propensity towards dogmatism. Similarly, the practice of nonviolence in fasting, sit-ins and the like can effect emotions in one's interlocutors or opponents. Cauchon sees this willingness to suffer as a way of shocking them into a response.

The last article in this part of *Inheriting Gadamer* is my own (a different version of an article which also appears in *Perspectives on Politics* (September 2015)), called "Philosophical Hermeneutics and the Politics of Memory." In it I explore the contribution that philosophical hermeneutics can make to overcoming gaps in the public memory of the United States. I begin by recalling some aspects of post-Civil War African American history and consider the American antipathy to confronting this history. Charles Mills calls the general failure of Europeans to recognize the histories and cultures of people of color "white ignorance"[18] and he looks to standpoint theory to overcome it. Standpoint theory looks to the epistemic consequences that different sorts of experiences characteristically have and it claims those of marginalized groups are likely to lead to more adequate accounts of their societies than those of more privileged groups.

Yet even if this causal account makes sense, it fails to account for the lack of uptake of the insights of marginalized groups. Here I argue for the same need for openness to which Mannies and Cauchon point. Under what conditions can we expect dominant groups to take up the testimony and insights of others? I think philosophical hermeneutics helps with this question by pointing to the virtues of recognizing that as historical beings our understanding is necessarily incomplete and that in this sense, we are necessarily ignorant. We can mitigate this ignorance by opening to the possible validity of the testimony and insights of others.

PART III: PLACE, PLAY AND THE BODY

In looking at the discussions in which Gadamer's work has been involved, I have thus far emphasized the connection between understanding and time. The unidirectional nature of time means that in understanding we take up the after and effective history of that which we are trying to understand. Yet in "Place and Hermeneutics: Towards a Topology of Understanding," Jeff Malpas emphasizes the equal importance of place and topology within both hermeneutics and, indeed, the temporality of understanding. He begins his contribution to *Inheriting Gadamer* by noting the prevalence of spatial and topological imagery and ideas in our speaking and thinking about understanding and he denies that these images and ideas are mere metaphors. Take the work of art. For both Heidegger and Gadamer, the work brings its situatedness with it. The Greek temple stands before us in a certain place and, moreover, establishes a place for what appears around it. It thus stands within what Malpas calls a dense web of relations, giving shape and focus both to other things and to itself. In focusing on the work, then, we are forced to focus on its placed character.

Malpas connects this placed character to the realm of openness with which the articles in Part II of the present volume are concerned and he connects openness to Gadamer's account of play. Openness belongs both to the "in between" character of play, insofar as it takes place between players and between players and the game, and to play itself, within the bounds of the space in which the play is defined. He also connects place to Gadamer's accounts of the Da of Dasein, human finitude and language. It may be in all these cases that Gadamer emphasizes the event of understanding and the temporality of the event. Yet, Malpas argues, events can only be understood in relation to place and he ends his article with the topological character of hermeneutics itself.

While Malpas turns to play to illuminate the importance of place in Gadamer's hermeneutics, Monica Vilhauer takes play up to question whether Gadamer sufficiently addresses the role of the body and the non-verbal aspects of understanding. In her essay "Verbal and Nonverbal Forms of Play: Words and Bodies in the Process of Understanding," she admits that throughout *Truth and Method*, Gadamer emphasizes the linguistic nature of what she calls the "play-process" of understanding, but she insists that in the first two parts of the book, his notion of language is expansive. It includes the communication of meaning through, for example, gestures, images, the movements of a dance and the sounds and rhythms of music. Hence, Vilhauer suggests, although Gadamer may not emphasize the body, it is crucial to his account of understanding. Indeed, much of the first two parts of *Truth and Method* shows that understanding can take place "body-to-body" without words and Vilhauer details how it does so in seeing and hearing, in our experience of non-verbal art, in everyday communication and in practical understanding.

Nevertheless, she argues that in the last part of *Truth and Method* Gadamer abandons his expansive conception of language and conceives of understanding's linguistic nature primarily in verbal terms. Although he concedes that body-to-body understanding remains possible in, say, learning a dance or seeing how a role is to be acted he now says this understanding is only complete when it becomes part of our verbal language. The upshot for Vilhauer is a kind of intellectualism that not only conflicts with the insights of the first parts of the book but also diminishes the importance of the body.

PART IV: SCIENCE, MEDICINE AND BIOTECHNOLOGY

Gadamer's skepticism about Habermas's attempt to fold hermeneutic understanding and empirical explanation into a critical social science is a feature of his skepticism about science and technology in general. Indeed, he writes about technology that "it leads to such a manipulation of human society, of the formation of public opinion, of the life conduct of everyone, of the disposition of each individual's time between job and family, and it takes our breath away." With regard to the sciences he concedes what he calls their "dedogmatization" in the course of the twentieth century. Nevertheless, he thinks it would be a mistake to overlook their connection to the domination of nature and society. The sciences, in his view, are irresponsible as long as they are steered by themselves and as long as they are not embedded in our hermeneutic-practical self-understanding of who we are and who we want to be.

In his contribution to the present volume, "On the Integration of Scientific Knowledge into Self-Understanding," Peter Fristedt notes the inroads that the sciences have made on precisely this sort of understanding. Fields such as genetics, neuroscience and evolutionary biology claim to provide better accounts of our bodies, thinking and behavior. How, then, should we think about them? Fristedt takes up Christine Korsgaard's strict division between first-person and third-person perspectives and Laszlo Tengelyi's equally strict distinction between naturalism and transcendentalism. Neither can account for the way scientific perspective stream into our everyday modes of thinking. Fristedt argues that scientific knowledge makes a kind of normative demand on us to be taken seriously as a source of truth about who we are. That is, we are not only practical identities but self-conceptions informed by scientific discovery. Hence, the question we need to face is one of integration.

Fristedt claims that it is Gadamer who, despite his skepticism about science, also sees hermeneutics as a mediating practice and, hence, can help us think through this integration. Here Fristedt works through four claims. First, integration is primarily one-way so that scientific knowledge will be integrated into the linguistically mediated world of our experience; second, scientific objectivism gives way to the plurality of perspectives, as a respected one of them. Third, science discloses truths about things in our world about things we care about and fourth, integration remains challenging. In closing his essay, Fristedt indicates just how challenging and just how Gadamer can nevertheless help.

In the second essay of this part of *Inheriting Gadamer*, "A Dialogic Approach to Narrative Medicine," Leah McClimans moves from science to medicine and to the attempt at integration represented by medical humanities. In specific her concern is the current interest in medical narratives as ways of allowing patients and their self-reports of their conditions to be heard. Unfortunately, McClimans thinks, narrative medicine can serve further to marginalize them. The promise behind narrative medicine is clear. With the institutionalization of medicine and its technologically-enhanced ability to probe, measure, and monitor, the patients' abilities to understand and communicate their own experience of illness gets lost while their caregivers become increasingly alien to them. Conversely, narrative medicine helps patients construct alternative understandings of their experience and helps health care providers conceive an alternative understanding of the ill experience. Rita Charon thus sees listening to patient stories as part of an enhanced medical epistemology while Arthur Frank sees listening as part of a simple moral response.

At the same time, McClimans thinks these authors fail to engage in a genuine conversation with their patients, one in which they open themselves up to the possible truth of what their patients say. Rather, for them listening tends to be a way of being with their patients or bearing witness to their suffering. In contrast, Gadamer's preconception of completeness directs itself at the possibility validity of the content of what others say. The doctor respects the patient as someone from which he or she can learn. Only in this way, McClimans argues is the patient brought into the healing process.

The last essay of this section and the volume, Lauren Barthold's "If Enhancement is the Answer, What is the Question?" takes on the question of bio-enhancement. Barthold points out that the idea of enhancement assumes that we know what enhances human life and what does not. To be sure, we also assume individuals hold different conceptions of the good life and hence that within the bounds of not harming others and athletic fair-play, they are free to decide for themselves what will and will not enhance their lives. Barthold is thus critical of those like Habermas who worry that bio-enhancement threatens an importance core of human nature. At the same time, like Gadamer, she is suspicious of the inclination toward domination and control built into science and technology. Neither nature nor human nature is something with an essence, she suggests; but neither is it a thing to be mastered. Rather, she argues that the history of hermeneutics allows us to see human nature in terms of the way finite human beings strive toward what is beyond them and, indeed, toward the infinite.

For Barthold what follows from this insight is the importance of the idea of equilibrium that Gadamer develops in his writings on medicine. Equilibrium defines the position of human beings between finitude and the striving for infinitude. As such, according to Barthold, it provides a measure for an ethics of enhancement that balances individual and community and that affirms both finitude and "the human urge for transcendence."

As this brief description of the contributions to this volume makes clear, they consider philosophical hermeneutics in relation to a wide variety of different interests: critique, critical sociology, anarchic multiplicity, written style, non-violence, standpoint theory, place, non- verbal language, neuroscience, medical narrative and bio-enhancement. Yet despite these differences certain themes appear and re-appear: among them: the importance of questions, the significance of Gadamer's conception of play, the question of bodies, the move beyond written and spoken language and inquiries into the future of science and technology. The contributions also cohere in their interest in considering both what we can learn from a philosophical hermeneutics and how we can extend it. I would like to take this opportunity to thank all the contributors for their essays.

NOTES

1. Hans-Georg Gadamer, *Truth and Method*, Second Revised Edition, trans. Joel Weinsheimer and Donald G. Marshall (New York: Continuum, 1989), p. 281.
2. Ibid. p. 281.
3. Theodore Abel, "The Operation Called Verstehen," *American Journal of Sociology*, Vol. 54, No. 3 (November 1948), pp. 211–18.
4. Ibid. p. 217.
5. See Honneth, "On the destructive power of the third: Gadamer and Heidegger's doctrine of intersubjectivity," *Philosophy and Social Criticism* (Vol. 29 no. 1), pp. 5–21. "In Gadamer's eyes, the morally problematic tendency of an 'authoritarian solicitude' results when a subject cognitively abstracts from the connection that it earlier already maintained with her or his interaction partner ... Gadamer would like to show that in both

cases it is an error related to cognition that must lead to the morally questionable assertion of a superior understanding (of the other)" p. 11.
6. Gadamer, "Text and Interpretation," Diane P. Michelfelder and Richard E. Palmer (eds.), *Dialogue and Deconstruction: The Gadamer–Derrida Encounter* (Albany, NY: State University of New York Press, 1989), p. 24.
7. *Truth and Method*, p. 297.
8. E. D. Hirsch, *Validity In Interpretation* (New Haven, CT: Yale University Press, 1967).
9. Ibid. p. 247.
10. Steven Knapp and Walter Benn Michaels, "Against Theory 2: Hermeneutics and Deconstruction," *Critical Inquiry*, Vol. 14, No. 1 (Autumn 1987), pp. 49–68, 57.
11. Steven Knapp and Walter Benn Michaels, "Intention, Identity, and the Constitution: A Response to David Hoy," Gregory Leyh (ed.), *Legal Hermeneutics: History, Theory, and Practice* (Berkeley: University of California Press, 1992), p. 193.
12. Terry Eagleton, *How to Read Literature* (New Haven: Yale University Press, 2013), p. 134; also see my criticism of Noel Carroll's intentionalism in *After Identity: Rethinking Race, Sex and Gender* (Cambridge: Cambridge University Press, 2001), pp. 92–3.
13. Jürgen Habermas, Josef Bleicher, *Contemporary Hermeneutics: Hermeneutics as Method, Philosophy and Critique*, p. 192.
14. See, for example, James Risser, *Hermeneutics and the Voice of the Other: Re-reading Gadamer's Philosophical Hermeneutics*, p. 168.
15. See "Text and Interpretation," p. 40 and Richard Bernstein, "What Is the Difference That Makes a Difference? Gadamer, Habermas, and Rorty," PSA: *Proceedings of the Biennial Meeting of the Philosophy of Science Association* 2 (1982), p. 335.
16. See Paul Ricoeur, "Hermeneutics and the Critique of Ideology" in Ricoeur, *Hermeneutics and the Human Sciences* trans. John Thompson (Cambridge: Cambridge University Press, 1981).
17. Hans-Georg Gadamer, "Subjectivity and intersubjectivity, subject and person," trans. Peter Adamson and David Vessey, *Continental Philosophy Review* 33 (2000) pp. 275–87, 284.
18. See Charles Mills, "White Ignorance," *Race and Epistemologies of Ignorance*, Shannon Sullivan and Nancy Tuana (eds.) (Albany, NY: State University of New York Press, 2007), pp. 11–38.

PART I
Critique and Causality

1 Critical Fusions: Towards a Genuine 'Hermeneutics of Suspicion'

LORENZO C. SIMPSON

I

This essay is drawn from a larger project in which I am now engaged, one in which I seek to develop a philosophical hermeneutics with critical intent and one that will consequently demonstrate the ongoing relevance of hermeneutic approaches to matters that are far beyond the field of literary and textual analysis to which hermeneutic strategies have all too often been restricted. As we know, hermeneutics embraces a distinctive family of approaches to linguistic and non-linguistic meaning, a set of approaches that grant central importance to the act and context of interpretation. When hermeneutics shifts its focus from understanding texts, utterances and deeds produced in the interpreter's own tradition to coming to terms with other, competing, cultures, traditions and epistemic regimes, then the question of its ability to provide genuinely *critical* understanding arises. Characteristic of hermeneutic approaches is an insistence upon taking as a touchstone the meaning or intelligibility of a text, utterance or action to an agent, be it the agent who seeks to understand or the agent who is to be understood. In the paradigmatic hermeneutic situation of the dialogue, ego and alter seek to forge a common language by "fusing" their respective contextual horizons or matrices of intelligibility. Indeed, dialogical acknowledgment on the part of the to-be-understood agent is a crucial moment in hermeneutic approaches. That the validity of a result of an act of dialogical understanding is so tightly indexed to an agent or to a community of agents seems to leave no space for rationally challenging the world as those agents know it. For this reason, hermeneutics has seemed to many to be unable to interrogate critically the status quo of a given tradition, given its overweening concern with understanding. Further, hermeneutics' emphasis on the contextuality of knowledge claims has just as often led to charges that it is a relativistic enterprise. Indeed, in its insistence upon the tradition-bound content and context of any putatively "critical" norms, hermeneutics is often opposed to the tradition of critical social theory, in particular to the form that social theory assumes in the work of Jürgen Habermas.

In my larger project, I make the case for hermeneutics' critical potential by pursuing hermeneutically-informed investigations primarily in three *topoi*, those of scientific theory choice, racial politics, and culture. Throughout, my brief for a critical hermeneutics takes the form of an extensive response to these commonly voiced charges of relativism and critical impotence. I urge that hermeneutics can be a critical philosophical enterprise as much as an interpretive one. My ultimate objective is to demonstrate the wide-ranging salience of hermeneutic approaches to philosophical issues and thus to show that the relevance and value of hermeneutic philosophy is by no means as limited as many of its critics maintain.

In this essay, I focus primarily on the practical/ethical domain to display the cogency of hermeneutically-informed social critique, to show that hermeneutically-informed conversation can be deployed with genuine critical intent. And by exploiting some of its heretofore insufficiently explored resources, I hope to demonstrate a role for hermeneutics in social and political contexts that, while remaining true to the spirit of hermeneutics, nevertheless goes beyond what Gadamer's writings explicitly provide.

In his influential anatomy of hermeneutics, *Freud and Philosophy*, Paul Ricoeur contrasts two genres: the hermeneutics of the recovery of meaning, associated with Dilthey, Heidegger, and Gadamer; and the hermeneutics of suspicion, whose masters were Marx, Freud and Nietzsche. In the latter the "true" or "real" meaning of actions, be they verbal or not, is presumably masked by a surface signification, and the "real" meaning gives the lie to what is manifest. As typically understood, the practice of the hermeneutics of suspicion depends for its legitimacy on what Richard Rorty called an *illegitimate* "theory hope," a view of the true that is vouchsafed to a *theoria*-like pure seeing, which is itself, Rorty averred, an anachronistic holdover of foundationalist philosophizing. In such foundationalist thinking, the ineliminable role of finitude and of the situated horizons from which interpretations of meaning necessarily emanate was overlooked, he claimed. The aspirations betokened by such a putative theory hope have been relentlessly ridiculed by many of the dominant philosophical movements of the twentieth and twenty-first centuries; the "negative dialectics" of Adorno, Heidegger's "destruction of metaphysics," Derrida's so-called "deconstruction" as well as by Rorty's own neo-pragmatism. And in many ways this was the central issue that animated the celebrated debates between Habermas and Gadamer. Indeed, in an essay bearing the title "The Hermeneutics of Suspicion," Gadamer dismisses this genre as but another species of foundationalism.[1] Another way of putting this, of course, is to say that the "hermeneutics of suspicion" is not sufficiently *hermeneutical*. On the other hand, because, to my mind at least, he never provided a clear and convincing account of the distinction between legitimate and illegitimate *sociopolitical* prejudices, one might say that hermeneutics, as Gadamer conceived it, was not sufficiently *suspicious*. Indeed, I find Gadamer's claim that his account of this distinction could serve as an effective stand-in for ideology-critique to be unconvincing.[2] So, in the discussion that follows I would like to address the question, how can critical suspicion be genuinely hermeneutic?

II

In our current moment of global modernity, I think that hermeneutics can make a unique contribution to critical social and cultural understanding. Given contemporary concern about questions of global justice and, in particular, the skepticism voiced by some "postcolonialist" and "multiculturalist" thinkers that any ethical regime with cosmopolitan intentions must inevitably founder on the shoals of a Eurocentric ethnocentrism, hermeneutic approaches to social justice may well be the best positioned simultaneously to do justice to cultural difference and to avoid situations where critique depends for its legitimacy on normative standards developed in and imposed by the West. To make this case, I highlight three conditions that allow for immanent or "internal" normative pressure to be brought to bear on social/cultural practices when hermeneutically understood. First are facts about culture and cultural identity. It is widely acknowledged that cultures are not monolithic, homogeneous wholes. Further, cultural identity itself can be understood to be what I would call a "cluster" concept, which means that certain elements of the set of features that collectively constitute one's social identity may be revised as a result of critical reflection without resulting in the loss of that identity. Second, I propose a conception of "second-order rationality," a mode of rationality that has a culturally-invariant purchase, and third, I elaborate a critical approach to cross-cultural understanding that is informed by what I currently call "counterfactual dialogical critique." In that both appeal to the possible acknowledgment on the part of the to-be-understood agent or agents, these conceptions of rationality and of critique provide, I would maintain, a more genuinely *hermeneutic* basis for what Paul Ricoeur has dubbed the "hermeneutics of suspicion" than do the critical strategies of those whom Ricoeur cites as its masters. For the self-understanding of Nietzschean, Freudian and Marxian theory does not unambiguously require that the validity of critique be subject to the acknowledgment of those to whom the critique is addressed.

My proposal for a dialogical method of critique will require no wholesale opposition to the actual options and choices of action available to, and sustained by, a given culture. It will allow us to split the difference, so to speak, between, and thereby potentially to reconcile, the emancipatory reflection championed by Habermas and others, on the one hand, and a hermeneutically sensitive consciousness, on the other. For the position that I develop here does not require – as Gadamer occasionally "falsely" alleged against Habermas – that emancipatory reflection dissolve all of the structures of intelligibility intrinsic to the culture in question. Ultimately, I suggest that the hermeneutic distinction between legitimate, or "true," and illegitimate, or "false" prejudice – a distinction that Gadamer famously invoked but for which, at least in practical/ethical contexts, a fully satisfactory account has yet to be provided – is not merely arbitrary. To leave it at this would be tantamount to a capitulation to the charge of relativism. On the other hand, the redemption of this distinction does not require an appeal to a discredited foundationalism. To avoid both, I propose criteria for making this distinction by a consideration of what is required for autonomous agency, by a consideration of what is meant by genuinely autonomous consent on the part of to-be-understood agents. In so doing, I offer a modality for bringing to bear critical perspectives that are both sensitive to cultural difference and that avoid an indiscriminate relativism.

III

Before pursuing further the idea of *critical* understanding, I want first to clarify my conception of understanding itself, in particular of what it means to understand another person or a culture other than one's own. To do so, I shall, briefly, address the social-epistemological problem of determining how genuine, that is, non-invidious, understanding of cultural formations that are not our own is possible, of determining what the conditions and limits of such understanding are. In general, I take the perspicuous *intelligibility* of the other to be a criterial property of an adequate hermeneutic understanding. This will involve the production of a perspicuous account of what the other takes her life to be about, that is, of her distinctive and fundamental aims and commitments, of the ways those aims are pursued or addressed, and of the assumptions she holds about the situation – structures or institutions – that provides the setting or context for those pursuits. If we pay adequate attention to these facets of interpersonal or intercultural hermeneutic understanding, we will discover that the potential for meaningful *critique* is an ineliminable *internal* feature of such understanding.

Dialogue between or across communities of intelligibility requires the identification of the *topic* or *Sache* that is being addressed in perhaps contrasting ways by the communities in dialogue. Here I believe we must consider the hermeneutic problem from a somewhat different angle than the one Gadamer was wont to adopt. His tendency was to focus on the tradition which both text and interpreter share, a focus that can occlude the problematic and deeply contested nature of topic identification in cases where one cannot rely upon the commonality provided by a shared tradition. By this I mean the problem of identifying the topic that will allow us to maximize the conspicuous intelligibility of a given response. So, my concern first is to "rotate" the relationship with which Gadamer is preoccupied, namely, the vertical relationship of an authoritative tradition to an interpreter, so that it becomes a horizontal relationship between interlocutors. This will mean that, in general, we will be unable to take for granted a shared tradition and the advantage that it gives us of already being "in" on the cultural conversation and the topics being addressed. In cross-cultural conversation, we may often be able to rely upon only our hermeneutic talents, and, crucially, the free response of intercultural interlocutors to our proposals. Accordingly, the presumption of authority that Gadamer accords tradition, I want to locate in the reciprocal recognition of interlocutors (though we must of course take care to remain sensitive to real asymmetries between dominating and dominated languages[3]).

There are general methodological constraints that condition our access to the fundamental concerns of others. It is in light of what are or could be concerns and issues for us that we are able to understand a form of life other than our own. When we understand, we invoke *Sachen* or dimensions of *our* experience, dimensions such as love, sexuality, religion, power, natality, and an awareness of our mortality. That is, unless we can identify the dimensions of experience which are addressed by the practices that are distinctive of the form of life we seek to understand, and we can do this only through modeling upon what can be logical spaces or dimensions of experience *for us*, we cannot understand it. The aim of a non-tendentious dialogical understanding of another is to produce an "ordered pair" – consisting of topic and response – exhibiting a "reflective equilibrium" that displays the most *compelling connection* between a topic and the correlative response to it.⁴ And here indeed, we would do well to heed Gadamer's advice. In the case of textual interpretation, Gadamer exhorts us to "anticipate completeness," "to interpret to the strongest case that can be made."⁵ And this will be a connection that, in the *final* analysis, will be viewed as compelling or not, *for us*.

There is thus a sense in which some degree of ethnocentrism is epistemologically unavoidable. To see others as engaged in, say, argumentative practices or in morally relevant practices requires *our* experience with those kinds of practice as a touchstone. And we can be sure, to pick morality, that if another culture's criteria for the application of moral terms demonstrated *no* overlap with ours, we would have no reason to think that they were engaged in moral discourse at all. The interpretation that yields a *Sache*, or topic, and contrasting approaches to it is, in the last analysis, ours. But I take this to be relatively harmless, and for two reasons. First, we can distinguish, on the one hand, what I would call the "transcendentally" necessary ethnocentrism of our unavoidable appeal to our notions of rationality and cogency, or to what we deem can be intelligibly related to them, from, on the other, the residue of a contingent, empirical and possibly invidious ethnocentrism. We can combat the latter by acknowledging the crucial importance of dialogue (with cultural others) aimed at mutually acceptable descriptions of the *Sache* and of its correlative contrasting practices. So, finding the appropriate topic of concern will require both my interpretive powers, which will by themselves yield only hypotheses, and the confirmational resources of dialogue.

So, a hermeneutically self-aware ethnocentrist – one who is aware of her transcendental ethnocentrism – would interpret others in accordance with the criteria that her lights reveal but not in a way that dogmatically precludes the possibility (or desirability) that her standards may change, i.e., that she could learn from others. Indeed, the relativist's refusal to judge can betray a refusal *to be judged*, a refusal both to make claims *on* others and to be claimed *by* those others.

Second, who "we" are is always subject to revision, for our identities are best viewed as being open to nonfatal contestation in that certain elements of the set of features that collectively constitute one's social identity may be revised as a result of critical reflection without resulting in the loss of that identity. Such a threat to cultural identity need not be feared if we acknowledge that identity is a cluster concept in that few if any beliefs or professions of value, taken singly, are essential to an identity. Our identities, then, need not be construed as being *identical* to our *prevailing* purposes, goals and projects. What counts as the proper description of the self is then open to contestable interpretation. Thus, the modification of one's matrix of intelligibility in response to an interpretive/dialogical challenge need not entail the risk of losing oneself. And, again, this holds for both sides of an intercultural dialogue.

IV

Given the hermeneutic account of intercultural understanding briefly outlined above, what resources does it offer for critical responses to differently cultured others? Or, to invoke a formulation recently used by Habermas, with what success can it mediate between, on the one hand, a "politics of identity" with its tendency to make *collective* rights of different social groups sacrosanct and, on the other, an "Enlightenment fundamentalism" that would in an invidious fashion abstract individuals from their identity-informing sociocultural milieux? To address this challenge, I show how my account licenses a form of immanent critique, and then I consider a conversational modality that takes advantage of the fact that, as my remarks on identity suggest, cultures are not monolithic, homogeneous wholes but are rather sites of contested interpretations, of competing interpretational narratives.

The model of understanding that I am proposing, emphasizing as it does hermeneutic charity, does not leave us powerless to respond critically to the forms of life that we wish to understand. That it does not promote, or even countenance, a promiscuous relativism can be demonstrated by way of a brief counter argument to a claim that Richard Rorty was wont to make, namely, that the only way to take seriously the distinction between the merely socially or culturally sanctioned, on the one hand, and the valid, on the other, is to adopt a discredited Platonic foundationalism. Lacking such a foundation to provide an "honest broker," there can be no non-question begging way, Rorty insisted, to critically evaluate or to referee conflicts between sociocultural practices.

Pace Rorty, I believe that there are grounds for critically assessing social practices that are *internal* to the cultural horizons that sustain those practices, grounds that make it unnecessary that critique appeal to anything beyond the standards of rationality and/or central vocabulary of a particular cultural group. The intuition that supports my conviction here is fed by the recognition that *we* can sometimes be brought to see that social practices and procedures of epistemic justification that *we* may have heretofore relied upon may prove to be unreasonable or untrustworthy, to us. And there is no reason to think that others cannot be brought to see this as well. Consider cases like that of the discovery of an unbalanced scale in an economic transaction, where the outcome of an accepted procedure for assessing relative value will have been *exposed* as having been an artifact of bias in the procedure itself, cases where it has been discovered that the procedures have been "loaded" in such a way as to prejudice their outcome. In such cases there are *reasons* to modify the procedure that can be acknowledged by *all* who engage in the practice.

My commitment to hermeneutic humanism entails, among other things, a disposition to genuinely respect differently situated others. And this will, I would argue, transcendentally demand that we treat differently-cultured others as being like us in that they, too, operate with an *ideal* of themselves wherein their actions can, if challenged in ways that are understandable to them, be held accountable to *reasons* that have a non-parochial purchase and that are binding for them. Now, given its identity, every culture implicitly makes the claim that its practices provide the best avenue for *its* flourishing, that they represent the best way for *it* to address the *Sachen*. Even the most insular forms of life can be understood implicitly to make the claim that their practices are the best way for *them* to flourish. This sort of culturally rooted validity claim provides the occasion or basis then for a non-question-begging cultural critique informed by the presumption of what I call second-order rationality.

What I am calling second-order rationality is obviously what is invoked when an experimental design in the sciences is criticized – for example, when a particular experimental setup is shown to be flawed in such a way that it cannot be dispositive for testing a given hypothesis, that it prejudices its outcome. But this mode of rationality can also be deployed in the interpretation of sacred texts and of political constitutions. The form of rationality that is implicit in my account here is a form of rationality that I take to have transcultural, or cross-cultural, or culturally invariant, standing. It is a disposition or mode of rationality that we are entitled to impute to everyone – that is, an inclination to reform one's practices in the direction of more rationality when one's lack of rationality is pointed out to one in terms with which one is conversant.

Accordingly, we can – without appealing to anything beyond the matrices of intelligibility, standards of rationality, and/or central vocabulary of any particular epistemic community or cultural group – intelligibly mark a distinction between what even everyone in a particular epistemic community *happens* to believe and what is, by their *own* lights, *reasonable* for them to believe, a distinction, moreover, that should command *their* attention. To *convince* someone of the questionability of their practices is *ipso facto* to provide them with a *reason* to consider alternatives.

The cross-cultural commitment to second-order rationality implies that social agents must, even if only pre-reflectively or implicitly, *anticipate* a relationship among their aims, beliefs and practices whose rational coherence differently situated others (including cultural "outsiders") could also appreciate. (I should emphasize, however, that this exploitation of the transcultural presumption of second-order rationality depends upon a prior hermeneutic *understanding* of the cultural context in which the disputed practices are situated; we would need to know what the aims of the disputed practices are, which topics they are addressing. Only such an understanding would allow the sort of critical representation that I have here elaborated.) In so providing members of a particular cultural tradition with an optic for recognizing and acknowledging what could be problems *for them*, the unavoidable presumption of this modality of reason also fully entitles critical outsiders to view "insiders" as being eligible, and in a way that begs no questions, to accept the burden of rational critique. In this sense, social agents, however implicitly, anticipate a dialogical confirmation of their rationality, granting an opening to potential critics.

I want to conclude my reflections here with a sketch of a third way in which hermeneutically informed approaches to intercultural understanding can allow us to navigate successfully between the Scylla of arrogant cultural imperialism and the Charybdis of impotent cultural relativism. I wish to make a case for a particular sort of conversational practice that can lay claim to being a genuine "development practice." Like the invocation of second-order rationality, these would be conversational practices whose *internal* normative pressure would perform critical work without the *imposition* of normative standards from cultural "outsiders."[6] I shall illustrate this conversational modality with primary reference to the practice of female genital cutting or excision in those parts of Africa, the Middle East, and Southeast Asia where women themselves seem to be part of the consensus in its favor. Now, while the existence of such a practice is clearly a matter of concern in and of itself, I am not claiming that the fact of its existence is the main problem to be addressed in these societies. Focusing on it, however, is useful for illustrating how resources for critique can be unearthed when careful attention is paid to the *autonomously* voiced preferences and concerns of those local cultural agents who are affected by such a practice, resources whose critical potential can be redeemed independently of any one-sided imposition of "Western" standards.

We begin by reminding ourselves that cultures are not seamless wholes, that, in the words of one observer: "[s]ince a culture's system of beliefs and practices, the locus of its identity, is constantly contested, subject to change, and does not form a coherent whole, its identity is never settled, static and free of ambiguity."[7] And further, as a United Nations report on justice and gender indicates: "the history of internal contestation reinforces [the premise] that cultures are not monolithic, are always in the process of *interpretation* and *re-interpretation*, and never immune to change."[8] These statements of course echo what I earlier referred to as the conception of culture as a cluster concept and the idea that cultures are in general sites of conflicting interpretations. If we further concede, as I have argued elsewhere we must, that the distinction between *intra*-cultural hermeneutic dialogue and *inter*-cultural hermeneutic dialogue is a matter of degree, not kind, then we should expect to find *within* many cultures traces of the tensions that we are more accustomed to noticing between them.[9] Consistent with this, it can be argued that many intercultural normative disagreements can be productively analyzed as *intracultural* conflicts.[10]

To take but one example, as Akeel Bilgrami, a philosopher who is himself Muslim, has argued, being a Muslim is not necessarily to accept the strategic framing of one's identity put forward by some of one's fundamentalist co-religionists;[11] such an identity can be critically reconfigured. He points out that Muslim communities are defined by competing values, of which Islam is one and, further, that Islamic identity is itself negotiable.[12] He goes on to make the point that given the spectrum of positions actually occupied by members of Muslim communities, critical pressure need not necessarily be viewed as an ethnocentric, imperialistic imposition from the outside, but rather it can be applied from the inside, where there are indigenous resources and aspirations that can fuel *internal* processes of critical response.[13] And, as the political theorist Yael Tamir has argued, "[a]lthough cultural choices are neither easy nor limitless, cultural memberships and moral identity are not beyond choice," and they can be made the subject matter for a politicized discussion oriented towards bringing these emotional processes to discursive consciousness.[14] I would argue that cultural identities are as much forged as found. They are fields of contestation and negotiation, often of struggles to expand existing and socially acknowledged logical spaces in order to accommodate the intelligibility of styles and forms of group membership that were previously marginalized.[15]

Given that cultures are not monolithic, homogeneous wholes such that none of their component parts, beliefs and practices can be altered without loss of integrity, it behooves us to be wary of taking at face value any *single* narrative purporting to capture definitively a culture's identity.

This suggests that we be attentive to ways in which cultural identity claims may be reified products. Categorically asserted cultural identity claims can be understood to be reified products in at least two ways: they may disingenuously veil strategic orientations, and they may belie conflicting interpretations of a culture's identity-defining structures, the fact that cultural identity is best seen as a cluster concept.[16] Cultural identity claims should not then be given carte blanche to function in such a way as to quarantine intracultural practices from discursive view, so as to immunize them from critical examination. As I shall presently suggest, the plurivocity of legitimate cultural narratives underwrites the hermeneutic intelligibility of a cultural agent assuming an oppositional stance vis-à-vis elements of her cultural matrix.

The central operative assumption behind the conversational practice that I am here endorsing, "counterfactual dialogical critique," is that cultural agents can be encouraged to consider social possibilities that, while currently unrealized, might actually be *preferred* by them, social possibilities whose realization is suppressed not because such realization would offend against all intelligible interpretations of cultural identity, but rather primarily because it would offend against *particular* interpretations, namely, those which may serve particular vested interests. For this reason, then, we should be on the lookout for interpretations of cultural identity that operate as cloaks or ideological veils concealing prudential, interest-based concerns.[17]

The interests that occasion such strategic representations are unlikely, except in unusual cases, to be distributed *uniformly* across individuals and groups within a culture. The *representativeness* of such strategic self-images can then be interrogated through dialogue with a representative variety of such individuals, acknowledging of course that what counts as a representative variety may be itself a matter for interpretive contestation. Nevertheless, it would be reasonable to start with representations parsed out in terms of standard demographic categories such as those of class, ethnicity and gender.

There are obvious overt signs that would trigger a "hermeneutics of suspicion," signs such as observed conflicts of interest within a society, observed indices of perceived or actual power asymmetries between categories of social membership, and so on.[18] But what if, as is not infrequently the case with female excision, there is no overt contestation of what seem to us problematic cultural practices? Here I should like to note that the *appearance* of asymmetrical or invidious treatment of identifiable demographic groups can serve to trigger *hypotheses* about the real interests implicated and about whether or not the interests of all cultural members converge in the way that prevailing cultural identity claims implicitly assert that they do.

It is useful here to consider a suggestion made by Habermas, indeed one that I have myself criticized in another context.[19]

> I make the methodological assumption that it is meaningful and possible to reconstruct (even for the normal case of norms recognized without conflict) the *hidden* interest positions of involved individuals or groups by ... imagining the limit case of a conflict between the involved parties in which they would be forced to consciously perceive their interests and strategically assert them, instead of satisfying basic interests simply by actualizing institutional values as is normally the case.[20] (Italics mine)

I would like to suggest here that we treat Habermas's comments as pertaining to what philosophy of science was wont to call the context of generation, the context within which hypotheses are proposed. Central now is the question, How to "test" these hypotheses concerning hidden or suppressed interests? Habermas makes reference to the possibility of indirect *empirical* confirmation based upon predictions about conflict motivations.[21] However, I want here to emphasize the extent to which the suspicion of potential dissensus can be *hermeneutically* redeemed (or, for that matter, falsified). We need not restrict ourselves to the social theorist's monologically produced picture of a counterfactually imagined conflict. The justification of the ascription of a potentially hidden interest can, indeed should, be a collaborative, dialogical project, one involving those whose interests are in question. With regard to the question of female excision, this means the affected and potentially affected women, whose perspective would be articulated under conditions that I shall now describe.

As an explicit *stylization* of the sorts of question that might, whether implicitly or explicitly, underlie such a dialogical engagement, capture its critical intent, and perhaps thereby prompt some of the processes of cultural self-reinterpretation alluded to above, I would suggest the following. When encountering some form of the practice of excision or genital cutting, a witness, whether sharing cultural membership with the affected women or not – one who failed to find the "general" acquiescence to the practice on the part of women to be perspicuously intelligible – might initiate conversations of a particular sort with them, conversations guided by the basic question: Armed with the knowledge of the all too likely physical and emotional consequences of the procedure, if the connection between undergoing the procedure (or the procedure in the concrete form that it now assumes) and your chances for flourishing in your society were virtualized, if that connection could be severed, would you still choose to undergo the procedure?[22] This is the sort of question that could be raised in the conversational modality that I refer to as counterfactual dialogical critique, a modality that, if practiced within a society, illustrates the plausibility of non-question-begging, non-invidiously ethnocentric, critical perspectives on practices within cultural formations that are not our own.[23]

Non-question-begging conversations with potentially affected social agents in "safe" spaces providing immunity from the threat of reprisal – aimed at eliciting fundamental or overriding interests – can be initiated.[24] Woven into such a conversation might well be discussions in which the agent is encouraged to engage in an imaginative variation of possible conditions on the realization of those interests, say, the interests in cultural solidarity and social flourishing; these are the virtualizations of counterfactual dialogical critique. This would entail consideration of scenarios in which the linkage between succumbing to the procedure of excision in the form that it currently assumes and being able to realize those interests is gradually severed. These counterfactual narrative scenarios may range from replacing clitoridectomy with lesser forms of mutilation, to a ritualized symbolic circumcision consisting of a small cut on the external genitalia performed under medical supervision and hygienic conditions, all the way to nothing at all.[25] If the agent, upon reflection, expresses a genuine *preference* for situations wherein her interests – chances for marriage and other important forms of social recognition, for example – and *foregoing* the procedure were jointly realizable, then this would count as her opting out of the putative "consensus." At the very least, we could say that a discussion that is informed by a consideration of these alternatives is more autonomously pursued – and that a life that is led in an awareness of them is more lucidly lived – than one which is not. This would be a means of conversationally interrogating the reasonableness of sociocultural configurations wherein women are faced with the forced choice between flourishing and bodily integrity; are confronted with the demand to choose "mutilation" or face "social death." It would foreground the possibility that the social forces which sustain this forced choice are a reflection of *one* particular cultural interpretation among others. Its aim is to effect a piercing of the epistemic/cognitive veil by raising the possibility of a way to extricate oneself from bondage to such a dichotomous conception of social options, thus enhancing the scope for autonomous agency.[26] My normative focus here is to try to deploy in this account some of our intuitions about the criterial conditions for the exercise of genuine autonomous agency. And minimally that involves the agent's *informed endorsement* of what she does. And the more this endorsement is given in the context of perceived alternatives, many of which can be understood to cohere with valid interpretations of the culture in question, the more *meaningful* that endorsement will be.

It might be objected that this conception of autonomy is too demanding to be of critical use, for none of us chooses all of our choices. Many of them are "thrust" upon us because of the nature of things or in situations that we would uncontroversially regard as "normal conditions." Everyone faces disjunctive situations not of their choosing, for example, "do your job or lose it". But some face situations of this sort that others do not, and do so for reasons that are more contingent than necessary, more "contrived" than "natural." The critical purchase of the concept of the restriction of autonomy takes as its background, then, what someone would otherwise – that is, absent arbitrary constraint – be capable of doing. The asymmetrical arrangement wherein one determinate group of mature agents must exercise a choice within a dichotomous or disjunctive framework – e.g., one structured by the alternatives of flourish or retain bodily integrity, but not both – while others are exempt from facing such a dilemma may be an arrangement that may well serve the interests of those who are exempt. This, I would argue, provides sufficient grounds to question the rational warrant of this arrangement and therefore to suspect the arbitrary, that is, *unreasonably* limited, and, hence, *criticizable* nature of the framework for choice for those who are constrained by it.

A second plausible objection to this critical deployment of autonomy is to claim that autonomy is but one value among other, perhaps competing, values.[27] Even if this can be persuasively demonstrated, the cultural practices we are considering, if challenged, tend to be defended in one of two ways: they are claimed to be essential to the integrity of the culture in question, and/or it is claimed that they are willingly endorsed by the cultural agents who participate in them. What I have said about the plurivocity of legitimate cultural interpretations addresses the former, while in the case of the latter, the *claim* to autonomous acceptance is precisely what serves to anchor the immanent critique that I have proposed.

It is important to note that this dialogical method of critique requires no *wholesale* opposition to the actual options and choices of action available to, and sustained by, a given culture. It is attuned more to the nature of the *distribution* of those social options and choices. And what about those cases where, even after such a conversation, some persist in holding to the view that such a ritualized procedure, in its current or traditional form, has an identity-constitutive character which is itself of overriding value? Consistent with the dialogical nature of the enterprise that I am here proposing, such a response may ultimately have to be acknowledged as a "falsifying" event. Prior to such acknowledgment, however, and given the heterogeneous constitution of culture, our questioning can be broadened to press the issue of social *interest*. We might pose the question, given the likely physical and emotional harms of undergoing such a procedure: Whose interest is served by the perpetuation of the practice? Given the conceived alternatives that our discussion has brought to mind, and in light of the hypothesis that the restricted alternatives in terms of which you originally chose were promulgated in the interest, or implicitly served the interests, of some as opposed to others, would you now *endorse*, in the sense of voluntarily choose, what you would have chosen before? The conception of autonomy that has informed my discussion is, I would argue, a distinctively hermeneutic one in that it is not conceived of as a property of a disembodied, acultural subject but rather of an agent who is *situated* within a particular concrete matrix of intelligibility.[28]

And that matrix of intelligibility is contingently expandable. This can happen when the semantic resources that would enable alternative legitimate cultural interpretations are enriched by the participation in the interpretive process itself of those whose interests had been marginalized. This expanded "hermeneutic" agency would remediate what was possibly a disguised unequal hermeneutic participation and ideally, at least, level the playing field.[29] I have described this within-group negotiation to expand the stock of generally acknowledged social meanings as a matter of expanding that group's moral horizon by advocating for the semantic authority or interpretive adequacy of alternative descriptions of a shared social world.[30]

Lest what I have proposed be dismissed as a "mere" armchair philosophical "thought experiment," consider some of the conversations about genital cutting that have recently begun to take place in a number of societies where it has been traditionally practiced. The conversations are just of the sort that I have proposed. In the African country of Mali, for example, they are pursued under the indigenous auspices of the COFESFA Women's Association and other NGOs. These conversations highlight the physical and emotional consequences of the ritual, the plurivocity of the cultural narratives deployed to justify the practice, and the patriarchal interests that it serves. And, though of course there are no guarantees, given that these conversations seek to engage opinion leaders and take place among both men and women in local communities, they may give rise to proposals that will be candidates for the sort of general social recognition, or what I have called semantic authority, that can foster cultural re-interpretation. It is useful to think of these conversations as a component of the within-group struggle to expand the group's moral imaginary by persuading members of dominant social groups to acknowledge the semantic authority of claims put forth by others. Indeed, such community-based discussion, sponsored by a NGO in Kenya (the Maendeleo Ya Wanawake Organization), has in some cases led to the implementation of alternative non-invasive rituals marking female rites of passage in local communities.[31] And similar developments are occurring in Senegal. It is worth noting that in the Senegalese case, where the issue of genital cutting was explicitly raised by Senegalese women themselves, care was taken in the discussion of this issue to avoid descriptors such as "barbaric" and other potentially question-begging cognates that would invidiously pre-judge the issue.[32]

What lessons can we draw from these examples, highlighting as they do the conversationally-underwritten and enhanced agency of local groups? Hermeneutics' emphasis upon the conversational negotiation and expansion of interpretive frameworks enables a distinctively illuminating analysis of the pragmatics and intelligibility of such conversational situations. And, this evaluative stance is I believe an inescapable aspect of intercultural understanding. This serves to underscore the status of my proposal as a model for mutually *critical* conversation and as a case of a genuine hermeneutics of suspicion.

NOTES

1. Hans-Georg Gadamer, "The Hermeneutics of Suspicion," *Man and World* 17 (1984), pp. 313–23.
2. Gadamer, "The Scope and Function of Hermeneutical Reflection," in *Philosophical Hermeneutics* (Berkeley: University of California Press, 1976), p. 31.
3. On the obstacles posed to intercultural translation by asymmetrical power relations, see Talal Asad, "The Concept of Cultural Translation in British Social Anthropology," in *Writing Culture: The Poetics and Politics of Ethnography*, ed. James Clifford and George E. Marcus (Berkeley: University of California Press, 1986).
4. See my *The Unfinished Project: Toward a Postmetaphysical Humanism* (New York: Routledge, 2001), p. 87.
5 Gadamer, *Truth and Method*, Second Revised Edition (New York: Continuum, 2002), pp. 293–4.
6. See, for example, Thomas McCarthy, *Race, Empire, and the Idea of Human Development* (Cambridge: Cambridge University Press, 2009), p. 243.
7. Bhikhu Parekh, *Rethinking Multiculturalism: Cultural Diversity and Political Theory* (Cambridge, MA: Harvard University Press, 2000), p. 148.

8. "Gender, Justice, Development and Rights," Report of the United Nations Research Institute for Social Development Workshop (2000), cited in Monique Deveaux, "A Deliberative Approach to Conflicts of Culture," *Political Theory* 31 (December 2003), pp. 780–807; emphasis mine.
9. See my *The Unfinished Project*, pp. 105, 109–10, 112.
10. See, for example, Monique Deveaux, "A Deliberative Approach to Conflicts of Culture."
11. Akeel Bilgrami, "What Is a Muslim? Fundamental Commitment and Cultural Identity," *Critical Inquiry* 18 (1992), pp. 821–42.
12. Ibid. p. 823. When we think of the controversy surrounding the so-called "Rushdie affair," we should note that, given the highly charged and contested nature of intracultural struggles to articulate and systematize expressions of cultural identity, the Muslim reaction to Salman Rushdie's *The Satanic Verses* and to the *fatwah* that followed its publication calling for his death, was hardly uniform (see Sadik J. Al-Azm, "The Importance of Being Earnest about Salmon Rushdie," *Die Welt des Islams* XXXI [1991], pp. 1–49, esp. 34).
13. Bilgrami, p. 823 and Akeel Bilgrami, "Rushdie, Islam, and Postcolonial Defensiveness," *The Yale Journal of Criticism* 4 (1990), pp. 301–11.
14. Yael Tamir, "Liberal Nationalism," *Philosophy and Public Policy* (Winter/Spring 1993), p. 4.
15. I have discussed the within group struggle to expand the moral imaginary in terms of persuading members of dominant social groups to acknowledge the semantic authority of claims put forth by others (on the concept of semantic authority, see my *The Unfinished Project*, pp. 110–11; and my "Humanism and Cosmopolitanism after '68," *New Formations* 65 [2008], pp. 57–8, 64–5). By this I mean to highlight the importance of ensuring that a claim made by a particular social group has a claim on all, that it be recognized as a general claim. This would compel interlocutors both to make perspicuous the hermeneutic and social contexts implicated in such a claim *and* to make a genuine and open-minded effort to assess the extent to which such a claim is generally compelling, that is, the extent to which it has purchase beyond the specific sociocultural context of its generation. Such a general claim would be one that *addresses* everyone, one that ultimately invites reply. It is a claim that is to be taken seriously by *all* as a *candidate* for a perspicuous description of the world, one that renders salient features that should command respectful attention. Such an acknowledgment involves treating the other's claim as making a claim on all, not by demanding acknowledgment or accession by force, but by getting each to recognize that it is addressed to them as a possible way for all to view the world that they share. And it might be discovered that mutual efforts to understand the heretofore marginalized or newly emergent descriptions may initiate social learning processes whereby what was previously seen as (merely) private becomes a matter of right and in need of public recognition and regulation.

To treat a claim as general in this way is to treat it as a speech act that imposes a mutual burden: the "addressee" assumes the obligation of taking the claim seriously enough to enter, along with the sender, a dialogically constituted space of reasons and reasoning in considering its general applicability; the "sender" assumes an obligation to justify the claim or a particular application of a term or to persuade the addressee, again in a mutually forged justificatory language, of the usefulness of so applying the term. To treat a claim as general in this way is to take it up in such a way that we are willing genuinely to risk having our view of things challenged, without of course there being any *guarantee* that we will be so persuaded. General claims remain defeasible, criticizable claims. But to fail to seek to understand, and to take such claims seriously *as claims*, is to fail to give the other her due. To take examples from our society, to treat, say, sexual harassment and police brutality as merely descriptions of social interaction from the points of view of women and blacks, respectively, with no presumption that these descriptions will have *general semantic authority* is to enact a restriction that would allow these issues to be understood as simply idiosyncratic matters of "their perception," where *their* perception has unfortunately become *our* collective problem, a problem to be handled perhaps strategically, rather than to be understood as a matter of what their perception *reveals* about our *common* social reality.

16. On the latter, see my *The Unfinished Project*, pp. 91–2.
17. Deveaux, p. 788.
18. On the occasion of a seminar that he offered at the Humanities Institute at SUNY Stony Brook on September 9, 1999, I understood Renato Rosaldo to offer the following methodological advice in response to a question that I put to him concerning strategic representation: one should in the first instance take what is said at face value, but be prepared to question it when, for instance, conversations with others seem to contradict it or when the respondent's own behavior seems to belie what s/he has said. Then go on to hazard interpretive projections of the form, "what would be the case if what the informant has said is true? or false?" Then, making the process recursive, return to engage the interlocutor in a confirmatory or disconfirmatory dialogue informed by what one has learned.
19. See my "On Habermas and Particularity: Is there Room for Race and Gender on the Glassy Plains of Ideal Discourse?" *Praxis International 6* (1986), p. 338.
20. Jürgen Habermas, *Legitimation Crisis*, trans. by Thomas McCarthy (Boston: Beacon Press, 1975), p. 114.
21. Ibid.
22. The health implications of female genital cutting have been well-documented. See, for example, United Nations, *Human Rights Fact Sheet 23: Harmful Traditional Practices Affecting the Health of Women and Children*, Geneva: United Nations, 1995 (cited in Sally Sheldon and

Stephen Wilkinson, "Female Genital Mutilation and Cosmetic Surgery: Regulating Non-Therapeutic Body Modification," *Bioethics* 12 [1998], pp. 263–85).

23. Here I am not concerned to address the putative inconsistency or hypocrisy of Western objections to such practices while apparently tolerating potentially dangerous forms of cosmetic surgery aimed at increasing sexual desirability (see Sheldon and Wilkinson, "Female Genital Mutilation and Cosmetic Surgery"). I am concerned to elaborate mechanisms for critical response to such practices that are untethered to "Western" views.
24. The idealization implied in the notion of "safe" spaces is deployed in the defense of the meta-ethical claim that non-question-begging, critical cross-cultural conversations can be meaningfully held. It does not address the equally important political question of how such spaces are to be created, maintained and respected as sources of proposals that are treated as candidates for semantic authority, that is, as candidates for general social recognition and acknowledgment.
25. On this spectrum of procedures, see Anna Elisabetta Galeotti's "Relativism, Universalism, and Applied Ethics: The Case of Female Circumcision," *Constellations* 14 (March 2007), pp. 91–111.
26. In her *The Politics of Our Selves: Power, Autonomy, and Gender in Contemporary Critical Theory* (New York: Columbia University Press, 2008), p. 2, Amy Allen provides a gloss on the concept of autonomy that is useful for the concerns of this chapter, namely that autonomy is the capacity of "critical reflection: the capacity to reflect critically upon the state of one's self . . . on the norms, practices, and institutions that structure [one's life] . . . and, on this basis to chart paths for future transformation."
27. See Marina Oshana, *Personal Autonomy in Society* (Farnham: Ashgate Publishing Limited, 1988), pp. 123–42, for a consideration of this issue.
28. My account of autonomy blends aspects of both what in the literature are referred to as internalist and externalist accounts of the phenomenon (see Oshana, 21ff). Though I concentrate here on "internalist" aspects of autonomy, namely on second-order endorsement of first-order choices and preferences, there are "externalist" aspects of my account as well (see Oshana, p. 87). For, even in cases where the requisite second-order endorsement is forthcoming, I ask whether or not the conditions governing what is available to particular social agents as a first order preference are invidious or arbitrary. Further, even if, for the sake of argument, we assume that endorsement *per se* is insufficient as a criterial property of autonomy and require that autonomous agents also assume the burden of discursively defending their choices (cf. Paul Benson, "Taking Ownership: authority and Voice in autonomous Agency," in John Christman and Joel Anderson eds. *Autonomy and the Challenges to Liberalism* (Cambridge: Cambridge University Press, 2005), such agents are obliged only to assume responsibility for responding to challenges that are appropriate and intelligible to them given their own evaluative standpoint or matrix

of intelligibility (cf. Benson, p. 113). So, this emendation would remain compatible with the hermeneutic account that I wish to develop here.
29. See Miranda Fricker, *Epistemic Injustice: Power and the Ethics of Knowing* (Oxford: Oxford University Press, 2007), pp. 152–3.
30. See note no. 15 above.
31. Maendeleo Ya Wanawake [2000] 'FGM – advocacy strategy for the eradication of female genital mutilation in Kenya', http://www.maendeleo-ya-wanake.org/ (last accessed March 25, 2011). See Chege, Askew et al., cited in Serene Khader, *Adaptive Preferences and Women's Empowerment* (Oxford: Oxford University Press, 2011), p. 72. The implementation of institutionalized alternatives to excision, access to those alternatives, and the *awareness* of the existence of and potential access to them on the part of female agents collectively address an important dimension of agency. They are illustrative of what I call conditions of second-order agency. I argue that we should distinguish between agential capacities of the first order, to wit, the capacity to produce an effect or to bring about a state of affairs (in the case under consideration, perhaps to lead a life that combines social flourishing and bodily integrity), and agential capacities of the second order, to wit, the awareness of and the ability to acquire or to avail oneself of the enabling or facilitating conditions of agency in the first-order sense. The latter, second-order capacities are then those that condition the exercise of capacities of the first order. Satisfaction of the conditions of second-order agency can be understood as an enabling condition of self-transformation in that it contributes to the motivational support requisite to the actualization of emancipatory self-transformation (see Allen, 12).
32. http://www.nytimes.com/2011/10/16/world/africa/movement-to-end-genital-cutting-spreads-in-senegal.html.

2 What is Interpretive Explanation in Sociohistorical Analysis?

ISAAC ARIAIL REED

The distinction between understanding and explanation, frequently used to make sense of the human sciences and their relationship to the natural or physical sciences, reliably destabilizes philosophical categorizations, because it is ontological, epistemological, and pragmatic all at once. "Understanding" can describe what historians and sociologists study, that is to say, a "sociology of understandings"[1] (ontology: people, with their understandings of the world and their wild and wonderfully weird subjectivities), how they study them (epistemology: methods of interpretation leading to understanding, routes to secure the validity of interpretation), and the inherently communicative nature of scholarly investigation and publishing as an accomplishable task (pragmatics: science is similar in some ways to all communicative action – for example, it has both a constative and performative dimension). It is tempting, then, to deconstruct the distinction between explanation and understanding itself. But this would be a mistake; instead an ill-fated but nonetheless useful attempt at sublation should be attempted. In what follows, I do so from a point of view defined by the line between sociology and history, a zone full of hermeneutic problems but surprisingly under-influenced by hermeneutic philosophy. I will refer to the research that occurs at this line as "sociohistorical analysis," and be concerned to show, in a concrete register defined by an arena of empirical study, how "interpretive explanation" works.[2]

For sociohistorical analysis, the debate about explanation and understanding matters because what it means to successfully explain (account for? retrodict? predict?) why people do what they do (or why they did, what they did) is both in dispute, and massively consequential for – to give just a few examples – policy proposals, the collective self-understanding of groups of people confronting their own violent histories, and the constitution of social movements as organizations both identity-bound and strategic. And, since the birth of the modern historical profession, the question of explanation and understanding has been part of thinking about the very possibility of doing history itself. What is an explanation? How does it work? When is it causal? And how do you make causal statements about particular historical transformations, full of willful agents engaged in contingent contests for power?[3]

Hermeneutics suggests, rather obviously, that explanation is subsumed under a broader category of human understanding, which can take many forms. Less obviously, hermeneutics suggests that *causal explanation itself* can be usefully reformed via a reconceptualization driven by hermeneutic approaches to meaning. In other words, not only is explanation a subcategory of understanding, but also explanation itself is simultaneously causal and interpretive in an interesting and underexplored way.

This idea of interpretive explanation – captured famously in Max Weber's definition of sociology in the opening pages of *Economy and Society* – can be better comprehended by expanding our purview on causality beyond the intent imitation of efficient causality in social theory.[4] This devotion to efficient causality is usually based upon one or another idealization of the causal theories of the natural sciences, but it lives in many forms, and is perhaps the ultimate sense in which Thomas Hobbes can be interpreted as the founder of modern social thought.

To move outside of thinking efficient causality, I present a necessarily degraded reading of Aristotle's four causes – degraded in the sense that it is bent towards the problems of twentieth-century and twenty-first-century social theory, and thus glides and glosses over major problems in the philosophical interpretation of Aristotle. With regrets, then, I propose a reformulation of Aristotle's schema of four causes so as to draw a distinction between *forming* and *forcing* causality which, in my view, would greatly enhance our comprehension of what is at stake in debates about causality in sociohistorical analysis. I show how this is the case by examining debates about the origins of the French Revolution.

ARISTOTLE'S FOUR CAUSES IN SOCIOLOGICAL THEORY: A HERMENEUTIC POSSIBILITY?

As is well known, in the *Metaphysics*, Aristotle gives the example of the casting of a bronze statue, and divides the causal aspects of this situation into four.[5] The material cause is the bronze (that is, the temperature at which it melts, its properties as a liquid and as a solid). The final cause is the endpoint of the process, "that for the sake of which other things are" – in this case, the finished statue. The efficient cause is that from which change comes, that is to say, the actual pouring of the bronze into the cast. And finally, the formal cause is, somewhat elusively "the whole, the synthesis, the form," the reference for which is the way in which a designed plaster cast gives shape to the bronze poured into it. I propose that by interpreting this schema with the problems of contemporary sociohistorical analysis in mind, this enigmatically given example can be useful for sorting through the causal confusion of social theory, and rendering somehow comprehensible the idea of interpretive explanation.

Though there are accounts in social theory of the relationship between Marx's concept of labor and Aristotle's metaphysics,[6] of the importance of the distinction between *zoe* and *bios* for understanding politics and state-society relations,[7] and even an attempt to base sociological research itself on the specifically Aristotelian concept of *phronesis*,[8] I here depart from the overwhelming emphasis in Aristotelian social theory on the constitution of human beings as practical reasoners in pursuit of good action or as political actors engaged in collective decision-making. This is because, in my view, for the problem of understanding/explanation in contemporary sociohistorical analysis, the dominant account of Aristotle's metaphysics and epistemology comes from Donald Levine, who developed an understanding of Aristotle's four causes as a means to comprehend a vast array of arguments in the history of modern social theory, and to argue against the reductionism inherent in many different approaches to explaining human life.[9] Levine's basic reading is as follows.

Levine begins by noting Aristotle's differentiation of the universal "theoretical" sciences from the "practical" sciences, thus lining Aristotle up with Max Weber, Wilhelm Dilthey, and the elements of Karl Marx's work that emphasize historical conjunctures and specificities.[10] This is because, unlike the "internal" dynamic of natural substances, human actions are subject to will, opinion, and how people construe the good. Thus the human sciences must strive for knowledge of "particulars."[11] Then, Levine argues that Aristotle distinguishes between that which is still "natural" about human action, and that which is "artificial." The passions (motivating emotions such as grief, hate, desire, and so on.) are "organismically grounded" (Levine's term).[12] "These provide the motivational energies for action."[13] Also, the faculties are also organismically grounded – sense perception, calculation, ability for thought, etc. All of this, then, is grounded in the "material cause" (or, we could say, the biophysical substrate of *being human*).

There are some social elements to the "material cause" of human nature in Levine's interpretation – humans naturally form associations, and the *polis*, in particular "exists by nature." This is because "(1) human beings by nature are endowed with the faculty of speech, by which they are disposed to discourse about good and bad, a disposition they can express only in the political community; (2) the component units of the *polis*, households and village, exist by nature; (3) the *polis* is the form of association towards which these unites aspire, the culmination of their existence – and that makes it their end."[14]

Thus, in Levine's reading, the human sciences are constituted or founded on an Aristotelian distinction between nature and artifice, with an understanding of *material* and *final* causes as "natural," and of *efficient* and *formal* causes as "artificial." Of these artificial causes, Levine suggests that we think of a political *regime* (e.g. as defined by Charles Tilly as "repeated, strong interactions among major political actors including a government"[15]) – as a formal cause, and the socialization and education that reinforces a regime as an efficient cause. In other words, formal causes refer to large social and state structures, whereas efficient causes are what we see "at work" in reproducing them, when we turn on the sociological microscope.

Levine uses all of this as a way to develop an anti-Hobbesian agenda for social and political theory. The idea here is that for Thomas Hobbes:

> ... the human world is constituted as a great field of interacting impulses, just as the mechanical world is constituted as a great field of interacting atoms, and their force is so strong that they perturb the workings of the only other natural phenomenon humans evince, reason. Analysis of these interacting motions, based on the natural propensities of atomic individualism, constitutes the alpha and omega of Hobbesian social science.

Hobbes thus "eliminates two other phenomena that Aristotle also assumed to be natural: the propensity of substances to actualize their potential in a certain direction, and the tendency of humans to organize themselves in enduring associations."[16]

Hobbes is, for Levine, the origins of the "modern" reductionism that he wants to avoid, and he does so by resisting both Hobbes' tendency to make causes in human life "natural," and his rather exclusive interest in "material and efficient causes." It is not hard to see that Levine's reading here is in fact part of the argument, in sociology, against rational choice theory, methodological individualism, etc. However, beyond this particular set of arguments, Levine's reading of Aristotle is useful because it locates quite clearly the links between Aristotle and the hermeneutic understanding of the human sciences in Dilthey, and because it shows how pre-modern schemas can be used to unsettle thinking about social causality in the contemporary philosophy of social science, and in sociological research itself.

I view Levine's argument as correct insofar as it finds and criticizes in contemporary social science a tendency to read material interests, on the one hand, and efficient social mechanisms, on the other, onto every social situation that is being analyzed, in a way that creates parsimony at the cost of external validity. If this is what we mean by reduction, then clearly Aristotle, and the hermeneutic tradition more generally, is its antidote. But to affirm and advance this antidote, I want to propose a different reading of the classic Aristotelian schema.

REREADING ARISTOTLE: FORCING AND FORMING CAUSES

My reading is less informed by the debates about classical and modern social theory which occupied Levine, and more informed by cultural sociology and, to some degree, science and technology studies. It also draws on Alasdair MacIntyre for its reconceptualization of formal causes. It is as follows.

Consider again the casting of the bronze statue as Aristotle's point of theorization for causality. The material cause, the properties of bronze, should be reconceptualized as the materiality of social life that participates in an *assemblage*. That is to say, there are material objects and technologies that are implicated in the heterogeneous networks and alliances that make up social life. Frequent examples of material causes in sociohistorical analysis include the built environment (including, famously for Bruno Latour, mechanical door closers), the "natural" environment, human bodies, and transportation, communication, and production technologies.[17]

The final cause is conceptualized elsewhere by Aristotle as telos or purpose, but here in terms of the image of final statue in the artist's mind, which is very close to saying the artist's *intention*. Final causes, then, should be read as referring to that set of causes we could call the motivation of human actors. Within the space of these sorts of causes, we find a set of debates about reasons, intentions, unconscious motives, and habituation, as well as the ubiquitous question of "interest" in social science explanations.[18]

Efficient causes are of course the most trouble, for a reason that is 400 years old. Since the attack on the scholastics in the scientific revolution, the pull to have one's own causal rendering of the world understood by the scientific community as an efficient cause is like intellectual gravity – you can fight it and build buildings that help you avoid crashing to the earth, but it does not go away. In social theory, this is central to the appeal of rational action theory and analytical sociology. But, from a hermeneutic perspective, we can see efficient causes as social mechanisms that are *one part* of the larger causal imagination. This, in particular, aids historical sociology, which has always been centered around questions about the conditions for, and pathways whereby, social life comes to be more "efficient" or "mechanistic." In other words, in historical sociology, we are in the business not only of identifying social mechanisms, but in trying to figure out the answers to questions such as when and how did state power become more *mechanistic* and *efficient* in its application and how did the *rationalization* of scholarship occur in relationship to the advent of bureaucracy and the market society? Thus, Aristotle's efficient causes should be reconceptualized as the repeatable, reliable, codified social mechanisms that can be triggered. These can be examined via "process tracing." Further examples are the triggering of the legal process by the filing of charges, self-fulfilling prophesies such as bank runs, and a variety of cause-effect mechanisms that we associate with market competition.

Finally, formal causes should be thought of indicating the dependence of human action on meaning, with an understanding that meaning includes referential, moral, and aesthetic elements. In other words, the references for actions, when they emanate from motives and participate in social actions, also include previous actions, not in themselves, but *as those previous actions are understood*. Those previous actions that are in the network of reference for an action thus make up its *meaningful context*. In his classic essay on the intelligibility of action, MacIntyre explains that if one considers different sequences of actions, of differing temporal expanse, one quickly finds that such sequences are also "of different types: conversations, feuds, enquiries such as those of the sciences, projects in the arts or politics, playing through a particular game and indefinitely many more long- or short-term individual or joint types of project and transaction."[19] What MacIntyre calls intelligibility, we might identify as the formal cause in action-reaction sequences, whose shaping of motive and mechanism makes both more concrete, and more comprehensible *as motives and mechanisms with force in the world*. Thus, for MacIntyre, "intelligibility is an objective property of actions or of sets of actions; it is not in the eye of the beholder" and includes in its purview both "the private world of the mental as well as the public world of the social."[20] MacIntyre then renders intelligibility as a property of everyday routines and of more consciously cultivated and rationally criticized practices (under which we can include sculpture).[21]

The colligation of different action sequences into types may vary significantly in the degree of generality that is possible while keeping a grip on the meanings that inflect action. So, if we take the intelligibility of action seriously, we will have to let the generality of an appropriate explanation vary by the research question as a well-defined why question about certain specific actions. For some research questions, the practice of sculpture in the classical tradition may be enough of a reference point to get at the formal cause; for other questions, important distinctions between different artistic schools will be significant. What all such explanations share, however, is this embedding of the push and pull of the world into a meaningful context.

At this point we have, then, a recharacterization of Aristotle's four causes that can be tracked in the following way:

1. Material: built environment, technology, materiality
2. Final: motives, interests, and intentions as the springs of action
3. Efficient: social processes that achieve regularity
4. Formal: the meaningful or intelligible background or context for action

One of the clear indications of several decades worth of work in science and technology studies is that the material causes are complexly intertwined with the formal in "giving form to" or "shaping meaningfully" how humans are motivated and navigate the social world. In other words, the way in which the world grants *agencement* to certain actions and not others, requires a comprehension of meaningful context, understood in a hermeneutic way, but also material semiotics.[22] I would, indeed, suggest that in a hermeneutic social science, the role of the material is paired well with formal causes insofar as both together constitute the *historically variable context for action*. The question then becomes how, if we understand these as types of causes, our understanding of and conduct of sociohistorical inquiry will change.

To begin with, a significantly different reading of the human sciences' relationship to the natural sciences than that proposed by Levine emerges. It now appears that, insofar as accounting for human action in its full efflorescence remains the goal of the human sciences in general and sociohistorical inquiry in particular, it is the material and formal causes that make up a complex of historical difficulties for the investigator that are relatively alienated from the image of natural science in Western modernity. Both the *meaningful context* for action and the *uptake of the material* into social life are the location of extensive work on the radical variation in the history of human social groupings, and, as I will shortly argue, extensive work on the formation of social kinds. That is to say, it is with material and formal causes that we find the core insights of hermeneutic philosophy to be directly at work in sociohistorical analysis: the relationship of part to whole as essential to understanding the environment for action; the emergence of new kinds, forms, and entities in the social world, including identities, systems of categorization, and sociotechnical objects such as options in options markets and derivatives.

It is still the case that motives and mechanisms, as those things to which the investigator is sometimes prone to attribute certain actions and outcomes, require interpretation – what is more interpretive than the problem of other minds? However, it would appear that final and efficient causes, understood in this way, are the sorts of things that investigators are prone to *put into* context. They are analogized, more frequently and more often with Humean bias, to causal forces. They are also, in well-known ways, the most frequent reference points for "reductionist" explanations, whether those reductions are done in terms of "interest," "status attainment," or some other moniker that, while of course being a useful part of the theoretical lexicon in the human sciences, is far too often leaned upon in the social sciences as the foundation of every explanation ("parsimony").

For this reason, I want to make distinction between *forcing causes* (final cause/motives, efficient cause/mechanisms), and *forming causes* (material cause/technological, formal cause/meaning) in sociohistorical analysis. It is, of course, an excessively crude distinction. But it is useful precisely because it captures and criticizes the central tendency of social science to focus on forcing causality, and, by implication, not to see forming causes as causes at all. Indeed, the overwhelming tendency in modern social science has been to see that which cannot be wedged into the efficient processes of mechanisms or the revealed or unrevealed preferences of interest to be outside the very possibility of explanation. This is a tendency shared, unfortunately, by some of the central thinkers in the hermeneutic tradition, who depart from the very possibility of explanation, and recede instead into the language of recontextualization and the addition of further accounts to the ones we already have.[23]

What differentiates forcing and forming causes from each other, *as causes*? If it is anything, it is that forcing causes take place as a kind of analogue of motion, where something, metaphorically speaking, "pushes" or "pulls" on something else. In contrast, forming causes work via a kind of *arrangement* – of signs, borders, boundaries, and other aspects of the "ground" for action. As such, these arrangements constitute a hermeneutic causality. The basic insights of the hermeneutic tradition apply to the grounds for action, the intelligibility of action, the "moral background" of action, and so on: these causes are collectively emergent, arbitrary, conventional, and historically variable; no actor can do without them; and to exert some control over these arrangements is, in part, to grasp at power. However, it should be noted that, precisely because of the emergent, social, and interpretation-dependent nature of these forming causes, attempts to influence them by this or that actor seeking an adjustment in power are subject to significant uncertainty and thus both unanticipated and unintended consequences. Action molded by the arrangements that are forming causes is inevitable qua action; changing this or that arrangement intentionally is quite difficult indeed. Finally, in the hermeneutic view, explanation rarely emerges at a high level of abstraction. For that reason, I now try to show what I mean by forming causes with reference to a specific problem in sociohistorical analysis.

PUBLIC OPINION, BOOKS, AND THE CAUSES OF THE FRENCH REVOLUTION

Explaining the French Revolution is a central occupation of Western historiography and of comparative-historical sociology; it looms in the background of classical social theory itself; two sociologists of science even claim that the French Revolution is the "model system" for historical sociologists studying social change.[24] Here I examine work from history and sociology on the lead up to revolution in the second half of the eighteenth century and on the very early stages of the "revolutionary situation," namely 1787–1789. I do not claim to offer an exhaustive review of the literature, or definitive evidence in favor of any particular interpretation of the French Revolution. Rather, I wish to use this extremely well researched topic as a testing ground for the distinction between forming and forcing causes. In particular, I will use the forming–forcing distinction to understand the relationship between the cultural historiography of the revolution and the widespread consensus, in comparative–historical sociology, that the fiscal crisis of the French state helped precipitate the revolution.

The very first thing to note is that the shift towards a cultural interpretation of the revolution's origins in the histories written in the 1980s and 1990s involved a tremendous amount of causal talk. Exemplary in this regard is the way in which two of the most important books in the cultural historiography of the Revolution contain sections titled "Do Books Make Revolutions?" and "Do Books Cause Revolutions?" (These authors were surely, also, two of the most self-aware concerning the conceptual problems they were opening up for social theory, hence the bluntness of the titles, which have a certain measure of irony to them.)[25]

This causal talk in Revolutionary historiography focused on changes in French (and especially Parisian) social life, and in particular the communicative aspects of that life, in the century before the revolution began in 1789, and especially after 1750. The messiness and difficulty of claiming causality here is intensely felt by historians – on the one hand, it feels absurd to say the revolution was Rousseau's fault; on the other, it is equally clear that in the years leading up to the revolution, *something* shifted in the meanings that *somehow* informed revolutionary action, and these meanings appear to bear some interesting resemblances to the core philosophical ideas of the Enlightenment. In sociology, the difficulty of making these sorts of causal claims is well known via the debate between Theda Skocpol and William Sewell, Jr. in the *Journal of Modern History* about the role of "ideology" in revolutions, and, in the French case, the role of Enlightenment ideologies in particular.[26] In what follows, I first elucidate how the explanation of the French Revolution via "culture" refers to forming causes. I then recapitulate the forcing cause explanation, well known in comparative–historical sociology, which traces the precipitation of revolution to the fiscal crisis of the French state. Finally, I discuss the potentially productive relationship between these two different causal analyses, and discuss a third option, a cultural forcing cause argument, which has been superseded in the literature.

Forming Causes in the Lead Up to the French Revolution

The forming cause story for the French Revolution has (as I will present it here) two parts: the formation of a new social kind, "opinion publique", and a shift in the arrangement of emotions, meanings, and status–ascriptions to royal authority. By describing these, together, we can depict the cultural atmosphere for action in the 1780s. And it was this atmosphere or context that gave shape and meaning to the fiscal crisis of the late 1780s.

Public opinion
In "Public Opinion as Political Invention," Keith Baker traces the invention of public opinion as a politically relevant object in pre-revolutionary France. He begins with a simple indicator of a change in meaning. In the *Encyclopédie* (1765), "opinion" is derided as the uncertain, subjective opposite of rational knowledge. And earlier in the

century, beliefs about fluctuations in uncertain opinion were mobilized as part of arguments for absolutist monarchy. However, in the parts of the *Encyclopédie methodique* that concerned finances and the police (published in subscription format in the 1780s), "opinion" is no longer defined, and instead there is an entry for "opinion publique." Strangely, this "public opinion" possesses the precise qualities that "opinion" lacked. Public opinion is, in this definition, universal, rational and objective, and it is a kind of court that judges people and governments. What happened?

In the ideologies of absolutism, the King was the only public person, and thus communication of advice to him could and should be secret, precisely to protect the King as the protector of the "public" or general good.[27] But over the second half of the eighteenth century, public opinion crept into politics and became a source of authority. First, French "notables" had to acknowledge developments in English politics, but in so doing they had to distance themselves from them, while also desiring reform of French government. Across the political spectrum, the French elite hated what was perceived as the chaotic, fear-based, irrational party politics of England after 1688. And yet, they articulated a desire for "liberty" of some sort, in opposition to the perceived despotism of the King's ministers, who spent the second half of the eighteenth century attempting to beat the regional *parlements* into submission. Simultaneously, another transfer occurred: from the early eighteenth century discourse concerning how an international "public" of Europe would judge the maneuvers of various absolutist regimes, to the possibility that a *domestic* "public" could discuss, and perhaps even judge, its own monarch – and especially the actions of his ministers. The result of this interwoven process was a thorough transformation of "public opinion." In 1750, Rousseau had used it to refer to collective values and customs and the source of the social standing of individuals. In contrast, "From 1770," explains Baker, "the term begins also to take on connotations of the Enlightenment and to acquire a more explicitly political resonance."[28]

What is particularly interesting for our purposes is that this new meaning of "public opinion" was a category of speech, and a frequently invoked justification for decisions, before any consensus was obtained on what it really referred to or on how to mention it. Hence, as Baker explains, "public opinion" emerged as an "abstract category" that political actors used to make their claims legitimate.[29] Furthermore, because of the desire to avoid English party politics, this category, though lacking a clear referent, acquired an association not only with "rationality," "enlightenment" and "the people," but also with stability. "Public opinion" became *both* "the enlightened expression of active and open discussion of all political matters," *and* "incompatible with divisions and factions."[30] And so, this complex set of associations and criss-crossing meanings were embedded in a category that was used in everyday political discourse and disputation, and, eventually, used by the King's ministers to legitimize state actions. For, the advocates and representatives of Versailles *also* began referencing public opinion in their attacks on the *parlements*. Jacob-Nicolas Moreau, defending monarchy, argued that the pamphlets decrying despotism and corruption in government failed because, when it comes to the pamphleteers, "neither their opinions nor mine will ever form what one means by 'public opinion' – unless one agrees that there can be an immense difference, in every sense, between public opinion and the unanimous wish of the nation" (in Baker 1990: 190; we will have reason to return to these pamphlets in a moment). Public opinion, though controversial and non-referential, is nonetheless real as a category at the middle of a constellation of meanings essential to the legitimation of domination. A new social kind has appeared on the political scene. It can be struggled over, reinterpreted, and even despised, but it cannot be erased. It is, as sociologists are fond of saying, "real in its consequences."[31]

At this point, a few comments are in order. First, note that the meaning of "opinion publique" emerges in the French/Parisian context *in relation* to other meanings that work in and around "public" and "opinion" and "politics," and especially in relation to those ascribed, by the French elite, to English politics. Second, the reality of the term precedes its reification. Indeed, the calling of the Estates General led, in Baker's view, to a set of actions which served to specify the referent for the term: "clarification was forced by the political process set in train by the calling of the Estates General."[32] Finally, this tracing of the formation of a social kind has an important material and technological shift as part of its arrangement: printing. Indeed, the lack of a clear "sociological referent" for the measurement of public opinion *does not* mean that the social kind "public opinion" was stranded – a category without support. Rather, public opinion came into being via an assemblage of different sorts of "stuff." Printing, as the material aspect of forming cause, was also essential to another shift, the "cultural atmosphere" in France.

Reading and delegitimation
What printed materials were people reading in eighteenth century Paris? And did what they read "make" or "cause" the revolution in some sense of the term?[33] We can begin with a set of basic empirical

theses, about the spread of print and reading in the second half of the eighteenth century.[34] Readership increased massively, and the product people were reading in Paris was qualitatively transformed. This applied to both the *Affiches* traced by Colin Jones,[35] and to the prohibited works that were not given the King's seal. The latter, the so-called *livres philosophiques* sold "under the cloak," exploded in popularity in the second half of the eighteenth century, and they included an overlapping typology of books: *libelles* attacking the depravity, lack of morality, and general self-indulgence of the King and those close to him (these could be of a scandal-mongering pamphlet variety, or of a longer, biographical nature); sheer pornography; works of political philosophy (e.g. treatises from Voltaire and Rousseau); and "utopian fantasy."[36] These genres bled into each other in complex ways. Furthermore, how people read changed, as well. A "new relationship between reader and text was forged; it was disrespectful of authorities, in turn seduced and disillusioned by novelty, and, above all, little inclined to belief and adherence."[37]

Subtle shifts of meaning occurred in these illegal texts. For example, later eighteenth century libels paint very different pictures of the King and his mistresses than did those that were popular during the reign of Louis XIV. One classic of the earlier era, *La France galante,* though scandalous, painted a picture of a powerful Louis XIV, "cutting a wide swath through the ladies of his court ... he is an imposing figure, the virile master of a powerful kingdom, usually referred to as 'le Grand Alcandre.'" In contrast, the *libelles* of Louis XV, especially those published after 1770, are quite different: the King is presented as having screwed up two foreign wars, perhaps because he "cares only for women," though he "is barely capable of an erection, so he falls under the spell of a common whore."[38] Simultaneously, Robert Darnton points to an important philosophical difference between the earlier texts and the later ones:

> The early *libelles* often protested against tyranny, a notion that goes back to antiquity and that underwent a revival during the Renaissance. But the late *libelles* accused the monarchy of degenerating into despotism, a concept that began to acquire a powerful new range of meaning at the end of the seventeenth century. Both terms conveyed the idea of the abuse of power, but tyranny connected it with the arbitrary rule of an individual, someone whose removal would eliminate the problem, whereas despotism indicated that it pervaded an entire system of government.[39]

Though this view of despotism began at the end of the reign of Louis XIV, by the end of the eighteenth century, despotism was central to the whole enterprise of libel: "From 1771 to 1789, despotism would be the main theme of *libelle* literature, one perfectly suited to the standard, scabrous details about royal orgies and *lettres de cachet*."[40]

Initial causal interpretations

The authors who reconstructed the meanings that made up the cultural atmosphere of Paris were clear in their conclusions that these meanings shaped the early moments of the revolution. Darnton explains that what the Marxist historians called the "aristocratic revolt" of 1787–88 was not, in fact, perceived as such in Paris. Rather, "contemporary Frenchmen ... did not perceive the 'aristocratic revolt'... Most of them despised Calonne and applauded the Notables' resistance to him ... the public took the parlements' side. And when [Brienne] tried to destroy the parlements, it took to the streets."[41] These events, in other words, fell into an interpretive framework developed by readers of the forbidden bestsellers of the eighteenth century. That framework centered on ministerial despotism, the incompetence of the King, and the overarching corruption of the system. It thus "helped contemporaries make sense of things" when the conflict with the *parlements* came to a head. And so, the final flourish: "That the Bastille was nearly empty and that Louis XVI desired nothing more than the welfare of his subjects did not matter in 1787 and 1788. The regime stood condemned. It has lost the final round in the long struggle to control public opinion. It had lost its legitimacy."[42]

Thus what happened in France in 1787–1789 is, according to the cultural historiography of the revolution, in part due to the invention of public opinion, and the reshaping and redefinition of the meaning and scope of royal authority. The question, however, is how to relate this kind of causal talk with the kind that prefers the more Humean, billiard-ball locutions of "triggers" and "forces."

The Force Given Form: The Financial Crisis of the State Reconsidered

Though debates over "culture" and the French Revolution continue, sociologists and historians are in fact relatively clear about one aspect of the causal explanation of the early moments of the revolutionary situation (1787–1789). That is the causal link between war, state debt, and the conflicts that ensued from the attempt by the King and his ministers to raise money to meet said debt. Here we find agreement:

> The debt accumulated by the French monarchy during the Seven Years' War and the War of American Independence precipitated the struggles of the French Revolution.[43]
>
> [R]oyal treasurers finally exhausted their capacity to raise loans from

financiers, and were forced (again) to propose reforms of the tax system. The usual resistance from the *parlements* ensued, and an expedient adopted in an attempt to circumvent it – the summoning of an Assembly of Notables in 1787 – only provided privileged interests yet another platform for voicing resistance. A last ditch effort to override the *parlements* (by Brienne in 1787–88) crumbled in the face of concerted upper-class defiance, popular demonstrations, and the unwillingness of army officers to direct forcible suppression of the popular resistance.[44]

Army and church did not cause the struggles of 1788 and 1789. All they did was contribute to the regime's feeble response. The cause lay squarely in the crown's inability to solve its fiscal problems.[45] The Old Regime state was thrown into crisis by impending bankruptcy, not by its split ideology.[46]

This is a clear example of a forcing cause, one that takes certain fixed entities to be real within the scope of the given analysis, and then watches as these entities push and pull on each other. As Tilly himself writes about his own work, "the arguments proceed as if each category were real, unitary, and unproblematic."[47] French society in 1787 has "particular structural characteristics" and these characteristics help explain what happens when tremendous "foreign pressures" are brought to bear.[48] The King can no longer borrow, so he and his ministers are "forced" to raise money by modernizing the finance system, and in particular by raiding areas of privilege that had been exempt. This leads to resistance ("push back") by the nobles.[49]

The consensus on this forcing cause is clear, but it is also incomplete. The obvious question is: what differentiates earlier financial crises from the one that precipitated the French Revolution? Tilly admits that the alliance that formed in reaction to the financial crisis was "odd": why, this time, did the opposition to the King take such a broad-based, popular form, knitting together "sinkholes of aristocratic privilege and purchased royal office … with peasants and bourgeois who railed against the expense, arbitrariness and corruption of government."[50]

The counterfactual that would be predicted by a *strictly* forcing cause account of French state finances and war-making is nicely implied by the historiographical expert on eighteenth-century French finance:

> The financial problems of the French monarchy on the eve of the Revolution might be seen, therefore, as a predictable consequence of long-standing institutional difficulties. What was not predictable was the path that the monarchy took. In 1788, instead of defaulting on part of its obligations, the monarchy convoked the Estates-General, the kingdom's representative body, which had not met for 175 years. It was this act, the calling of the Estates-General to solve a financial crisis, and not impending bankruptcy

per se, that was novel in French history. This fateful decision opened the way to a whole new era of politics, in fact, to revolution.[51]

I submit that this eventful pathway occurred because of the way the events of 1787–1789 were *shaped and formed* by the existence of "public opinion" as a politically relevant object – which had *not* been part of the landscape in 1750 or 1770 – and the atmosphere into which this latest attempt by the King's ministers to shore up the state's finances was thrust – an atmosphere of delegitimized and pornographically ridiculed royal authority. This "made the difference" between, for example, the outcome of the financial crisis of 1770 and that of 1787. More generally, it provided the arranged and significant background for action as the events of the revolution began to be strung together as a series of cause-and-effect, pushes-and-pulls.

The importance of the background for action is causal in the sense that it refers to a difference that made a difference, to a shift or change in meaning consequential for an outcome as we have identified it. Indeed, the essence of the cultural historiography of the revolution is that several shifts in the meaning of French politics had emerged, along with a rapid change in the network of pamphlets and books, and that the books themselves contained a shift in meanings and attitudes towards the monarchy. The pamphlets and books were, moreover, read with an increasing intensity as they were produced at great rates in the later eighteenth century. This intense reading shifted the cognitive and emotional relationship of many of the people in Paris towards the King; simultaneously, "public opinion" became a potential source of political legitimacy for French notables, even if no one yet knew how to measure it.

But as I describe the shift, note that none of these make sense without the whole, and they certainly could not have *forced* anything to happen *inside the state* by themselves. Rather, they are parts of the whole atmosphere of meaning that could give shape to "social forces": first during the resistance of nobles to the King and his ministers that was supported by the lower parts of the social hierarchy in Paris, and again when the Bastille was stormed, thus "inventing" revolution by combining popular violence with reasoned legitimacy in the name of "the people."[52]

Note, finally, how this cause that "gave form to" the events of the French Revolution came to be: through an assemblage of heterogeneous things, not a regularized process or even a conjunction of regularized processes. Rather, some mechanistic things happened, some manifestly singular things happened, some "material" things happened, some "ideal" things happened, and it was all networked together via a series of "alliances" – between printing, pornography, and philosophy, for example. Out of the whole mess came an assemblage, an arrangement of meaning and material that guided the actions that became the French Revolution.

Culture as a forcing cause?

At this point, it should be relatively clear that under the rubric of "culture," many historians of the French Revolution arrived at a conclusion concerning what I am here calling "forming causes." And an unsympathetic reader might be inclined to read this entire debate/debacle as really one between economics and culture, or perhaps between Marx and Durkheim. But in fact, there is one final note to make about the cultural turn in the historiography of the French Revolution, and it is one that speaks directly to the distinction between forcing and forming causes, and the possibility of a hermeneutic approach to sociohistorical analysis.

The authors of the cultural turn in studies of the French Revolution (Baker, Darnton, Chartier, Sewell, Hunt) have many theoretical differences between them.[53] What they share, however, is an overwhelming tendency to reach for a form of causal talk that is explicitly *non-mechanistic*. Chartier, for example, attacks any notion of a "direct" causal connection between the *content* of the works of forbidden literature and a shift in beliefs that undermined the legitimacy of the *ancien régime*. He writes:

> The images in the libels and in the topical pamphlets were not graven into the soft wax of their readers' minds, and reading did not necessarily lead to belief. If a connection existed between the massive distribution of an aggressively disrespectful pamphlet literature and the destruction of the image of the monarchy, it was doubtless neither direct nor ineluctable.[54]

Darnton, for his part, claims that Baker is insufficiently subtle because he imposes a model of discourse that is overly determinate and perhaps anti-humanistic.[55]

To what is all this critique directed? It is relatively clear, in fact, that it is directed at an earlier cultural historiography that posited culture as a *forcing* rather than *forming* cause. For this earlier work, the causal importance of culture was to be identified by the push-and-pull of "values" on "action." And in this particular understanding, the cultural hypothesis failed. For, while intellectual historians have long been fond of noting certain "writer-philosophes" or men of letters who also participated in the Constituent Assembly, a careful analysis of the writings of the members of the Assembly led to the conclusion that "in the end, the Constituents who had participated in the 'Republic of Letters' prior to 1789 represented only a small minority, about one-twelfth of the Assembly's membership." Timothy Tackett thus casts significant doubt upon the degree to which, say, the "values" of the Enlightenment were direct, *forcing* motivators of what assemblymen did, or, say, whether "reading Rousseau" could *force* someone to "become revolutionary." Note, however, that even Tackett admits that references to "reason" and "natural rights" began to appear later on in 1789 in certain member's writings, and thus concludes that there may have been some influence on the Assembly by "their more intellectual colleagues."[56] This indicates a movement *away* from attempts to render meaning a forcing cause, and an embrace of an understanding of its work as inhering in forming causality.

DISCUSSION: HOW TO THINK ABOUT FORMING CAUSES[57]

In pointing to these arrangements of materiality and meaning, the analysts of the French Revolution articulated precisely that which, in one way or another, has been the occupation of hermeneutic philosophy, interpretive sociology, and symbolic anthropology for many academic generations. The invention of public opinion is the "condition of intelligibility" for calling the Estates General; the delegitimation of the King via printed pornography provides part of the moral and aesthetic background against which the storming of the Bastille can occur and be lauded as an expression of popular sovereignty. In this sense, these historians operate in the universe of Clifford Geertz and Susan Bordo, examining the public documents of discourse to infer the anatomy of a shifting worldview. However, they do so in a way that engages the enduring questions of causality and plausible worlds of sociohistorical analysis. As such, their work is particularly useful for understanding the possibility of interpretive explanation. What does their analysis reveal about the difference between forming and forcing causes, as I have termed them here? I see four essential ways in which these causes depart from the standard understanding of cause in social science.

Lack of Fixed Entities

Forming causes address not how kinds, objects, and forces push and pull on each other, but rather how kinds, objects and forces came to be in the first place, or have their meaning and significance fundamentally changed. Public opinion *becomes* a social kind – first as a category of politically inflected language, and then as the disputed reference for that category. Meanwhile, what it means to *have a fiscal crisis in the state* is fundamentally different in 1789 than it was in 1750, because the "atmosphere" created by the pamphlets and forbidden bestsellers inflects crisis with a new set of meanings, including the system-wide corruption and despotism of the King's men.

An Eventful Approach to History

In examining the formation and modulation of kinds, one is presented with a world subject to an "eventful" revision of its causal laws, precisely because the entities and the atmospheres in which they act are fundamentally variable. Thus the calling of the Estates General to solve the fiscal crisis, and the "invention" of revolution at the Bastille opens up a new political ontology, with very different meanings, definitions, and possibilities.[58]

Assemblage

The forming cause piece of the causal story of the French Revolution is not reliably tractable as "micro" or "macro," or as following rules of aggregation and emergence familiar from social theories that take the individual as the fundamental unit of analysis. Rather, the atmosphere of the revolution was created by a network of objects (printing presses, pamphlets in circulation), meanings (the content of such pamphlets, the emergent legitimacy of "public opinion"), political devices and tools available within the current system (the calling of the estates general), and beliefs in certain sectors of the French nobility (the entitlement to "liberty" felt deeply by "notables"). In forming causes, in other words, the *emergence* of new kinds is not something that happens from a lower level to a higher level so much as it occurs across "levels," it is, when it comes to levels and entities, ontologically promiscuous.

Dynamic Nominalism

Ian Hacking refers to his species of investigation as one in which he traces the interaction between the name and the named, and Baker's argument about public opinion certainly fits with this.[59] This interaction is evident at key moments in the revolution: the calling of the Estates General was interpretable in terms of, but also gives new meaning to, "public opinion;" while Jones argues about the *Affiches* that the papers could "could claim to embody as well as represent that 'public opinion' whose importance recent historians have not been slow to emphasize."[60] That "public opinion" could be so contested in its referents and meanings is precisely the point of Hacking's dynamic nominalism.

BREAKING THE BREAK: HERMENEUTICS AND SOCIOHISTORICAL ANALYSIS

In the Anglophone tradition of thinking about the history, causality, and society, the legacy of J. S. Mill dominated that of William Whewell in the twentieth century. The mirror image of this is the break Hans Georg-Gadamer made with the project of Wilhelm Dilthey in *Truth and Method,* thereby eschewing the project of explanation, and with it, most of social science. This reading was reinforced because it was shared, in its broad outlines, by Gadamer's debating opponent Jürgen Habermas. The essence of this reading of Dilthey was that, first, Dilthey's hermeneutics was a psychologism that rested on an unsustainable concept of empathetic feeling; second, Dilthey's hermeneutics alternated wildly between an implausible capturing of the subjective soul or intention of the author and an "objectivist" or even "Cartesian" attempt to develop a sovereign perspective on all of history; thirdly, that, trapped inside these nineteenth-century prisms, Dilthey expressed a devotion to "method" that was scientism by another name.[61]

Through the work of Austin Harrington, this understanding of Dilthey has been revealed as flawed in the sense that it grasps *neither* the relational meaning of Dilthey's work vis-à-vis his contemporaries *nor* the core ideas of his vision for the human sciences. In particular, Dilthey, first, countered psychologism with an understanding of *Geist* which was a prologue to the twentieth century view of cultural or discursive formations as text-analogues; second, did engage in the idea of using general theory, but did so to articulate a project of historical explanation that we would recognize now as concrete and historically bounded – connected to questions such as "What were the origins of the French Revolution?"; third, did not really mean *method* in the sense that was fetishized in American social science in the twentieth century.[62]

This suggests an opening in hermeneutics to ask questions about meaning, cause and effect. Interestingly, a parallel opening may be emerging in sociology. Certainly, the field of comparative-historical sociology has expressed deep discontent with Millsian conceptualizations of social science. In sociology more broadly, there has been a partial unsettlement of the notion of causality. In a variety of recent texts, sociology is understood to have reconsidered its overwhelming dependence on specific statistical techniques, and in particular, logistic regression, to make causal or quasi-causal claims. Thus, in the field today, there is a reconsideration of a wide variety of philosophical issues concerning how to think about explanation, including events and eventfulness, the meaning and utility of counterfactuals, necessity and sufficiency in causal analysis, and different understandings of what constitutes explanation.[63]

This unsettlement means that the line between history and sociology can no longer be easily assimilated into a simple version of the ideographic/nomothetic distinction. And it is precisely in such a moment that the core ideas of hermeneutics can be helpful. For example, hermeneutics provides a language with which to think about how in human science the goal is often to "illustrate the general significance that resides *within* each chosen case."[64] Furthermore, the concept of a virtuous hermeneutic circle offers an alternative to hypothesis testing in social science that does not dispense with responsibility to evidence or the idea that one interpretation can be judged to be superior to another.

Given these shifts in intellectual context, the issue of explanation and understanding looks different. Since Max Weber, much of the debate about interpretation and explanation in the human sciences has focused on the action inside the actor's head; on what I have here termed final causes as motives. A vast literature exists here, which concerns the possibility of interpreting individuals in a way that gets at the core of their subjectivity. Hence the essential questions: Are reasons causes? Should we start with the presumption of rationality, and infer the degree to which actors' understandings depart from it? If we say that someone is driven by an unconscious motive, are we in effect telling them they have false consciousness? In contrast to this, the questions I have asked here are: How can we characterize discursive formations as causal? What sort of power do we want to ascribe to them? And how does materiality play a role? In my view, this is part of the way forward for hermeneutics in the twenty-first century.

It is towards this end that I have drawn a single, and crude, distinction between forcing and forming causality in this chapter. In doing so, I hope to have rendered explicit something that is implicit in the best sociohistorical practice. To grasp the vagaries of causality in human life, we need an understanding of causality far more expansive than has heretofore been dominant. For human action is too weighted with significance to be understood only as subject to efficient causes. To put the matter paradoxically, for hermeneutics, arrangements of meaning may be efficacious without being efficient.

NOTES

1. Andreas Glaeser, *Political Epistemics: The Secret Police, the Opposition, and the End of East German Socialism* (Chicago: University of Chicago Press, 2011).
2. Paul Ricoeur, "What is a text? Explanation and Understanding," in *Hermeneutics and the Human Sciences: Essays on Language, Action, and Interpretation* (New York: Cambridge University Press, 1981); Paul Roth, "Interpretation as Explanation," in David R. Hiley, James Bohman, and Richard Schusterman, eds., *The Interpretive Turn: Philosophy, Science, Culture* (Ithaca, NY: Cornell University Press, 1991). Gurpeet Mahajan, *Explanation and Understanding in the Human Sciences* (Delhi: Oxford University Press, 1997).
3. William H. Dray, "'Explaining What' in History," in May Broadbeck, ed., *Readings in the Philosophy of the Social Sciences* (New York: Macmillan, 1968), pp. 343–8.
4. Max Weber, *Economy and Society: An Outline of Interpretive Sociology* (Berkeley: University of California Press, 1978).
5. Aristotle, *The Basic Works of Aristotle*, edited by Richard McKeon (New York: Random House, 1941).
6. Howard Engelskirchen, "The Aristotelian Marx and Scientific Realism: A Perspective on Social Kinds in Social Theory" (Ph.D. diss., State Universtity of New York at Binghamton, 2007).
7. Georgio Agamben, *Homo Sacer: Sovereign Power and Bare Life* (Palo Alto: Stanford University Press, 1998).
8. Bent Flyvberg, *Making Social Science Matter: Why Social Inquiry Fails and How it Can Succeed Again* (New York: Cambridge University Press, 2001).
9. Donald N. Levine, *Visions of the Sociological Tradition* (Chicago: University of Chicago Press, 1995).
10. Levine writes that, "methods geared to the demonstration of universal propositions are therefore out of place in the practical sciences," *Visions*, p. 109.
11. Ibid. p. 108.
12. Ibid. p. 112.
13. Ibid. p. 112.
14. Ibid. p. 113.
15. Charles Tilly, *Regimes and Repertoires* (Chicago: University of Chicago Press, 2006).
16. Levine, *Visions*, p. 124.
17. Bruno Latour, *Reassembling the Social: An Introduction to Actor-Network-Theory* (New York: Oxford University Press, 2007); Jim Johnson, "Mixing Humans with Non-Humans: Sociology of a Door-Closer," *Social Problems* 35, pp. 298–310 (1988). [Jim Johnson was a pen name for Bruno Latour.]

18. Donald Davidson, "Problems in the Explanation of Action," in *Problems of Rationality* (New York: Oxford University Press, 2004), pp. 101–16; Isaac Ariail Reed, *Interpretation and Social Knowledge: On the use of theory in the human sciences* (Chicago: University of Chicago Press, 2011), pp. 135–53.
19. Alasdair MacIntyre, "The Intelligibility of Action," in J. Margolis, M. Krausz and R. M. Burian, eds., *Rationality, Relativism, and the Human Sciences* (Boston: Martinus Nijhoff Publishers, 1986), p. 64.
20. Ibid. pp. 64–5.
21. Ibid. p. 66.
22. John Law, 2007. "Actor Network Theory and Material Semiotics." http://www.heterogeneities.net/publications/Law2007ANTandMaterialSemiotics.pdf (last updated 25th April 2007); Manuel DeLanda, *A New Philosophy of Society: Assemblage Theory and Social Complexity* (New York: Bloomsbury, 2006).
23. Richard Rorty, "Inquiry as Recontextualization: An Anti-Dualist Account of Interpretation," in David R. Hiley, James Bohman, and Richard Schusterman, eds, *The Interpretive Turn: Philosophy, Science, and Culture* (Ithaca, NY: Cornell Univeristy Press, 1991), pp. 59–80; Clifford Geertz, "Thick Description: Toward an Interpretive Theory of Culture," in *The Interpretation of Cultures* (New York: Basic Books, 2000).
24. Monika Krause and Michael Guggenheim, "How facts travel: The model systems of sociology" *Poetics* 40(2), pp. 101–17 (2012).
25. Roger Chartier, *The Cultural Origins of the French Revolution* (Durham, NC: Duke University Press, 1991), pp. 67–91; Robert Darnton, *The Forbidden Best-Sellers of Pre-Revolutionary France* (New York: W.W. Norton & Co., 1995), pp. 169–246.
26. Theda Skocpol, "Cultural Idioms and Political Ideologies in the Revolutionary Reconstruction of State Power: A Rejoinder to Sewell." *Journal of Modern History* 57 (1) pp. 86–96 (1985); William Sewell, Jr. "Ideologies and Social Revolutions: Reflections on the French Case." *Journal of Modern History* 57 (1) pp. 57–85 (1985).
27. Keith Baker, *Inventing the French Revolution* (New York: Cambridge University Press, 1990), p. 170.
28. Ibid. p. 187.
29. Ibid. p. 172.
30. Ibid. p. 188, 194.
31. W. I. Thomas and D. S. Thomas, *The Child in America: Behavior problems and programs* (New York: Knopf, 1928), p. 572.
32. Baker, *Inventing the French Revolution*, p. 172.
33. The initial model of "intellectual origins" of the revolution was, as both Chartier and Darnton agree, "diffusionist" and top down. In his classic *The Intellectual Origins of the French Revolution*, Daniel Mornet traced the spread of philosophical ideas, and ultimately what he liked to call "intelligence," through various institutions, examining, for example,

what was taught in schools, increases in readership, and the growth of the Freemasons. Lacking a concept of "field" or "discourse," however, Mornet dichotomized "ideas and principles" and "pragmatic action" in an unfortunate way; the inheritors of his project in the 1990s set themselves the task of reconsidering these "origins" from an updated theoretical perspective.

34. For printing and the theory of ideological infrastructures and its applicability in pre-revolutionary France, see Michael Mann, *Sources of Social Power, volume 2* (New York: Cambridge University Press, 1993), pp. 175–6 and 36–7; For printing and distribution structures in the provinces for "under the cloak" literature, see Darnton, *Forbidden Bestsellers*, pp. 22–82; For the growing importance of a literary market and its consequences, see Geoffrey Turnovsky, *The Literary Market: Authorship and Modernity in the Old Regime* (Philadelphia: University of Pennsylvania Press, 2010); For quantitative figures on the orders of clandestine literature in the run up to revolution, see Robert Darnton, *The Corpus of Clandestine Literature in France, 1769-1789* (New York: W.W. Norton & Co., 1995).
35. Colin Jones, "The Great Chain of Buying: Medical Advertisement, the Bourgeois Public Sphere, and the Origins of the French Revolution" *American Historical Review* 101 (1), pp. 13–40 (1996).
36. Darnton, *Forbidden Bestsellers*, pp. 115–36.
37. Chartier, *Cultural Origins*, p. 91.
38. Darnton, *Forbidden Bestsellers*, p. 213.
39. Ibid. p. 213.
40. Ibid. p. 214.
41. Ibid. p. 243.
42. Ibid. p. 246.
43. Charles Tilly, *Coercion, Capital, and European States: AD 990–1992* (Cambridge MA: Blackwell, 1992), p. 186.
44. Theda Skocpol, "France, Russia, China: A structural analysis of social revolutions," *Comparative Studies in Society and History* 18(2), pp. 175–210 (1976), p. 188.
45. Michael Mann, *Sources of Social Power, Volume 2*, p. 179.
46. Sewell, "Ideologies", pp. 66–7. Anticipating the kinds of arguments I make here based on the cultural historiography of the revolution, Sewell continues on to write that "once the crisis had begun, ideological contradictions contributed mightily to the deepening of the crisis into revolution." Forming causes are a useful category, in part, because they help specify how something could "contribute mightily" to a revolution without *forcing* it to happen.
47. Tilly, *Coercion, Capital, and European States*, p. 35.
48. Skocpol, "France, Russia, China," p. 182.
49. This forcing cause is itself the product, in these accounts, of the *conjuncture* of two earlier forcing causes (and thus the utility of conjunctural

causality to historical sociology becomes quite concrete): (1) the imperial war-making of the French state in competition with other European states (a cause which became more powerful as England developed economically (see Skocpol "France, Russia, China," 179–80)), and (2) a series of money-raising procedures, such as venality, that worked in the short term but which, over the longer term, were disastrous: "each time the state raised money in one of these ways, furthermore, it created another walled-off pool of privilege that would be harder to drain for new money in the future" (Charles Tilly, *European Revolutions: 1492–1992* [Wiley-Blackwell, 1996], p. 162).

50. Tilly, *European Revolutions*, p. 163.
51. Gail Bossenga, "Financial Origins of the French Revolution," pp. 37–66 in Thomas E. Kaiser and Dale K. Van Kley, editors, *From Deficit to Deluge: The Origins of the French Revolution* (Palo Alto: Stanford University Press, 2011), p. 38.
52. William Sewell, Jr. "Historical Events as Transformations of Structures: Inventing Revolution at the Bastille" in *Logics of History: Social Theory and Social Transformation* (Chicago: University of Chicago Press, 2005), pp. 225–70.
53. Specifically, Darnton takes a more Geertzian position vis-à-vis "culture," Baker prefers arguing for the autonomy of "discourse" (thus implicitly engaging Althusser and Marxism), Chartier uses a theory of "representation" and is influenced by Habermas' theory of the public sphere, Sewell identifies a dialectic between action and structure taken from the social theory of Anthony Giddens, and Hunt focuses on the Durkheimian notion of "collective representations."
54. Chartier, *Cultural Origins*, p. 83.
55. Darnton, *Forbidden Bestsellers*, p. 176.
56. Timothy Tackett, *Becoming a Revolutionary: The Deputies of the French National Assembly and the Emergence of a Revolutionary Culture (1789–1790)* (Princeton: Princeton University Press, 1996), p. 65.
57. The following fourfold distinction was developed by myself and Daniel Hirschman, and thus this section is in dialogue with Daniel Hirschman and Isaac Ariail Reed, "Formation Stories and Causality in Sociology," *Sociological Theory*, 32 (4), pp. 259–82 (2014). The discussion here emphasizes the hermeneutic dimensions of the concept and their relationship to cultural history, whereas Hirschman and Reed are more concerned with the formation of objects and kinds, engaging field theory and Actor Network Theory directly.
58. Francois Furet, *Interpreting the French Revolution* (New York: Cambridge University Press, 1981), pp. 77–9; Sewell, "Historical Events as Transformations of Structures," p. 267.
59. Ian Hacking, *Historical Ontology* (Cambridge, MA: Harvard University Press, 1996); Ian Hacking, "The looping effects of human kinds," in Dan Sperber, David Prernack, Ann James Premack, editors, *Causal cognition:*

A multidisciplinary approach (New York: Oxford University Press, 1995), pp. 351–83. In the twentieth century, public opinion became a classic instance of a "looping kind." Sarah E. Igo, *The Averaged American: Surveys, Citizens, and the Making of a Mass Public* (Cambridge, MA: Harvard University Press, 2007).

60. Jones, "Great Chain of Buying," p. 39.
61. Wilhelm Dilthey, "The Construction of the Historical World in the Human Studies," in H. P. Rickman, ed., *Dilthey: Selected Writings* (New York: Cambridge University Press, 1976), pp. 170–245. Wilhelm Dilthey, *Selected Works, Volume 4: Hermeneutics and the Study of History* (Princeton: Princeton University Press, 1996); Hans-Georg Gadamer, *Truth and Method* (New York: Continuum Publishing Company, 1989, Second Edn). Jürgen Habermas, *Knowledge and Human Interests* (Boston: Beacon Press, 1971).
62. Austin Harrington, explains that, by *Geist*, Dilthey meant, "not some reified mental substance but a complex of relationships between practices, experience and signifying activities." Austin Harrington, "Dilthey, Empathy and Verstehen: A Contemporary Reappraisal," *European Journal of Social Theory* 4(3), pp. 311–29, p. 323. See also Austin Harrington, "Objectivism in Hermeneutics? Gadamer, Habermas, Dilthey." *Philosophy of the Social Sciences* 30, no. 4 (2000), pp. 491–507; Austin Harrington, "In Defence of *Verstehen* and *Erklären*: Wilhelm Dilthey's *Ideas Concerning a Descriptive and Analytical Psychology*." *Theory and Psychology*. 10(4), pp. 435–51, 2000.
63. Andrew Abbott, *Time Matters: On Theory and Method* (Chicago: University of Chicago Press, 2001); Richard Biernacki, *Reinventing Evidence in Social Inquiry: Decoding Facts and Variables* (London: Palgrave-Macmillan, 2012). Gary Goertz and James Mahoney, *A Tale of Two Cultures: Contrasting Qualitative and Quantitative Paradigms* (Princeton: Princeton University Press, 2012). Kristin Luker, *Salsa Dancing into the Social Sciences: Research in an Age of Info-glut* (Cambridge, MA: Harvard University Press, 2008); George Steinmetz, editor, *The Politics of Method in the Human Sciences: Positivism and Its Epistemological Others* (Durham, NC: Duke University Press 2005).
64. Harrington, "In Defence of *Verstehen* and *Erklären*," p. 446.

3 The Anarchy of Hermeneutics: Interpretation as a Vital Practice

SANTIAGO ZABALA

> *Hermeneutics is "anarchic" in Reiner Schürmann's sense of this word; it does not try to assault its Sache but rather tries to grant what is singular and unrepeatable an open field.*
>
> Gerald L. Bruns, *Hermeneutics*, 1995

The twenty-first century has inherited from Hans-Georg Gadamer a philosophical stance that is continuously overcoming itself, that is, whose applications and consequences he could not have foreseen. While some interpreters[1] consider hermeneutics recent feminist,[2] political,[3] environmental,[4] or aesthetic[5] postmodern developments foreign to Gadamer's philosophical project, others instead believe they are bound to his thought. After all, there are several indications in his writings that he predicted and probably also wished to see these developments for hermeneutics. One of these signs is his definition of the classics. As he pointed out in *Truth and Method*[6] it's not the source or origin that makes a classic but rather its effects and consequences, that is, those uncontrollable features that also constitute its nature. For those of us who consider the effects and consequences of hermeneutics, like classics, more significant than its origin, inheriting Gadamer's philosophy of interpretation does not mean conserving the discipline's established history and essence but rather developing new directions in order to continue the dialogue (or conversation)[7] he always sought.

This is also evident in the different interpretations that have been given to Gadamer's own history of hermeneutics and that reveal how its origins cannot be established once and for all but must always be sought through diverse interpretations.[8] While some histories situate the creation of philosophical hermeneutics in the seventeenth century, when Johann Dannhauer introduced for the first time the Latin word "*hermeneutica*" as a necessary requirement for those sciences that relied on the interpretation of texts, others proclaim that it was formed two centuries earlier by Flacius, in *Clavis scripturae sacrae*, or even centuries earlier by Aristotle, in his treatise *Peri hermeneias* (*De interpretatione*). It is probably for these reasons that Gianni Vattimo recently pointed out how:

> The history of modern hermeneutics, and, so far as we can imagine, also its future, is a history of 'excess' – of the transgression of limits, or, to use another idiom, the history of a continuous 'overflowing.' From its origins as an inquiry into the understanding of the texts of the past, it developed into a general philosophy of existence, and then into the only possibly ontology.[9]

While this analysis might raise doubts that there is such a thing as an origin, a history, or any unified development of hermeneutics, it also indicates the discipline's anarchic essence, its opposition to the established Gadamerian historical canon. Even though this canon allowed hermeneutics to become a respected philosophical discipline, it has also restricted its militant or anarchic nature. This restriction has allowed the discipline to expand and to be protected within the academy, but it is also attributable to the conservative political views of its major representatives (Heidegger, Paul Ricoeur, and Gadamer).[10] Nonetheless, now that hermeneutics has become an established philosophical arena whose history and essence have been studied substantially, its anarchic nature can finally be analyzed without damaging its academic reputation.

The goal of this essay is not simply to craft a new interpretation of the origins of hermeneutics but also to outline its anarchic essence. Anarchy, as Reiner Schürmann explains, means absence of rule, but not absence of rules.[11] This is why as a resistance to principles, conventions, and categories anarchy is not the end of hermeneutics but its foundation. The plurality of interpretations that hermeneutics relies upon is not a metaphysical foundation but an ontological condition where achievements are measured not in relation to factual truths but to ontological events. As an existential stance, hermeneutics in the twenty-first century becomes a philosophy that creates alterations, shocks, and disruptions that allow us to overcome metaphysical impositions. In this way, Gadamer's philosophy of interpretation has given birth to an interpretation of philosophy, that is, a concern not only for those concepts we cannot overcome (Being, truth, identity) but also for those we must endorse (difference, alterity, emergency).

While very few authors have described hermeneutics as an anarchic venture, there are several thinkers throughout history who have used interpretation to revolt, to alter social conditions. Even though not all of these examples justify interpreting the essence of interpretation as "anarchic," an investigation of their works may well open the way

The Anarchy of Hermeneutics: Interpretation as a Vital Practice 69

to new fruitful directions for philosophic disciplines as well as politics and culture at large. I will explore the hermeneutic dimensions of three historical figures – Martin Luther, Sigmund Freud, and Thomas Kuhn – whose hermeneutic operation was meant to overcome ecclesiastic and scientific impositions and disclose their militant ethos. I will complete this brief exploration of a hermeneutic anarchy with the thought of Gianni Vattimo, who explicitly emphasized interpretation's "militant," "terrorist," and "communist" vocation in his recent work.[12]

Luther's hermeneutic operation was directed against the hegemony of the Catholic Church's magisterial establishment, which pretended to be the only valid interpreter of the biblical text. His *Ninety-Five Theses* (1517) and translation of the Bible into German (1534) provoked a general political revolt against the papacy because until then the ecclesiastical hierarchy had forced every believer to turn to its officials for readings, interpretations, and elucidations of the text. Against such spiritual, cultural, and political dominion Luther instead believed that the literal meaning of the Bible contained its own proper spiritual significance, which should be interpreted by each believer: the Bible is *per se certissima, apertissima, sui ipsius interpres, omnium omnia probans, indicans et illuminans*; that is, "it interprets itself." In asserting this, Luther was valorizing both the linguistic text and one's own linguistic practice, the interpreter's capacity to judge for herself. If, as Luther said, "Scripture is not understood, unless it is brought home, that is, experienced," then interpretation cannot be dictated from above and must be experienced from within. Interpretation is part of existence because by bringing new vitality to the text, it also reinforces the interpreter's own faith.

For these among other reasons, Luther decided to translate the Bible, a translation that brought about a revolutionary political operation through hermeneutics, that is, from the vital nature of interpretation. He transformed it from a foreign book in a foreign tongue, accessible only through an establishment imposed from above, into a document that could be read without the permission or intervention of the Catholic Church and was open for all literate people's interpretation. With Luther's impact in Germany comparable to, if not greater than, that of Dante in Italy or Rousseau in France, Hegel could affirm that if Luther had done nothing besides this translation, he would still be one of the greatest benefactors of the German-speaking people. Although the traditions of the Church should not be put aside, since they are also an effect of the Bible's history, Luther should be recognized for his political action, that is, for depriving for the first time the Roman pontifex of his absolute authority over the Bible. By recognizing everyone's right to interpret for himself, Luther exercised the latent anarchic nature of interpretation.

As Luther's hermeneutic operation began as a rejection of ecclesiastical imposition, so Freud's psychological revolution was set in motion in order to overcome the imposed facts of the positivist scientific culture of the early twentieth century. One of his chief targets was the empiricist theory of modern science, which conceived the human mind as a *tabula rasa*, a blank surface upon which impressions could be inscribed and from which descriptions could be made. This scientific understanding of the mind, common also to Descartes, presupposed certain moral values that were supposed to find a correlative in the social world the mind inhabited; in other words, objectivity prevailed over the subject, which was considered merely a mirror of nature. Against these common beliefs of modern science, Freud suggested that our actions are motivated not by pure, rational, and logical mechanisms but rather by many different unknown forces, motives, and impulses constantly clashing within and between our conscious and unconscious minds. For these reasons, familiar forms of irrationality such as self-deception, depression, ambivalence, or even weakness of the will, all of which were problematic in the Cartesian model of invisible unitary consciousness, became in Freud part of the normal manner of human beings. Freud anarchically transgressed the accepted line of demarcation between the "rational/normal" and the "irrational/abnormal" human being.

However, Freud did not limit his discoveries to explaining the normality of the "abnormal," which by itself produced great progress for civilization. He also emphasized how the dynamically interchangeable relation between the conscious and subconscious is the same as that of the human being and his society. In this structure, problems might emerge from oppressed instincts (imposed from above by society), from unconscious determinations (death or sexual drives upwelling from within), or from their objective interpretations, in other words, from the positivist psychologies of the time. These psychologies held that a patient's suffering came only from objective ignorance, in other words, from a lack of information about his own life. If this were actually true, then a better description of the patient's dreams would be enough to cure him. But the mind implies unconscious factors that not only determine conscious ones but also reject the expression of certain mental states. In this condition, interpretation is required to inform the patient of those memories he has repressed. Therefore, interpretation is the only available approach to the human mind and to those non-objective, unconscious factors that demonstrate that the mind cannot be considered a *tabula rasa*. Against the traditional "dream book" mode of interpretation in terms of fixed symbols, Freud applied "free association," which obliged the patient (not the interpreter) to report hidden or forgotten thoughts. The emancipation that Freud brought about by stressing unconscious mental processes and the analysis of the human psyche through the vital exercise of interpretation spread irreversible doubts about the objective formation of human rationality.

In opposition to the rationalist psychologies of the epoch, in 1900 Freud published *The Interpretation of Dreams*, which recognized, among other things, how conscious, reflective meditation cannot be imposed on dreams because they are "the royal road to knowledge of the unconscious." This is a road that descriptive psychologies are incapable of traveling because they limit themselves to present, consciously recalled expressions of the dream. Even though Freud has not received enough recognition in the histories of hermeneutics, his project was really a development and radicalization of the previous psychological hermeneutics of Schleiermacher and Dilthey, who doubted that the author of a work would be able to reconstruct its meaning if informed of all the techniques used to produce it. Just as a complete reconstruction of a patient's life would not necessarily solve his problems, the history of the production of a work of art could not explain the meaning of the work to the author. As Jürgen Habermas rightly notes, Freud goes beyond the art of interpretation insofar as his system of analysis must grasp "not only the meaning of a possible distorted text, but the *meaning of the text-distortion itself.*"[13]

American scientist Thomas Kuhn also used the anarchic vein of interpretation to free his field of research from objectivism. But unlike Luther and Freud, neither of whom defined their own work as "hermeneutic," Kuhn explicitly recognized in various autobiographical passages the fundamental effects that the philosophy of interpretation exercised over his innovative view of scientific revolutions. For this reason, Richard J. Bernstein saw in Kuhn one of the first examples of "the recovery of the hermeneutical dimension of science," that is, its interpretative nature.[14]

When Kuhn published *The Structure of Scientific Revolutions* in 1962, logical empiricism's dominion over the philosophy of science was unquestionable. Scientific innovation could come only from an accumulation of knowledge, that is, as a closer approximation to the truth than any earlier theory achieved. But this normative orientation, by presupposing truth as the only common measure of scientific development, not only discredited the history of science but also considered it useless because it just indicated past errors. For logical empiricism, these historical changes were nothing more than the account of uniform progress toward better science, but for Kuhn they were a confirmation that science is not uniform but shifts through different phases. But in these shifts, the sciences are not so much making "progress toward truth" as "changing paradigms"; in other words, older theories become different rather than incorrect. Kuhn explained this relation to previous scientific theories with his idea of "incommensurability," which he shared with Paul Feyerabend: sciences driven by different paradigms do not share any common measures because the standards of evaluation are themselves subject to change. Incommensurability, then, is interpretation. If this were not the case, then ancient, medieval, and contemporary scientists would all have deduced the same results when looking at the moon. Instead, every epoch has brought about its own scientific progress through different, incommensurable paradigms.

For Kuhn scientific progress is really an alternation between what he called "normal," "revolutionary," and "extraordinary" phases of science. While "normal science" is very much like puzzle solving, where success depends on whether the rules are strictly followed, "revolutionary science" instead involves the revision of these beliefs and methods, and this inevitably detaches it from normal science and shifts science into its "extraordinary" phase. This detachment (or revolution) takes place when a dominant paradigm is left behind and when universally recognized scientific achievements that for a long period of time provided the model of problems, methods, and solutions for a community of scientists to reach a crisis. Such crises become evident when anomalies and discrepancies resist the expected solutions of normal scientific experiments, making progress impossible. In this condition, the very paradigm that has guided normal science until then is questioned, and when a rival paradigm emerges, "extraordinary science" is the result. But Kuhn does not consider this rival paradigm a mere substitution for the previous one because at first it will allow only a certain amount of progress, which must still be accepted by the community of scientists. Kuhn calls this phase a "pre-paradigm," that is, a paradigm lacking the consensus the previously normal science could depend upon. But once a larger number of scientific communities begin to accept the new paradigm, collective progress will again be possible, making science ready for new puzzle solutions. The conclusion that derives from Kuhn's hermeneutic intuitions is twofold: first, truth is not the main concern that drives scientific progress, and, second, scientific knowledge does not change through confrontation with hard facts but through a social struggle between contending interpretations of scientific communities.

As we can see, Luther's revolt against the Roman pontifical authority and Freud's dismantling of traditional psychology's rational constitution of the mind are not very different from Kuhn's transgression against the dominion of logical empiricism over science's unilinear development. Interpretation, for these three authors, was not a tool to revolt, dismantle, and transgress but rather the very practice of revolution, dismantling, and transgression. Their theoretical operation was both anarchic (for resisting conventions, structures, and principles) and hermeneutic (because they presuppose the possibility and project of interpreting differently and right to interpret differently). For these thinkers, together with other radical figures such as Friedrich Schleiermacher and Luigi Pareyson, interpretation is a vital practice, that is, an action in contrast to the conservative impositions that constituted the beliefs, ideologies, and philosophies of an epoch. For this reason, Wilhelm Dilthey (who was the first to trace systematically the history of hermeneutics) saw in the vitalist essence of hermeneutics the priority of interpretation over scientific inquiry, theoretical criticism, and literary construction.

In the twenty-first century the anarchic origins and essence of hermeneutics I have been trying to expose have not only aligned themselves with Heidegger's ontology of event but also become politically militant. This is particularly evident in the work of Vattimo. In his latest books and essays the Italian philosopher has moved further away from Gadamer's canon in order to recuperate the transgressive and anarchic vein of hermeneutics.[15] According to Vattimo, the emphasis on religion and politics one often sees in contemporary hermeneutics is not only a development of Gadamer's extra-methodical experience of truth but also of the original transgressions of hermeneutics, as Plato pointed out in the *Ion* (534e) and *Symposium* (202e). Although Plato presents hermeneutics as a theory of reception and as a practice for transmission and mediation, Hermes is accused of anarchy because the messages he transmitted were never accurate; in other words, his translations and interpretations always altered the original meanings. But more than an error, Vattimo believes, Hermes' alteration is the real contribution of interpretation, which, unlike descriptions that pursue the ideal of total explanation, adds new vitality to the original meaning.

Even though in the past hermeneutics always had a significant weight as the theory and practice of the interpretation of laws and sacred scriptures, today it "can no longer be presented . . . as an innocent theory of the interpretative character of every experience of truth"; there is much more at stake according to the Italian thinker.[16] For example, instead of pointing out the difference between the "*Geisteswissenschaften*" (the "human" or "spiritual" sciences) and the "*Naturwissenschaften*" (the natural sciences), hermeneutics must display to what extent it can provide vital answers against the exclusive and violent impositions of neoliberal policies in our framed democracies. The problem of these democracies and policies is that they are determined by the triumph of technology in which science becomes an instrument of oppression, control, and policing:

Here "policing" takes many different forms: the "policing" of thought (notably the proponents of analytic epistemology), the "policing" of the leading classes (consider the "neorealism" of the major academic journals, as well as of the international "mainstream" media), the "policing" of governments (in the form, for instance, of cultural policies "compliant with the current order'" "neutral" audit and assurance exercises and processes, or "objective" evaluation of scientific productivity – the latter, starting from the privilege of English, represent a continuation of old imperialist and colonialist policies by other means).

While many find that this metaphysical organization of the world has created a state of exception, Vattimo, following Heidegger, instead believes we are in a condition where "the only emergency is the lack of emergency," that is, of events. In this condition hermeneutics, understood as an ontological stance striving for existence, takes the form of a political or, at least, existential commitment, meant to stir and shake those who obstruct our own involvement in the world. The fact that this project does not offer itself to descriptions but rather involves us from the beginning as interpreters – concerned human beings – is an indication of its existential nature. This is why outside the prejudice of knowledge as the mirror of nature one can no longer imagine a world given objectively but only through events.

As we can see Vattimo, following Nietzsche's and Heidegger's ontologies, suggests that interpretation must be understood from an ontological point of view, that is, in order to hold Being open to different events. This is why hermeneutics, like certain oppressed political, ecological, or social movements, "is committed to defend[ing] the survival of the human species on earth [because the] continuation of life requires that the event of Being is held open." Although hermeneutics is becoming the philosophy of the absence of emergency, contributing to our social, political and cultural well-being, its thinkers will be "explicitly accused of being crypto-terrorist[s] and fomenters of social disorder."[17] While some might consider this a negative feature, Vattimo instead believes this accusation to be central in the transformation of hermeneutics from a Gadamerian philosophy of dialogue to one of anarchic excess. After all, the intolerance of any form of anarchic hermeneutics within the academy rises from these accusations, which have always marginalized its thinkers:

Hermeneutics is forbidden from transgressing the proper limits of academic 'good manners,' limits that are essentially those of 'descriptive' metaphysics: there is a thing in front of me, 'the world out here', I describe it, I analyze it; I also judge it and condemn it (as absurd, false, morally unacceptable ...); limits that depend always on assuming the validity of the distinction between subject and object – the very distinction which does not hold within the *Geisteswissenschaften,* the human sciences, and whose rejection gives rise to the 'excess' of hermeneutics – an excess that has an impact like that of a 'terrorist' attack, even if an attack of ideas.[18]

This excess is not very different from Luther's revolt, Freud's dismantling, and Kuhn's transgression of the conservative impositions on religion and science in their epochs. As we can see, interpretation is a vital practice, a philosophy of *praxis*, where Being's event is always held open for existential purposes. But as a vital practice interpretation provides a contrast not only for the passive acceptance that characterizes descriptions but also for those limits that Vattimo refers to in the passage above. This is why the "hermeneuticist, if they are to become serious, must also become, fatally, a militant – the question is: for which cause?"[19]

Vattimo responds to this question by choosing those marginalized social, cultural, and intellectual sectors that battle for survival against neoliberal economic constraints. These are not simply the weak and oppressed but also the humanities non-instrumentalist disciplines, which have so much difficulty in obtaining research funds. The problem is not that these groups are incompetent but that they are both useless and dangerous to the "absence of emergency" that liberalism has achieved. Particularly dangerous from a neoliberal point of view are also those political causes, such as communism and Marxism, which have recently reemerged after the financial crisis of 2008. This is why Vattimo believes that to be a communist is not very different from being a hermeneuticist; both are fighting against those objective and realist constraints that have become increasingly indistinguishable from the laws of corporate capitalism. What is at stake here is a "reformation of the world" that must be "undertaken by a militant hermeneutics with all the tools of the humanities at its disposal – philosophy, theology, fine arts, law, politics."[20]

In sum, hermeneutics cannot be reduced to a philosophical discipline such as aesthetics or to a philosophical school as such positivism. There is more at stake in the process of interpretation, which transcends disciplinary parameters and schools' ambitions. The works of the authors I have examined show it to be a thought in progress, constantly developing in different directions and for diverse problems. This is why hermeneutics, as the possibility to interpret differently, is not simply revolutionary but rather a way of thinking that leads to revolt, alteration, and change. If it were only a revolutionary thought, then it would have to pretend to be absolute, complete. But hermeneutics does not pretend to have discovered the true meaning of a text, truth, or Being; rather, it discloses the different interpretations of these features. The world of hermeneutics is not an "object" that can be observed from different points of view and that offers various interpretations. It is a thought-world in continuous movement. If this world does not reveal itself to the perceptions of human beings as a continuous narrative, it is because we are not passive describers but engaged performers who must strive – through interpretation – for existence.

NOTES

1. Jean Grondin, among others, is concerned that contemporary hermeneutics has lost touch with Gadamer's original project. See his "Vattimo's Latinization of Hermeneutics: Why Did Gadamer Resist Postmodernism?" in *Weakening Philosophy*, ed. S. Zabala (Montreal: McGill-Queen's University Press, 2006), pp. 203–16, and also his "Must Nietzsche Be Incorporated Into Hermeneutics? Some Reasons for a Little Resistance," Iris: European Journal of Philosophy and Public Debate 2, no. 3 (April 2010), pp. 105–22.
2. Georgia Warnke, "Hermeneutics and Feminism," in *The Routledge Companion to Hermeneutics*, ed. J. Malpas and Hans-Helmuth Gander (London: Routledge, 2014), pp. 644–59.
3. Gianni Vattimo and Santiago Zabala, *Hermeneutic Communism: From Heidegger to Marx* (New York: Columbia University Press, 2011).
4. Forrest Clingerman, Brian Treanor, Martin Drenthen, and David Utsler, eds, *Interpreting Nature: The Emerging Field of Environmental Hermeneutics* (New York: Fordham University Press, 2013).
5. Santiago Zabala, *Emerging Aesthetics: Only Art Can Save Us* (forthcoming, 2016).
6. Hans-Georg Gadamer, *Truth and Method*, trans. Joel Weinsheimer and Donald G. Marschall (London: Continuum, 2014), pp. 286–91.
7. The difference between "dialogue" and "conversation" is explored in my "Being Is Conversation," in *Consequences of Hermeneutics*, ed. Jeff Malpas and Santiago Zabala (Evanston: Northwestern University Press, 2010), pp. 161–76.
8. Gerald Bruns, Maurizio Ferraris, Jean Grondin, Patxi Lanceros, Andrés Ortiz-Osés, Gayle L. Ormiston, Richard Palmer, James Risser, Alan D. Schrift, Joel Weinsheimer, and others have written extensive histories, introductions, and dictionaries of hermeneutics that all disagree about where to situate the origins of the discipline.

9. Gianni Vattimo, "The Future of Hermeneutics," in *The Routledge Companion to Hermeneutics*, ed. Jeff Malpas and Hans-Helmuth Gander (London: Routledge, 2014), p. 722.
10. See Vattimo and Zabala, *Hermeneutic Communism*, chap. 3, for a detailed analysis of conservative representatives of hermeneutics.
11. R. Schürmann, *Heidegger on Being and Acting: From Principles to Anarchy* (Bloomington: Indiana University Press, 1990), p. 295.
12. See Vattimo, "The Future of Hermeneutics," and Vattimo, "The Political Outcome of Hermeneutics," in *Consequences of Hermeneutics: Fifty Years After Gadamer's* Truth and Method, ed. J. Malpas and S. Zabala (Evanston: Northwestern University Press, 2010), p. 282.
13. J. Habermas, *Knowledge and Human Interest*, trans. J. J. Shapiro (Boston: Beacon Press, 1971), p. 220.
14. R. J. Bernstein, *Beyond Objectivism and Relativism: Sciences, Hermeneutics, and Praxis* (Philadelphia: University of Pennsylvania Press, 1983), p. 31.
15. Vattimo and Zabala, *Hermeneutic Communism*; and Vattimo, *Della realtà: fini della filosofia* (Milan: Garzanti, 2012), English translation forthcoming from Columbia University Press; Vattimo, "The Political Outcome of Hermeneutics," p. 282; and Vattimo, "The Future of Hermeneutics."
16. Vattimo, "The Political Outcome of Hermeneutics," p. 282.
17. Ibid. pp. 284, 286.
18. Vattimo, "The Future of Hermeneutics," p. 723.
19. Ibid. p. 25.
20. Ibid. p. 727.

PART II

Hermeneutics and Openness

4 Elements of Style: Openness and Dispositions[1]

WHITNEY MANNIES

Openness is an essential political virtue. After all, consider what happens to our political life when we fail to exercise it. For one, we tend to avoid or gloss over encounters that would challenge our beliefs or worldviews. Thus insulating ourselves, we often become more convinced of our rightness, ultimately leading to more ideological polarization.[2] Often, we engage only with people or information that reinforces what we already think, with the result that we become less informed and more ideologically extreme.[3] American television viewers choose to watch news programs that reinforce their pre-existing worldviews, and they avoid programs likely to challenge their ideas.[4] When people *do* encounter information that challenges their misconceptions, they will often avoid or diminish its importance.[5] Alarmingly, for some groups of ideologues, being confronted with factual information that challenges convictions only further *increases* their radicalization, resulting in a backfire effect.[6] Evidently, under certain conditions, humans become less likely to alter their viewpoints, and more likely to think up ever more improbable justifications for why they remain right.

Perhaps most alarmingly, a lack of openness exacerbates structural inequalities by diminishing the voices of the less privileged: in discussion groups, subjects generally give less weight to the views of low-status group members, often women or people of color.[7] This deficit of recognition is an injustice in and of itself. As Miranda Fricker has argued, rationality is a central component of each individual's humanity, so failing to duly acknowledge this quality in others constitutes an "epistemic injustice."[8] In the process, we may do ourselves epistemic harm by depriving ourselves of a valuable and interesting perspective. What is more, these personal harms often give rise to greater social harms: insofar as knowledge is necessary for the good-functioning of society, its suppression can only make our collective life worse. John

Stuart Mill, arguably the most enthusiastic supporter for openness in political life, averred that:

> The peculiar evil of silencing the expression of an opinion is, that it is robbing the human race ... If the opinion is right, they are deprived of the opportunity of exchanging error for truth: if wrong, they lose, what is almost as great a benefit, the clearer perception and livelier impression of truth, produced by its collision with error.[9]

Lack of openness, then, leads to polarization, exacerbates inequality, inflicts personal epistemic harm, and interferes with our capability to discern the truth and our common good.

Yet it is not entirely clear how we achieve openness. Our reliance on the familiar persists even in situations where we encounter new, more accurate information, and even – or perhaps especially – when we consider ourselves informed. In order to begin to address this issue, I turn to the consummate philosopher of openness, Hans-Georg Gadamer. Gadamer sees openness as following from our recognition that we have something to learn from the Other. I expand on his analysis, however, by arguing that openness also requires emotional, social, and reflective dispositions, which Gadamer ignores. In addition, I consider how the style and form of texts have the power to influence the kinds of dispositions with which we approach texts, influencing our ability to be open to the content of the texts' messages.

OPENNESS

What is openness? How can we know that we are *actually* being open, instead of lingering in our unexamined prejudices? How might we discover which of our beliefs are warranted, and which are illegitimate? Even those with the most unjust and polarized views seem to think of themselves as fair and balanced. How can we be sure that we really are giving every perspective its due?

Openness, Gadamer maintains, begins from the premise that all new understanding is grounded in prior understandings. There is no Archimedean point whence we objectively perceive the world as pure fact; we cannot issue neutral descriptions of the raw data of experience. Indeed, claiming objectivity for one's views is a sure way to disallow the legitimacy of any competing views. Thus while it holds out the hope of being supremely right, it eliminates the motivation to be open to other perspectives. In place of objectivity, Gadamer posits that all perception is "prejudiced" by prior understandings – "prejudices" simply denoting the totality of our prior understandings, both good and bad.[10] According to Gadamer, prejudices have a constructive role to play in the process of understanding since they orient all new information within the totality of one's extant prejudices – what Gadamer calls a "horizon of understanding."[11] Individuals' horizons, while not perfectly commensurate with one another, do overlap: two people will have different notions of freedom, for example, but their notions are probably not so entirely alien that they cannot talk about freedom at all.

Though all understanding is prejudiced, the inevitability of prejudiced understanding is not a license to persist uncritically in it. On the contrary, it compels one to approach the task of understanding more critically than ever. We can start by assuming an interrogative stance towards the world, actively cultivating a consciousness that is willing to be, as Gadamer put it, "pulled up short."[12] When we approach the world in a questioning rather than a defensive manner – in other words, with openness – we become less likely to gloss over information that threatens to cause uncomfortable cognitive dissonance. Instead, actively seeking out those points of dissonance, we become sensitized to even the smallest fissures of unintelligibility. This is the "hermeneutically-trained consciousness" – a mind not content with assumptions, but which searches for, instead of avoids, inadequacies and inconsistencies in understanding.[13]

Gadamer argues that openness also requires a sincere expectation to learn something from the Other. This seems obvious, but so many of our exchanges lack this expectation: we talk with someone merely to confirm our own rightness; we read a text with psychoanalytic suspicion, seeking to unearth the author's subterranean motivations; we are interested in an artwork for its historical importance or financial value. These approaches are not inherently *wrong*. If an author seems pathological, for example, it is certainly appropriate to employ a psychoanalytic method, looking past potential truth claims to explain the content of a message as a symptom of underlying pathologies.[14] Still, Gadamer argues, the possibility of psychosis does not mean that we should not at least *begin* by taking others at their word.[15] If we eventually find pathology lurking there, it will not be because we began with the assumption that we would find something pathological. Sincere openness, according to Gadamer, requires us to approach an idea with a presumption in the Other's favor, precisely so that the Other may better highlight and dispel our own prejudices.

In the same way that a psychoanalytic approach may cause the reader to bypass the claims of a text in order to arrive at an underlying pathology, a radically historical approach may cause us to look past a text's immediate claims in favor of an historical truth. In doing so, readers "have given up the claim to find in the past any truth that is valid and intelligible for ourselves."[16] While it is perfectly reasonable to want to avoid imputing anachronistic meanings to a text by placing it in its historical context, the hermeneutical approach to interpretation, unlike a radical historical approach, does not reject the possibility that a text contains truth relevant to our present situation. Could it not be the case, however, that an historical approach yields extremely relevant realizations? After all, by demonstrating the dependence of all belief systems on their historical contexts, historical approaches reveal the ultimate artificiality and contingency of all truth – a most transformative understanding indeed. But when historical scholarship leaves us with *only* this realization, and indeed, when we begin historical scholarship with this expectation, we find ourselves with, as Margaret Leslie writes, "the dust of scholarship."[17] While frequent denaturalization of our ideas may be a constructive exercise, the historical realization of the contingency of all beliefs does not exhaust the universe of possible meanings. We ought to approach the text with the sincere expectation that it may impart relevant and transformational understandings, and we ought not to assume in advance what those understandings will be.

Finally, Gadamer argues that openness requires that we not content ourselves with a perfunctory understanding of the Other. Ostensibly engaging with others in order to learn, but nevertheless proceeding to content ourselves with a weak and unconvincing iteration of their ideas, we may feel justified in rejecting them, however prematurely. "Dialectic," Gadamer reminds us, "consists not in trying to discover the weakness of what is said, but in bringing out its real strength."[18] If we encounter only straw men, not only do we end up convinced of the superiority of our arguments, we compound the injury by flattering ourselves for being so open-minded. Sincere openness, in contrast, obliges us to do our best to encounter the claims of the Other in their strongest possible light.

Openness thus begins with an awareness of our prejudiced condition. It obligates us to cultivate sensitivity to fissures of unintelligibility, to maintain the sincere expectation that the Other has something to teach us, and to be willing to transform our understanding as a result. Moreover, we ought not to content ourselves with a weak portrayal of the Other, but seek to see the claims of the Other in their strongest possible light. This version of the Other is most capable of challenging us, of compelling us to examine our prejudices, and of highlighting the inconsistencies and inadequacies in our prior understandings. By operationalizing openness in these ways, we can diminish – though perhaps not eliminate – the risk of persisting in our errors.

DISPOSITIONS

I want to add nuance to Gadamer's explanation of openness, however, by further exploring how it is that the claims of the Other come to appear in their strongest, most intelligible light. Truth claims, after all, present themselves in a variety of ways, compelling us to diverse ways of thinking, so shouldn't we likewise expect varieties of openness? Does openness look the same when we encounter Ludwig Wittgenstein's claim that "The world is everything that is the case" as when we read Emily Dickenson, "I reason, earth is short/And anguish absolute/And many hurt;/But what of that?"[19] Surely, a reader who seeks to bring Dickenson's truth claims into sharpest relief will be doing something quite different when she seeks to do the same with Wittgenstein. Openness, it turns out, is not a fixed outlook or an unvaried attitude, and it does not take place on a merely linguistic plane. The claims of the Other, I submit, appear more or less intelligible depending on the emotional, social, or reflective dispositions with which they are encountered. If we take seriously the obligation to strengthen the arguments of the Other against ourselves, we will have to adjust our dispositions.

I am not suggesting that we attempt to empathically transport ourselves into the speaker's or author's affective state in order to authentically understand their message. Rather, I am arguing that uncritically importing our own emotional, social, and reflective dispositions to a dialogue may result in a less than generous hearing or reading, and consequently we may miss out on the best challenge to our convictions and expectations. For example, a blithe attitude might cast Montaigne's reflections in their most plausible light, while a legalistic remove might find Kant most convincing, but to approach either with the disposition appropriate to the other may handicap their texts' dialogic power even before we begin to consider the content of the truth claims. If we are to make the Other our most effective dialogical partner, it follows that we ought to try to meet it with the dispositions in which its message appears most formidable.

Yet how can we know *which* kinds of dispositions cast ideas in their strongest, most intelligible light? While social cues may be forthcoming in oral communication, texts, being just words on a page, seem at a particular disadvantage when it comes to encouraging the non-linguistic disposition that could frame their ideas in the most intelligible light. How can we encounter anything except stark knowledge claims, since in a text all we find (at least ostensibly) is language? Socrates, of course, never wrote anything down; texts could not convey the non-linguistic dispositions he felt were required for the activity of philosophy. Amélie Rorty explains, "[P]hilosophy is not merely a reading of the world, it is a turning of the soul. It is precisely because he saw the dangers of contextless thought that Socrates refused to write."[20] According to this line of thought, *writing* philosophy would be a vain endeavor, since a static text could never bring about the dispositions and actions that make philosophy transformative.

Contra Socrates, I do not think that texts are powerless to bring about the emotional, social, and reflective dispositions necessary for genuine, transformative dialogue. Texts actively encourage us to encounter their truth claims from within certain social, emotional, and reflective dispositions – not merely as a result of their content, but also as a consequence of their style and form. The style and form of writing help to orient the reader in certain emotional, social, and reflective dispositions that bring the text's truth claims into sharp relief. It follows, then, that *if we are to be open to ideas, we ought to encounter ideas from within the dispositions that reveal them in their most intelligible light,* and *we ought to be attentive to the ways in which the style and form of a text may encourage us to adopt certain dispositions.*[21] By encouraging the dispositions that would help us to encounter the claims of the text in their strongest possible light, the style and form of a text become, as Martha Nussbaum argues, "a part of content – an integral part, then, of the search for and the statement of truth."[22]

In what follows, I concentrate on written texts, and how their style and form can serve to encourage the emotional, social, and reflective dispositions that strengthen the text against us so that it may be a more effective dialogical Other, better highlighting and dispelling our prejudices.

Openness and Emotional Dispositions

"You are surprised not to find in me the transports of love," Roxane declares in the final epistle of Montesquieu's *Persian Letters*. She concludes:

> If you had known me well, you would have found there all the violence of hate. But for a long time you have had the good fortune to believe that a heart like mine was submissive to you. We were both fortunate: you thought I was deceived, and I was deceiving you. My language, no doubt, seems new to you. Could it be that after having overwhelmed you with sorrow, I should even yet force you to admire my courage? But it is finished. The poison consumes me. The pen falls from my hands. I feel even my hatred weaken. I am dying.[23]

Thus the end of Roxane, Usbek's favorite harem girl. After following their relationship through hundreds of letters, readers are likely just as overwhelmed by the injustice of Roxane's situation as she is, just as convinced that even the most benevolent of arbitrary powers is ultimately demoralizing and corrupting. Furthermore, readers' emotions – their sympathy with Roxane and regret for her death – may be transferred to the political sphere, where they feel by analogy the precariousness of dignity and virtue under an absolutist regime. For readers to feel the force of Montesquieu's argument, they must be willing to trade in nostalgia for benevolent absolutism for dignity and self-respect, they must forgo dependence and flattery for moral courage and genuine love. Without these emotions, they will remain under the sway of a slavish delusion, nursing nostalgia for a benevolent absolute ruler. The emotions to be cultivated in *The Persian Letters* are part and parcel of the political logic to be grasped, and they are crucial to becoming the kinds of citizens that Montesquieu's self-governing regime requires. Emotions, in other words, are not just icing on the cake.

Here the style and form of *The Persian Letters* are central. Its epistolary form is intimate, as Montesquieu notes in his personal correspondence: "[T]he characters themselves recount their actual experiences, and this makes us feel their passions better than any mere narration could."[24] Montesquieu reorients the affective reality of readers so as to bring his arguments for limited, lawful power into sharpest relief, and he does so by means of a style that nurtures the attachments and emotions appropriate to a self-governing people.

Love, to take another example, specifically love of *patria* or our fellow citizens, has often been cultivated in readers as a prerequisite for their political theorizing, and, here again, the style and form of texts has played a crucial role in how those emotions cause us to theorize. Martha Nussbaum's examination of Rabindranath Tagore argues that his poetry and narratives are meant to establish and sustain the shared emotions that would support new, democratic political principles and political institutions.[25] By writing in the form of personal narrative he rejects traditional forms of expression, evincing skepticism about engrained rituals and cultural traditions and proposing, radically, that all of humanity can be communicated in the exploration of an individual life. Tagore's style and form is an attempt to replace parochial ways of knowing and feeling so that the reader might realize a new, universal citizenship through the contemplation of individual experience. Through the style and form of Tagore's writing, the emotional connection a reader has to Tagore's individual's life is extended to all of humanity.

On the other hand, an author may desire to embed the reader's contemplation of politics in a passionless state, and so employ a style and form of writing meant to quell emotions, as with Baruch de Spinoza's *Theological–Political Treatise*. Spinoza thought that fear, especially religious fear, was actually what caused people to cling helplessly to superstition and rendered them unable to evaluate claims using reason.[26] Full of ponderous historical and scriptural summary, the logical presentation of his *Treatise* borders on the mathematical, but its style and form is suited to the task of encouraging the reader to the kind of unsuperstitious, detached emotional disposition that Spinoza identifies as absolutely necessary for the good functioning of reason.

Understanding is always grounded in an emotional orientation. These examples indicate that there is not only one, all-purpose emotional disposition suitable for approaching all kinds of claims. It is impossible to see the logic of Montesquieu's self-government if we do not love autonomy more than easy dependence; we will never find Tagore's democracy reasonable if we fail to feel a transcendent connection to our fellow citizens; and in Spinoza's view, we could never embrace the logic of a secular government while at the same time harboring an intense fear of eternal punishment. Emotional orientations may be subtle, or we may be accustomed to overlooking or minimizing the emotional components of our thinking, but they are nonetheless present. Style and form are crucial in encouraging the particular kinds of emotional responses that can cast the text's claims in the strongest possible light.

Openness and Social Dispositions

Recent empirical research has demonstrated that feeling secure in a social existence helps to allay the risk of entertaining radical notions and questioning cherished ideas and beliefs. Cohen et al. (2007) show that people resist information and compromise when they feel a threat to a valued identity and sense of self-integrity, but that people who feel secure in a valued identity exhibit greater openness to arguments as well as a greater willingness to trust negotiation partners and make compromises.[27] Evidently, feeling secure in a valued identity causes us to be more open to arguments, even when that identity seems antagonistic to the idea at hand.[28] In addition to feeling socially secure, feeling socially connected is often a boon to openness. Aristotle noted as much in his *Rhetoric* when he considered the effect of a speaker's character on our judgment. The rapport that exists between the speaker and audience is a crucial element of persuasion, since, Aristotle explains, "things do not appear the same to those who feel friendship as to those who are hostile."[29] He adds later that "we like those who are not frightening to us, with whom we feel confident, for no one likes a person he is scared of. Companionship, living in the same place, ties of kinship, and all such things are forms of friendship."[30] Aristotle's insight is reflected in contemporary empirical research that demonstrates that social proximity to people who think differently than us can help to motivate us to consider more thoroughly our previously unexamined beliefs.[31] For example, people who come to know gays and lesbians are more likely to become supportive of gay rights issues.[32] As important as good reasons and logical arguments may be to philosophers, it is often the sense of social trust, connection, and security that make understanding possible.

Texts can and do encourage social connection and affirmation that cause the reader to be more open to the ideas in the text, and they often accomplish this through the style and form in which they are written. When David Hume asked his readers to radically reevaluate the concepts of perception and causation in his *Essay Concerning Human Understanding*, he employed a style and form that embedded his audience in a shared cultural and moral order. By stylistically linking the reader to the text by way of a familiar social ontology, Hume helped his readers to remain open to the content of his text despite its radical epistemology.[33] Michel de Montaigne used a similar strategy: invoking a shared oral tradition, he promoted a sense of camaraderie that made his readers more amenable to the zigzags of his loose, essayistic style.[34]

It is not always the case that the shared social connection that facilitates openness is between the readers and the author; sometimes the text cultivates a social connection between the readers and the characters in the book itself. Genevieve Lloyd remarks that Montesquieu's *The Persian Letters* accomplishes an expansion of moral and political sentiment by allowing us to occupy and sympathize with multiple points of view. The letters, "offer a plurality of epistemological and moral perspectives, clearing conceptual space for the enactment of cosmopolitan consciousness."[35] Lloyd argues that Montesquieu, "by drawing us to imagine the situations of his characters and to observe European customs and assumptions from their perspectives, his narrative still illuminates our attitudes toward the uninvited others at our border and in our midst."[36] Attention to the literary elements of an historical text, in other words, has contemporary relevance as a practice through which modern readers can cultivate reflective and other-regarding attitudes, expanding their moral and political sentiments to cultivate in themselves a cosmopolitan consciousness. Martha Nussbaum makes the case that Henry James's qualitatively rich, third-person narrative form embeds the reader's subjectivity in a complex matrix of social connections, causing the reader to feel the experience of others more keenly by provoking a profound analogizing between one's self and the Other. In this way, certain rich, narrative styles cause the reader to be less individualistic and thus bring about more profound ethical deliberation.[37] Indeed, Kidd and Castano's (2013) cognitive research supports Nussbaum's interpretation. They show that reading literature can actually enhance our ability to understand the mental states of others by contributing to our capacity for engaging in complex social relationships. Literary fiction's deviation from the mundane and scripted convention causes readers to engage with social experiences, albeit fictional ones, that disrupt their expectations, thus challenging them to expand their socio-cognitive skills.[38] The style and form of texts turns out to be crucial to the deliberation of justice and moral knowledge.

Yet while Hume, Montaigne, Montesquieu, and James arguably bring about the reader's understanding by inspiring social connection, what if it is the case that, instead of finding social connection a spur to ethical contemplation or philosophical risk-taking, we instead experience it as an oppressive field of multiple, intersecting structures of power? What if we find that a thickly-elaborated social field simply introduces more constraints, restricting our emancipatory or ethical possibilities?

This is Michel Foucault's critique of these kinds of thickly-elaborated Nussbaumian dialogical situations in "What is an Author?"[39] Instead of encouraging our ethical imaginations, thinking from within such social ontologies limits our emancipatory and ethical possibilities by constraining the scope of our own potential subjectivities. Because of this, Foucault employs a style that attempts to explode the reader's notion of subjectivity: readers are not singular, unitary individuals embedded in a particular social situation, but rather the reader herself must experience her own subjectivity as a field of diffuse, intersecting regimes of power.

Nor is it only our notions of our own subjectivity that limit us, but also our notions of others' subjectivities as singular origin-points. In "What is an Author?" Foucault argues that, oftentimes, idiosyncrasies in writing style are construed to validate our intuition that there *is* a subject behind the words. Hence style in writing is perceived to indicate an identity, an essence, or origin that would limit the pluralities of meaning. But Foucault's style is designed to disabuse us of this notion of a unitary subject: he writes in a passive voice and avoids pronouns. Without an "I" or "We" or "One" upon which to hang a thought, Foucault denies his sentences the clarity of a unitary subject, and communicates a diffuse field of subjectivity both for himself and the reader. Exposing the author figure as a myth woven by intersecting disciplines suggests at once their artificiality *and* possibilities for their alteration, which for Foucault is their emancipatory potential. In the introduction to *Archaeology of Knowledge*, Foucault himself makes the link between his writing style and the effacing of subjectivity:

> What, do you imagine that I would take so much trouble and so much pleasure in writing, do you think that I would keep so persistently to my task, if I were not preparing – with a rather shaky hand – a labyrinth into which I can venture, in which I can move my discourse, opening up underground passages, forcing it to go far from itself, finding overhangs that reduce and deform its itinerary, in which I can lose myself and appear at last to eyes that I will never have to meet again. I am no doubt not the only one who writes in order to have no face. Do not ask who I am and so do not ask me to remain the same: leave it to our bureaucrats and our police to see that our papers are in order. At least spare us their morality when we write.[40]

Foucault "writes in order to have no face," so as to decenter our norms of authorial unity and our own subjectivity. Foucault's style, then, is crucial to the point he is making; the disorientation, cognitive dissonance, or the loss of self effected by his labyrinthine style *is* an emancipatory mode of unmasking. For the reader, the act of inhabiting unfamiliar subjectivities becomes a task that is also fundamental to being open to Foucault's message. Without challenging our own self-perception as a unitary individual, without experiencing the free-floating disorientation of a subject-denying style, we are not engaging with the text in a way that allows its truth claims to appear to us most convincingly. Refusing to experience the decentering effects of an unorthodox, labyrinthine, self-effacing style diminishes the dialogical potential of Foucault's text.

Though their conclusions diverge, both Foucault and Nussbaum argue that the reader's understanding of the text is bound up with the reader's understanding of her own subjectivity and orientation in a social ontology. Indeed, it is actually an integral part of what the text is attempting to accomplish. If we sincerely want to encounter the text's message on its own terms and at its most intelligible, we ought to seek to view it from within the kinds of subjectivity and social connection that the text suggests to us.

Openness and Reflective Dispositions

Finally, what is the effect of our reflective dispositions on our ability to be open to the claims of a text? *How* we arrive at the truth of a text is often just as important as the truth we arrive at – sometimes more so. To that end, the style and form of a text can encourage the reader to undertake the kinds of reflective actions essential for encountering the text's truth claims. Nussbaum, for example, argues that the shape of Henry James's narrative style embodies the text's truth claims, "setting up in the reader the activities that are appropriate for grasping them."[41] Nussbaum argues that this unique cognitive exercise causes the thoughtful reader to perform an empathic exercise, and this reflective exercise is critical – indeed, indispensible – to gaining the kind of ethical knowledge to which James aspires.

By "reflective dispositions," then, I refer to the rhythm and meter of our thinking. Is our deliberation quiet and brooding, calm and considered, quick and jarring? Does a confusing style necessitate sustained reflection, or do fragments of language, barely enough to articulate a thought, demand our own independent creative thought? Or perhaps a text's style and form is meandering and essayistic, lulling us into comfortable contemplation? Foucault could not have simply *informed* readers that their notions of subjectivity need to be decentered because this approach would likely have reinforced precisely the kinds of subjectivities he sought to dismantle. Likewise, Hannah Arendt could not have instructed us directly about the dangers of system-building. Rather, following the ebb and flow of her experimental and tentative essay style, she manages to convey her point without simultaneously undermining it.[42]

One very clear example of the effect of style and form of writing on our reflective dispositions is Nietzsche. Take one of his most obvious and talked-about styles: the aphorism. For example, number 83:

> "*Instinct.* – When the house burns one forgets even lunch. – Yes, but one eats it later in the ashes."[43]

Or perhaps number 160:

> "One no longer loves one's insight enough once one communicates it."[44]

Short, sometimes shocking, and always chthonic, what are we to make of this style? How ought we to reflect in the wake of Nietzsche's aphorisms? Commentators are hardly united. Walter Kaufmann argues that his aphoristic style is meant to express his anti-system tendencies, and that it is also grounded in a holistic experimental mode: the short stabs at wisdom mimic hypotheses to be tested, and their abrupt endings leave the reader to evaluate them.[45] Sara Kofman interprets the aphorisms as metaphors in an obscurantist code that would exclude the vulgar but include elite members of a certain class.[46] Alexander Nehamas argues that, by being so disconnected from one another, the aphorisms resist being woven into a coherent narrative or logical argument.[47] Moreover, he argues, when we zoom out to survey Nietzsche's œuvre as a whole, the proliferation of different styles and forms turns out to be a method for resolving a central problem in Nietzsche's work: how to preach against dogmatism without being dogmatic himself.

> [H]e wants his readers to accept his views, his judgments and his values as much as he wants them to know that these are essentially *his* views, *his* judgments, and *his* values ... [He desires] to have as readers only those who will always be aware of the nature of his views, and of all views in general.[48]

Conspicuous styles highlight the interpretive quality of Nietzsche's messages, implicitly conveying the message that all views are only interpretations.

So the style and form of Nietzsche's aphorisms inspire different kinds of reflective dispositions. But what if there is no style at all? Jacques Derrida's estimation of Nietzsche's aphoristic style is that there is none: style requires context, but because aphorisms are isolated, they therefore have no context for reference.[49] Aphorisms, for Derrida, cannot even be "fragments" because that would be to conceive of them as part of a totalizing whole. Yet Derrida's deconstructionism is so utterly focused on the text that it neglects to see that the reader, too, brings context. Though texts may exert an exogenous, independent effect on the reader, texts do not exist completely independent of the reader. Aphorisms cannot lack style because the reader already brings with her a tradition of style – in Gadamerian terms, a "horizon of understanding" that includes notions of the appropriate readerly responses to texts' styles and forms – within which even fragments are interpreted according to some notion of style and form. This means that no fragment will leave us utterly at a loss. "I have forgotten my umbrella" – arguably Nietzsche's most talked about and least intelligible marginalia – yields no meaning and has no style, according to Derrida. But while this fragment may be inscrutable, it is not *utterly* so. The power of "I have forgotten my umbrella" to throw us into confusion is not a testament to its nothingness. Indeed, it has generated more than its fair share of interpretations.[50] Labeling a text style*less* imperils openness: we fail to recognize the effect of our own expectations and experience on interpretation, allowing our "tyranny of hidden prejudices" to pass unnoticed.[51] Instead, by recognizing that we bring our own interpretations of style and form to a text, we can acknowledge our prejudiced condition and, being thus aware, become all the more critical of how we approach the style and form of a text.

In other words, readers are not blank slates. Our own stylistic expectations and experience shape our encounters with the style and form of a text; our experience and expectations influence what kinds of emotional, social, and reflective dispositions we might feel compelled to develop in response to a text. Clearly, Kaufmann, Kofman, Nehamas, and Derrida encounter Nietzsche from within their own horizons of understanding, and as a result, they draw different conclusions about the consequences of Nietzsche's style and form. My own hermeneutical perspective of style and form does not arbitrate between these different interpretations. Rather, it suggests that we ought to recognize the embeddedness of our own stylistic understanding, and that we ought to be attentive to how a text's style and form may suggest dispositions that cause the text to be our most effective dialogical Other.

Gadamer reminds us that the mutual autonomy of the dialogic partners precludes the possibility of commensurate understanding, but the overlapping traditions within which text and reader are oriented hold out the promise of a productive fusion of understanding.[52] We are *not* blank slates who perfectly absorb the autonomous Other; similarly, texts are not blank slates onto which we project our autonomous understanding. One does not, as Warnke notes, "simply experience the other as one experiences oneself."[53] And indeed, how monotonous to simply assimilate the text to ourselves! Installing the reader as sovereign over the text's meaning – a kind of Barthian coup – is not only an exercise in subjectivism that violates the text's autonomy, it is also, ultimately, boring.[54] An omnipotent reader eventually confronts her pyrrhic victory in the dull, repetitive solipsism of her own projections.

STYLE AND DOMINATION

Hence hermeneutical dangers loom large: we may forfeit a critical opportunity by assuming that a text has no style at all or by failing to recognize that we bring an interpretive context with us. There is also the danger that we may so completely deliver ourselves over to a style that it overcomes our own thought. Kathleen Merrow, for example, argues that Nietzsche's rhythmic style is calculated to overpower his audience's reason by imbuing his prose with a sense of occult ritual: "Rhythm has a physiological basis as a pulse or beat that over time was transposed into more abstract forms. This is the source of its compelling power, first in ritual and dance, later in poetry and prose."[55] In Merrow's view, Nietzsche's rhythmic style is a negation of freedom, a method of brainwashing by engendering, "an unconquerable urge to yield and join in; not only our feet . . . but the soul."[56] To take the claims of Nietzsche's style seriously, need we submit ourselves to hypnotization? Ought we to allow ourselves to be swept along with this undeniable occult compulsion? What do we do when a text's style and form actively promote the suppression of the reader's interpretive ability? If the style and form of a text seem to encourage us to forgo all independent thought, would we not be left dangerously vulnerable to manipulation?

I do not think so. I argue for an approach to style and form that can help us to be *more* open, not less, and that is committed to the autonomy of dialogic partners. By strengthening the Other against ourselves, we come to a more critical evaluation of the legitimacy of our prior understandings. Accordingly, we are never obliged to follow the intimations of a style and form so far that we relinquish our autonomous interpretive power. Even if we were to agree with Kathleen Merrow that Nietzsche's style evokes an "unconquerable urge to yield," we ought not to let ourselves be thus hypnotized.

If we find that a certain interpretation of style and form does hypnotize us or undermine our autonomous interpretive power, however, we need not accept this as the only, final interpretation. In an illuminating discussion between Jean-Francois Lyotard and Jean-Loup Thebaud in *Just Gaming*, Thebaud remarks that the style of Lyotard's *L'Economie libidinale* allows very little negotiation with the reader, such that its take-it-or leave-it quality excludes the possibility of dialogue.[57] Lyotard concedes that, "insofar as it does not lend itself to dialogue, it perpetrates a kind of violence," but Lyotard defends himself, arguing that his style was never intended to suppress dialogue:

> [T]he regulating of dialogic discourse, even of dialectical discourse in the Platonic sense, seemed to me to be associated with power, since ultimately it aims at controlling the effects of the statements exchanged by the partners of the dialogue; I was trying, on the contrary, to limit myself to the delivery of a mass of statements barely controlled in themselves, and, insofar as the relation to the addressee is concerned, they were drawn up more in the spirit of the bottle tossed into the ocean than in that of a return of the effects of the statements to their author.[58]

Thebaud felt that Lyotard's style perpetrated a kind of violence on the reader insofar as his style diminished the reader's interpretive ability, but here we see that Lyotard had actually intended for his style to *challenge* the violence of a previous style. Nevertheless, Thebaud remains unconvinced. Ultimately, their perspectives on the emancipatory consequences of this particular style are irreconcilable.

What can we conclude about style, form, and openness from this exchange? First, the dispositions that a text's style and form evoke will vary according to each person's interpretation, and will sometimes even starkly contrast – as is the case with Thebaud's and Lyotard's contradictory interpretations of Lyotard's style. Still, we are not so utterly alienated from each other's traditions that we find our different interpretations of style and form mutually unintelligible. After all, Thebaud and Lyotard, for all their disagreement, were able to communicate their perspectives to one another. Second, we need not arrive at a consensus for how to interpret style and form. Rather, debating the consequences of style and form for our thinking may disclose new and critical perspectives of a text, and we may hit upon new ways to approach the text that strengthen its ability to serve as a dialogical Other. Lyotard offered a new interpretation of his style and form, interpretations that Thebaud might have seized upon to better encounter the truth claims of the text.

In light of this, I argue that a commitment to openness obligates us to follow the intimations of style and form so that the claims a text make on us might be most keenly apprehended. The traditions of interpretations in which we live are not inert, and we are not bound inextricably to our previous stylistic prejudices. When one approach to style and form leaves us none the wiser regarding a certain text, we can alter our approach so as to understand the text's claims more fully. Thebaud has not *mis*interpreted Lyotard's style when he experiences it as violence, but, in light of their conversation, he might try to re-approach the text, this time trying to experience the style as a spur to interpretive freedom, as Lyotard indicates was his intention. If Thebaud tries and still experiences Lyotard's style as a kind of epistemological violence, he may put the book down and read another. I would recommend that he not put the book down too conclusively, however.

When we encounter a style and form that is unusual or difficult, we ought not to dismiss it as valueless – or worse, noxious. Openness requires that we suppress the tendency to skip over what we do not immediately understand and resist the urge to dismiss a form and style of writing that does not fit comfortably with our previous experience. When we dismiss the stylistic value of a text, we forfeit a portion of its ability to provoke us to further investigation. The critical potential of style and form lies in its ability to strengthen the text's claims, highlight and challenge our prior understandings, and thus encourage us on to more coherent understandings of the world. This is not a call to embrace completely and uncritically the text's stylistic implications. The experience of style and form is always in service to the maintenance of an open, interrogative orientation towards the text. We ought to embrace the implications of style and form for our dispositions only insofar as those dispositions bring out the text's strengths as a productive foil for our understanding.

Because our interpretations of style and form are historically grounded, we cannot say that there is a *correct* style. Nussbaum, for example, so privileges the thickly contextualized narratives that point, in her view, to an Aristotelian ethics that she fails to recognize how other styles and forms of writing may also lead to valid and valuable ethical insight. A commitment to openness, however, obliges us not to dismiss unexpected, disturbing, or unintelligible styles and forms. Instead, we ought to let style and form be yet another element of the text that can pull us up short. Then, we might find ways to approach the style and form of a text in ways that better dispose us to the claims the text is making. When, for example, Nussbaum finds that Samuel Beckett writes in an ethically bankrupt style and form, a hermeneutical approach to style might first question how Beckett's style and form might move us to a better, more coherent understanding of the truth claims he is presenting. Taking this approach, each reader may still arrive at different conclusions: we might conclude with Stanley Cavell that Beckett's style and form fragment the coherence of our social and ethical visions, thereby affirming our ability to create meaning, or we might agree with Nussbaum that Beckett is ethically bankrupt. What is important is that we approach style and form with a presumption in its favor, that is, with the presumption that it is an important element in arriving at the truth claims in the text.

CONCLUSION

I began this essay claiming that openness is a political virtue: it prevents us from becoming convinced of our rightness, it makes us more likely to consider the perspectives of others, and in the process it can lead to less polarization and more justice. Openness, however, is not merely a matter of being open to the content of ideas, but also of meeting those ideas on the emotional, social, and reflective registers that portray them in their most intelligible lights. Oriented in certain emotional, social, and reflective dispositions by the style and form of a text, we allow the text to be a more autonomous and effective dialogic Other. A stronger Other is a better challenge to our prejudices, helping us to sort out the legitimate from the illegitimate prior understandings, and compelling us on to more coherent understanding. However, we need not inhabit dispositions that would overwhelm our interpretive autonomy.

This perspective implicitly acknowledges that there is a range of emotional, social, and reflective dispositions that can be justly considered "philosophical" or "political." The scope of our thinking and of our public debate is limited when we insist that we meet truth claims only on a particular emotional plane, or only as detached thinkers, or according to one particular reflective practice. When we allow style and form to inform our dispositions so that the claims of a text appear most convincingly, we maintain philosophy's critical ability and are driven to stronger and more creative philosophic enterprises. This is, ultimately, an exercise in pluralism.

NOTES

1. E. B. White and William Strunk, Jr., *The Elements of Style*, illus. Moira Kalman (New York: Penguin Press, 2005).
2. Campbell et al. argued in their landmark study of American voting behavior that voters were strongly motivated to avoid cognitive dissonance. See Angus Campbell, Phillip E. Converse, Warren E. Miller, and Donald T. Stokes, *The American Voter* (Chicago: University of Chicago Press. Reprint edition, 1980) [1960]; These political consequences corroborated the social psychological insights of Leon Festinger who argued that individuals seek to avoid the psychological discomfort that results from an inexplicable or unrationalizable inconsistency in their beliefs or actions, and that individuals will actively seek to avoid situations or information that make such inconsistency salient. See Leon Festinger, *A Theory of Cognitive Dissonance* (Stanford: Stanford University Press, 1957).
3. Silvia Knoblock-Westerwick and Jingbo Meng, "Reinforcement of the Political Self through Selective Exposure to Political Messages," *Journal of Communication* 61 (2011), pp. 349–68. Also see Cass Sunstein, *Why Groups Go to Extremes* (Washington, DC: American Enterprise Institute, 2008).
4. Kevin Arceneaux and Martin Johnson, *Changing Minds Or Changing Channels?: Partisan News in an Age of Choice* (Chicago: University of Chicago Press, 2013).
5. See Charles S. Tabor and Milton Lodge, "Motivated Skepticism in the Evaluation of Political Beliefs," *American Journal of Political Science*, 50.3 (2006), pp. 755–69.
6. Also see the experiments of Nyhan and Reifler. They placed individuals in ideologically homogenous groups, and observed that the more ideologically extreme the group, the more willing individuals would be to avoid the cognitive dissonance that challenging information causes, even inventing unlikely counter-arguments to counter the factual information with which they were presented. Brendan Nyhan and Jason Reifler, "When corrections fail: The persistence of political misperceptions," *Political Behavior* 32, no. 2 (2010), pp. 303–30.
7. Sunstein, p. 17.
8. Miranda Fricker, *Epistemic Injustice: Power and the Ethics of Knowing* (Oxford: Oxford University Press, 2007).
9. John Stuart Mill, *On Liberty and Other Writings* (Cambridge: Cambridge University Press, 1989).

10. Hans-Georg Gadamer, *Truth and Method* (New York: Continuum, 1975), pp. 272–3. Hereafter cited as *"Truth and Method."*
11. Jean Piaget elaborated a similar model of understanding in the field of child development, arguing that all new information was attached to certain pre-existing "schemas." Jean Piaget, *A Child's Conception of the World* (London: Routledge and Kegan Paul, 1928).
12. *Truth and Method*, p. 270.
13. Ibid. p. 271.
14. Jürgen Habermas, for example, argues that we ought not to take all truth claims at face value. Jürgen Habermas. "On Hermeneutics' Claim to Universality" in *Contemporary Hermeneutics: Hermeneutics as Method, Philosophy and Critique*. Ed. Josef Bleicher (Boston: Routledge and Kegan Paul, 1980).
15. Georgia Warnke, "Experiencing Tradition versus Belonging to It: Gadamer's Dilemma," in *Review of Metaphysics*, 68 (December 2014)
16. *Truth and Method*, pp. 302–3.
17. Margaret Leslie, "In Defense of Anachronism" *Political Studies* 18.4 (1970), pp. 433–47, 433. Leslie further articulates the objection to a radical historicism: "A recognition of the very otherness of past ways of thought can be profoundly educative, shaking the complacency of our own assumptions ... We can gain in self-awareness and modesty by appreciating the vast differences between other times and our own. But this lesson, however valuable, is very different from the one that historians of political thought originally set out to learn. Once again, the historical scholarship which was undertaken in the first place largely because its object was believed to have relevance for us now, itself appears to demonstrate that this object can have nothing immediate to say to us," p. 435.
18. *Truth and Method*, p. 361.
19. Ludwig Wittgenstein, *Tractatus Logico Philosophicus*, in *The Wittgenstein Reader* (Oxford: Blackwell Publishing, 1996); Emily Dickenson, *The Complete Poems of Emily Dickenson* (Back Bay Books, 1976), p. 142.
20. Amélie Oksenberg Rorty, "Experiments in Philosophic Genre: Descartes' 'Meditations'" *Critical Inquiry* 9.3 (1983), pp. 545–64, 563.
21. By "style," I refer to all those elements that one might learn from Strunk & White or from high school English teachers: diction, syntax, sentence structure, rhythm, tone, imagery, hyperbole, active/passive voice, punctuation, point of view, etc. "Form" refers more specifically to the type or genre of writing: novels, essays, aphorisms, epic poems, treatises, etc.
22. Martha Nussbaum, "Introduction: Form and Content, Philosophy and Literature," *Love's Knowledge: essays on philosophy and literature* (Oxford: Oxford University Press, 1990), p. 3.
23. Baron de Montesquieu, *The Persian Letters* (New York: Meridan Books, 1961), p. 280.
24. Montesquieu's personal correspondences, cited in Elizabeth Cook,

Epistolary Bodies: Gender and Genre in the Eighteenth Century Republic of Letters (Stanford: Stanford University Press), p. 66.
25. Martha Nussbaum, *Political Emotions* (Cambridge, MA: The Belknap Press, 2013).
26. Baruch de Spinoza, *Theologico-Politico Treatise* (Cambridge: Cambridge University Press, 2007), see especially section 5, p. 5.
27. G. L. Cohen, D. K. Sherman, A. Bastardi, L. Hsu, M. McGoey, and L. Ross, L., "Bridging the partisan divide: Self-affirmation reduces ideological closed-mindedness and inflexibility in negotiation," in *Journal of Personality and Social Psychology* 93:3 (2007), pp. 415–30.
28. Also see Correll, Spencer and Zanna who demonstrate that self-affirmed individuals are less biased and more likely to be persuaded by an argument because of their attending to the argument's strength. They show that being made to feel secure in one's identity does not merely induce agreeableness, it actually increases a person's attention to evaluating the argument. Joshua Correll, Steven J. Spencer, and Mark P. Zanna, "An affirmed self and an open mind: Self-affirmation and sensitivity to argument strength." *Journal of Experimental Social Psychology* 40:3 (2004), pp. 350–6.
29. Aristotle, *Rhetoric,* in *Plato* Gorgias *and Aristotle* Rhetoric. Trans. Joe Sachs (Newburyport, MA: Focus Publishing, 2009), Book II, Chapter 1, ll. 32–3, p. 189.
30. Aristotle 2009, Book II, Chp. 4, ll. 34–7, p. 199.
31. Richard E. Petty, "The Elaboration Likelihood Model of Persuasion," *Advances in Experimental Social Psychology,* 19 (1986), pp. 123–205.
32. Lewis (2011) shows that people who know lesbian, gay, and bisexual individuals are more likely to support gay rights. Gregory B. Lewis, "The Friends and Family Plan: Contact with Gays and Support for Gay Rights," 39.2 (2011), pp. 217–38.
33. John J. Richetti, *Philosophical Writing: Locke, Berkeley, Hume* (Cambridge: Harvard University Press, 1983).
34. Dilys Winegrad, "'Maistrise Engendre Mespris': Montaigne and the Generative Power of Language," *Symposium: A Quarterly Journal in Modern Literatures* 35.2 (1981), pp. 168–80.
35. Genevieve Lloyd, "Imagining Difference: Cosmopolitanism in Montesquieu's *Persian Letters,*" *Constellations* 19.3 (2012), pp. 480–93.
36. Lloyd 2012, p. 492.
37. Nussbaum 1990.
38. David Comer Kidd and Emanuele Castano, "Reading Literary Fiction Improves Theory of Mind," *Science* 342.6156 (2013), pp. 377–80.
39. Michel Foucault, "What is an Author?" In *The Foucault Reader,* ed. Paul Rabinow (New York: Vintage Books, 2010).
40. Michel Foucault, *The Archaeology of Knowledge* (New York: Vintage Books, 2010), p. 17.
41. Martha Nussbaum 1990, p. 6.

42. Ari-Elmeri Hyvönen, "Tentative Lessons of Experience: Arendt, Essayism, and 'The Social' Reconsidered," *Political Theory* 42.5 (2014), pp. 569–89.
43. Friedrich Nietzsche, *Beyond Good and Evil* in *Basic Writings of Nietzsche* (New York: The Modern Library, 2000), p. 271.
44. Nietzsche 2000, p. 281.
45. Walter Kaufmann, *Nietzsche: Philosopher, Psychologist, Anti-Christ* (Princeton: Princeton University Press, 1950), see especially chapter 2, "Nietzsche's Method."
46. Sara Kofman, *Nietzsche and Metaphor* (Palo Alto: Stanford University Press, 1993).
47. Alexander Nehamas, *Nietzsche: Life as Literature* (Boston: Harvard University Press, 1985), p. 23.
48. Ibid. p. 35.
49. Jacques Derrida, *Spurs: Nietzsche's Styles* (Chicago: University of Chicago Press, 1979).
50. For a few recent contributions to the umbrella debate, see Quentin Skinner, "Lectures Part Two: Is it still possible to interpret texts?" *The International Journal of Psychoanalysis* 89.3 (2008), pp. 647–54; Chung-Hsiung Lai, "Nietzsche's Forgotten Umbrella – Memory, Life and History," *Euramerica (Institute of European and American Studies Academia Sinica)* 34 (2004), pp. 203–29; Samuel A. Chambers, "Foucault's evasive maneuvers: Nietzsche, interpretation, critique," *Angelaki: Journal of Theoretical Humanities* 6.3 (2001), pp. 101–23.
51. *Truth and Method*, p. 272.
52. Ibid. p. 367.
53. Georgia Warnke, "Literature, law, and morality," in *Gadamer's Repercussions: Reconsidering Philosophical Hermeneutics*, ed. Bruce Krajewski (Los Angeles: University of California Press, 2004), pp. 82–102, 94.
54. Barthes argues in his essay "The Death of the Author," that the author is dead because the reader is the sole origin of interpretation. Roland Barthes, "The Death of the Author," *Image, Music, Text*. trans. Stephen Heath (New York: Hill and Wang, 1977), pp. 142–8.
55. Kathleen Merrow, "'The Meaning of Every Style': Nietzsche, Demosthenes, Rhetoric" *Rhetorica* 21:4 (2003) pp. 285–307, 298.
56. Ibid. p. 299.
57. Jean-François Lyotard and Jean-Loup Thebaud, *Just Gaming: Theory and History of Literature* (Minneapolis: University of Minnesota Press, 1985).
58. Lyotard and Thebaud 1985, pp. 4–5.

5 Openness to Critical Reflection: Gandhi beyond Gadamer

STEVEN PAUL CAUCHON

In *Truth and Method,* Hans-Georg Gadamer argues that interpretation is always bounded by one's prejudices and fore-meanings, which he calls "horizons." A genuine understanding of individuals, texts, and traditions therefore requires one to endeavor to see beyond the particularity of one's own horizons. Indeed, when we are *open* to the truth claims put forward by our interlocutors, we can examine critically the prejudices that make up our horizon and potentially "fuse" them with those of our interlocutor. However, in contemporary political discourse, openness to the claims of one's interlocutors is not always forthcoming. Political discourse can lead to the ossification, if not exaggeration, of one's prejudices, rather than opening them up to critical reflection as Gadamer suggests. It is therefore puzzling that Gadamer's account of hermeneutic understanding claims to be *descriptive* rather than *prescriptive*. This essay argues that if hermeneutics is to fuse horizons, it needs to be prescriptive. It ought to clearly endorse openness as a normative value-commitment that encourages a willingness to change in light of what we learn while engaged in dialogue. The vulnerability and willingness to be open to transformation is not merely a description of what understanding is, but rather a critical and conscientious step in its process.

Gandhi's idea of *ahimsa*, non-violence, and his encouragement of *satyagraha*, nonviolent political action, are prescriptive in this way as they link the requirements of hermeneutical understanding with clear moral commitments. Thus, *satyagraha* requires that those practicing nonviolent political contestation be open to their interlocutor's claims. Moreover, while a *satyagrahi's* use of non-violence and suffering often yields political leverage, its ultimate goal is to make the practitioner's truth *apparent* to her interlocutors by eliciting affective dispositions (such as love, empathy, compassion) though the process of self-suffering.

In order to understand the significance Gandhian thought has for hermeneutics, this essay first addresses Gadamer's argument concerning the process of dialogue and its relationship to hermeneutics. The following section discusses Gandhi's epistemology and its relationship to *satyagraha,* and considers how one might apply the latter without adopting Gandhi's religious convictions. The third and final section brings Gadamer and Gandhi into conversation to illustrate how *ahimsa* and *satyagraha* provide a practical model for engendering openness.

HERMENEUTICS AND THE PROCESS OF UNDERSTANDING IN DIALOGUE

In *Truth and Method,* Gadamer argues that the epistemological and ontological assumptions embraced by the Enlightenment and natural sciences are inapplicable to the "human sciences." Kant's response to "what is Enlightenment," emphasized *thinking for oneself* through one's capacity to reason, rather than relying on the authority of tradition. However, according to Gadamer, the move to circumvent the fore-meanings inculcated by tradition fails to take into account the "ontologically positive significance" that they bring to understanding. Drawing on Heidegger's *Being and Time,* Gadamer explains fore-meanings as our "practical pre-understanding" and "ongoing engagement with things themselves."[1] Indeed, without them, we have no means to make sense of the world in which we live. Although understanding always requires the use of our fore-meanings and prejudices as a starting point, they are by definition provisional in nature and are, or at least ought to be, subject to revaluation and revision when applied to new situations.

Gadamer thus concludes that the Enlightenment was erroneously "prejudiced against prejudice itself, which denies tradition its power," creating a false antithesis between reason and tradition.[2] It is not our prejudices that blind us, but rather our inability to recognize them as necessary (but also conditional) aspects of understanding. Gadamer argues that removing this prejudice against prejudice inherited from the Enlightenment will bring us to an "appropriate understanding of the finitude which dominates not only our humanity but also our historical consciousness."[3] Indeed, contrary to the Enlightenment perspective, the history of tradition does not belong to us, but rather we to it. The prejudices and fore-meanings of the interpreter, which the Enlightenment sought to eliminate, actually constitute one's historical reality and cannot be eliminated.

Gadamer admits that our fore-meanings and prejudices may lead us to erroneous conclusions. However, as one "cannot separate in advance the productive prejudices that enable understanding from the prejudices that hinder it and lead to misunderstandings," the prejudices that occupy one's consciousness must be "worked out" during the *process* of understanding.[4] Gadamer thus sees the primary task of the hermeneutic scholar to be on guard against the potential arbitrariness of the fore-meanings she brings to the process of understanding and to direct her gaze "on the things themselves" as persons trying to understand texts and individuals are always projecting.[5] Gadamer suggests that a *hermeneutically trained consciousness*, that is sensitive to "an other's" alterity, helps guard against misunderstanding and allows one to critically examine one's own prejudices concomitantly. Thus, the hermeneutic task is that of fostering a degree of openness in the interpreter that will allow the text to speak to her. Indeed, Gadamer states that hermeneutics is not "knowledge as domination," but rather consists "in subordinating ourselves to the text's claim to dominate our minds."[6]

However, this argument does not mean one should uncritically accept the text's message, but rather approach it with an explicit awareness of being prejudiced. Indeed, by approaching a text with an initial position of openness, we assume that the text has something to say to us and that this might affirm or oppose what we already believe to be true. Therefore, when a text presents us with information ostensibly incongruent with our prejudices, we must not be defensive, but allow the text to assert its own truth against our own fore-meanings. When we are sensitive and open to the text's alterity, we are in a better position to locate, examine, and appreciate areas in which we are "pulled up short by the text"[7] as they are the locus of genuine understanding.

Gadamer uses dialogue to explain this process. Nevertheless, rather than outlining a technique for how one should go about conducting such a dialogue, Gadamer *describes* the ways in which we can be blind to what another has to tell us. Specifically, Gadamer outlines three ways in which intersubjective relations between "I" and "Thou" operate, the first two of which are indicative of such blindness. In the first instance the "I" treats the "Thou" in instrumental terms: we treat the person with whom we are in conversation as an object that can generate knowledge (e.g. of human behavior) for our own ends. For example, when a scientist brackets her prejudices, and excludes everything that is "subjective" in order to predict the actions of another human being, she not only reflects herself out of this interaction, but also treats her interlocutor in a purely instrumental fashion.[8] Gadamer rejects this approach to engaging with another, as it is "purely self-regarding and contradicts the moral definition of man," *à la* Kant's categorical imperative.[9]

Gadamer also rejects the second way he claims that an "I" encounters a "Thou" in dialogue. In this instance, the "I" claims to "understand the other better than the other understands himself" and approaches the other strictly through the *I's* own cognitive framework.[10] Even though the other is treated as a person, and not an object as in the previous interaction, the understanding of the other is still conducted in a self-relating fashion. Specifically, the other has no existence separate from the *I* and the *I* therefore assimilates its knowledge to her own. In this case, the other's claims are kept at a distance. Only in the third instance is the "I" open to the "Thou" and is thus able to genuinely understand what she has to say. Gadamer claims that when one understands another in the terms of this third instance, she thinks "along with the other from the perspective of a specific bond of belonging" and is prepared to listen to what the other has to say.[11] In Gadamer's words, "[o]penness to the other, then, involves recognizing that I myself must accept some things that are against me, even though no one else forces me to do so."[12] Therefore, it is only when we are *open to and take seriously the claims of another* that we are able understand them and critically reflect on our own fore-meanings.

However, is this how understanding generally takes place (that is, leaving ourselves open to the claims individuals make), especially when we engage in political dialogue? Put differently, if the process of understanding that Gadamer outlines is a deviation from ordinary political dialogue, and assuming that a fusion of horizons (i.e. understanding others) is a desirable phenomenon, should hermeneutics be framed as a prescriptive argument about how one *ought* to go about understanding individuals, and not merely a description of how this process is possible? As Georgia Warnke points out, dialogue for Gadamer is not arguing, but a discussion with the end of evaluating claims that can be accepted and revised based on an encounter with "the other."[13] However, she also points out that dialogue can conversely reinforce and even exaggerate our fore-meanings. Indeed, it is not difficult to see how individuals in contemporary political discourse are reluctant to be open to the examination of their prejudices and political dispositions.

Take a study by Brendan Nyhan and Jason Reifler that Warnke uses to illustrate this point.[14] Their study tested the effects of counter-information on preexisting political prejudices and found that when presented with evidence that undermined their preexisting political beliefs, subjects nevertheless stood fast in their beliefs, and in some instances adhered to them more fervently. Evidently, citizens engage in "motivated reasoning," seeking information that confirms prior beliefs while ignoring information contrary to them.[15] Rather than being open to counter-information that might help us to critically evaluate our prejudices, we develop "elaborate rationalizations" that allow us to hold on to them.[16] With this study in mind, how might we avoid the potential for the hermeneutic circle to become "vicious," one that reinforces, rather than helps us re-evaluate our fore-meanings?

It is difficult to find a satisfactory answer to this question in *Truth and Method* as Gadamer frequently stresses that his goal is to clarify the conditions under which understanding takes place, not to develop a procedure for understanding that might address such a concern. Indeed, Gadamer states that the conditions he outlines for understanding "do not amount to a 'procedure' or method which the interpreter must of herself bring to bear on the text; rather, they *must be given*."[17] However, throughout this section, Gadamer also suggests the hermeneutically orientated mind is *trained* and *willing* – "a person trying to understand a text is *prepared* for it to tell him something. This is why the *hermeneutically trained* conscious must be, from the start, sensitive to the text's alterity."[18] This passage paradoxically suggests that a "cultivated mind" is a skill to be fostered, not something to which one might be naturally predisposed. However, one also gets the sense that Gadamer is reluctant to offer a technique that could fall prey to the limitations he associates with the Enlightenment and natural sciences vis-à-vis interpretation and objectivity (that is, being prejudiced against prejudice).

Gadamer uses Aristotle's idea of *phronesis* as a foil to explain why no such technique is available for the hermeneutic process. *Phronesis* is the capacity to consider the best mode of action in order to enhance one's quality of life; it involves not only the *ability* to decide how to achieve this end, but the *capacity* to reflect on it. Gadamer argues that Aristotle's treatment of moral decision-making (making the right choice), like understanding, depends on its *application*. Because understanding is always application, it follows that just as we cannot be trained to make the "right choice" independent of the situation in which moral principles are applied, we cannot be trained to understand or interpret in a correct way, as what constitutes "the right interpretation" will always be contingent on contextual factors.

For instance, in legal hermeneutics, understanding "the spirit of the law," rather than "the letter of the law," depends on the situation in which the former is applied. Indeed, we do not expect judges to apply the letter of the law verbatim, but rather come to a conclusion about how the spirit in which the law was created applies to a particular circumstance. The sensitivity that we expect judges to exercise in this process, and their willingness to let the text of the law *tell them something,* mirrors the conditions needed for genuine understanding between individuals. This result underscores the difficulty that Gadamer finds in prescribing a technique of hermeneutic understanding, as a judge's capacity to interpret and be sensitive to the spirit of the law is the result of years of experience, not any technique per se.

However, the fragility inherent in this situation is exacerbated in dialogue as, at least ideally, two parties must be open if *mutual understanding* is to be realized. The way this process plays out in contemporary political discourse is more akin to the way prosecution and defense attempt to interpret the law in trial, not the judge that Gadamer employs. Rather than being open to what the letter of the law has to say to them, prosecution and defense are actively trying to bend the letter of the law to their own purposes. The lack of openness by prosecution and defense in this scenario is arguably a function of their motivation to win the case, not letting the truth prevail per se. We can think of this instance as similar to Gadamer's first instance of dialogue between the *I* and the *Thou* in which the latter is *instrumental* to the ends of the former. Thus, the lawyer's "motivated reasoning" can override what the letter of the law might be trying to tell her, as she is not necessarily open to what it, or the opposing counsel, has to say. Gadamer would likely suggest that such lawyers are not attempting to understand the law, but are rather attempting to dominate it. Indeed, such individuals would seem to lack the "self-mastery" Gadamer argues as necessary for the kind of understanding that the experienced judge is able to enjoy.

With this in mind, I argue that if we want our interlocutor to understand us, we cannot assume, as in Gadamer's third way of dialogue, that they possess the requisite self-mastery and openness. Indeed, we regularly assume that what we say can often produce an initially defensive disposition, rather than one of openness, in our interlocutors. This result leaves us with two practical questions: if we are to achieve Gadamer's ideal third situation, how do we develop the self-mastery necessary for understanding that he outlines? Furthermore, as this is a dialogical process, how do we encourage our interlocutors to exercise a similar openness of mind? In the following section, I address this set of questions through a Gandhian lens by examining the importance of the body and emotions for evoking openness in interpersonal dialogue.

GANDHI, EPISTEMOLOGY, AND THE UTILITY OF SELF-SUFFERING

Gadamer writes that "[t]o reach an understanding in a dialogue is not merely a matter of putting oneself forward and successfully asserting one's own point of view, but being transformed into a communion in which we do not remain what we were."[19] I argue that a key element to realizing this communion resides in the affective dispositions (for example, love, empathy, compassion) that one is able to foster though the process of self-suffering outlined by Gandhi. In order to makes this case, I turn to Gandhi's account of *satyagraha*, or nonviolent political action, and *ahimsa*, or non-violence, and the epistemological conviction on which their legitimacy is predicated.

For Gandhi, Truth is God; truth is the sole justification for human existence and all human activities should be concerned with its pursuit. Indeed, he declared that his life had consisted of nothing but experiments with the truth.[20] At the same time, Gandhi claims that because absolute Truth alone is God, absolute Truth is ultimately beyond his or any of our reach. Neither he nor anyone else can possess an Archimedean point in which one could see objective 'truth.' Rather, "we will always see Truth in fragment and from different angles of vision."[21] Or, as he also puts the point, "what appear to be different truths are like the countless and apparently different leaves of the same tree."[22] Yet truth is not relative for Gandhi; rather one's perception of truth is either impaired or enhanced by their ability to listen to their conscience. Indeed, he remarks:

> There are innumerable definitions of God because his manifestations are innumerable. They overwhelm me with wonder and awe and for a moment stun me. But I worship God as Truth only. I have not yet found Him, but I am seeking after Him ... But as long as I have not realized this Absolute Truth so long must I hold by the relative truth as I have conceived it. That relative truth must, meanwhile, be my beacon, my shield and buckler.[23]

Thus, Truth is universal, but like the horizons of interpretation in hermeneutics, truth appears to individuals in various forms. Indeed, our *relative* truth claims constitute our reality and our view of *universal* Truth is fragmented, partial, and incomplete. Our inability to see beyond relative truth underscores the epistemological limitations Gandhi associates with human understanding and seeking Truth. Although Gandhi suggests that it is impossible to transcend this limitation, he nevertheless argues that we can *discipline* ourselves in order to overcome certain aspects of it. Specifically, he claims that in order to gain even a fragmented view of Truth, we must cultivate our soul in which one's conscience resides. In his words, conscience "is the ripe fruit of strictest discipline" and "can reside only in the delicately tuned breast."[24] Everyone possesses a conscience, but effectively listening to it requires a strict series of disciplines – *ahimsa* being central among them.

For Gandhi *ahimsa* is a synonym for truth and is as simple in theory as it is difficult to practice.[25] In the minimal sense, *ahimsa* means not injuring any living being, whether by body or mind.[26] However, like the absolute truth that Gandhi claimed was beyond his reach, so is the practice of perfect *ahimsa*.[27] Thus, the practices of not injuring any being, and the pursuit of truth, are both continuous undertakings that are constantly reinforcing one another. Gandhi underscores this reciprocal relationship when he states, "*[a]himsa* is my God, and Truth is my God. When I look for *ahimsa*, Truth says, 'Find it out through me.' When I look for Truth, *ahimsa* says, 'find it out through me.'"[28] In other words, the practice of *ahimsa* will lead one, and those they engage with, to the truth and the pursuit of truth will lead one to accepting *ahimsa* as truth. Gandhi argues that one's true self-interest consists in the good of all and that one must engage in self-purification in order to realize this truth.

For Gandhi, the process of practicing *ahimsa* requires a great deal of self-suffering and self-purification, or *tapas*. The inclusion of *tapas* within his notion of *ahimsa* is not only a departure from the latter's source in Hindu tradition, but can also strike those unfamiliar with Gandhian thought as a logical contradiction (i.e. the idea of *ahimsa* embracing self-violence). However, Gandhi prides himself in not being a philosopher in the systematic sense. Indeed, his teachings are riddled with a number of seemingly logical contradictions as he was constantly changing his views based on his experiments with truth. For example, despite claiming the central importance of *ahimsa* to his teachings, Gandhi does not categorically reject violence and frequently suggests that violence is preferable to cowardice.[29] This is because Gandhi understood much of the violence in the world as a function of cowardice and fear, which he argued could be tempered through the processes of self-suffering.

Therefore, Gandhi's synthesis of *tapas* and *ahimsa* is meant to test a *satyagrahi's* courage and commitment to truth, which also serves as an ascetic tool for self-realization and self-discipline. For instance, Gandhi was constantly trying to reduce himself to zero, be "humbler than dust" and believed that *ahimsa* was the farthest limit of human humility. To the extent that one becomes "humbler than dust," one is less likely to engage in the kind of self-centered motivated reasoning that hinders their capacity to seek truth and understand the point of view of others. Thus, the requirement of epistemic humility for Gandhi is twofold: first, human fallibility dictates that we must never take any truth as beyond question. Second, understanding is always bound by one's ability to listen to one's conscience and thus partial and necessarily incomplete. For instance, alluding to motivated rationality, Gandhi remarks, "people will turn and twist the [interpretation of the] text to suit their own purposes ... *Selfishness* turns them blind, and by a use of the ambiguous middle they deceive themselves and seek to deceive the world."[30] Put differently, our deep-seated selfishness hinders our willingness to admit when we are in error and thus fulfill our duty, which is the relentless pursuit of truth. It is through self-suffering and purification that one is able to temper the proclivity toward self-regarding means of engaging in the world, specifically political dialogue, and instead seek truth and common understanding with those that we engage with. Gandhi thus argues that self-suffering makes us humble, and that when we are humble enough, we will realize we are no more important than any other living being.

However, it would be a mistake to think that the practice of *ahimsa* is essentially negative and that the requirement of self-suffering is inward in nature (that is, being consumed with one's own pain). Although in its negative form, *ahimsa* dictates that we refrain from action (i.e. non-violence), in its positive form it requires love, compassion, and forgiveness for all living beings, which indicates the need for outward action. Rather than renouncing social life, Gandhi alternatively stressed the need for the ascetic to immerse themselves in the service of others. Specifically, the ascetic's suffering should not be conducted in isolation, but rather utilized in the services of others. Therefore, it is not enough to abstain from injuring any living being, one must love every living being by helping them pursue truth as well. It follows that one must also engage in political discourse as Gandhi claims, "the quest for Truth, cannot be prosecuted in a cave."[31] Indeed, by participating in political discourse one is able to legitimize and/or scrutinize one's respective political dispositions while also conveying one's truth claims to the world. Gandhi argued that the process of practicing *ahimsa* and the truth that it leads one to is not limited to the individual seeker, but is also a means of *converting those who have yet to acquire a clear vision of it.*[32] Gandhi refers to this process of conversion based on *ahimsa* as *satyagraha*, political action based on non-violence.

Satyagraha literally means insistence on truth, but for Gandhi it also meant "pure soul-force."[33] The term soul-force implies the fortitude accorded to one with epistemic conviction and is consequently able to act without fear. If one is abused through another's ignorance, one must be resolute in one's truth, be willing to suffer for it, and in doing so demonstrate to the aggressor one's love for and certitude of the truth. Gandhi remarks, "[i]f someone gives us pain through ignorance, we shall win him through love."[34] However, Gandhi also realized that our interlocutors might not share our truth and might therefore be *closed off* to what we have to say. Indeed, even amongst the most "conscientious persons, there will be room for honest differences of opinion," as we only see truth in its fragmented form.[35] Being aware of this limitation, Gandhi constantly stressed the need to facilitate an interlocutor's openness to our truth claims. The key to evoking such a disposition lies in the *satyagrahi*'s willingness to suffer and the emotions, such as empathy, admiration, and even confusion, elicited by fasting, "sitting-in," etc. Although *satyagraha*'s potential lay in the political leverage commonly associated with civil disobedience, it is also a means of communicating ideas and feelings insofar as watching voluntary suffering can cause a change in the heart and mind.

To be sure, despite contemporary appropriations of Gandhi's idea of *satyagraha*, his practice of non-violence is more than civil disobedience. However, while it is possible to practice civil disobedience without embracing Gandhi's epistemology, it is impossible to employ and understand *satyagraha* without engaging in Gandhi's process of truth seeking. Gandhi frequently advised his followers that they could not understand truth by mimicking his actions and teachings alone; rather one must struggle and suffer oneself in order to see the truth and convey it to the world. Gandhi claimed that *satyagraha* was an infallible remedy because it was centered on the process of truth seeking and self-transformation; absent this process, *ahimsa* and *satyagraha* become wooden lifeless dogmas that enable hypocrisy, distortion, and ultimately yield the practice as ineffective. This is because absent a transformation in thought by both interlocutors, the victories a *satyagrahi* may realize are at risk of being short lived.

Gandhi is widely known for his nonviolent campaign of gaining independence from Great Britain. However, this campaign was also part of a larger, more ambitious project. Indeed, Gandhi argued that for India to become an independent civic nation, a fundamental transformation needed to take place in India's mindset that would facilitate the necessary self-development embodied by *swaraj*.[36] It is no coincidence that *swaraj* generally means self-rule[37] – Gandhi argued that any gains toward Indian independence would be exceedingly difficult, and or ephemeral, if the Indian population did not acquire individual self-mastery first. Hence, rather than focusing only on the imperial occupation by the British, Gandhi claimed that true independence required both internal and external change in both parties. A long-lasting and peaceful independence required epistemic humility and openness on the part of the Indian population and it required eliciting openness in the British population, appealing to their hearts and minds. In other words, although the practice of civil disobedience may compel an adversary to change her course of action, absent a change of mindset, the victory is at risk of being superficial and/or temporary.

The requirements for attaining the epistemic humility necessary for the practice of *ahimsa* and *satyagraha* often strikes those unfamiliar with Gandhian thought as daunting and/or exclusive to those who share his metaphysical/religious convictions, as they include temperance/chastity *(brahmacharya),* truthfulness *(satya),* justice (or freedom from greed), and courage. Indeed, even some of his closest followers often criticized Gandhi for setting unrealistic expectations for the practice of *satyagraha*.[38] Nevertheless, dwelling on Gandhi's religious convictions obfuscates the insight he offers into the demanding process of critical dialogue. Although the conclusions Gandhi draws vis-à-vis the utility of *ahimsa* are firmly grounded in religious texts, specifically Vedic teachings, Gandhi himself claims, "though my views on *ahimsa* are a result of my study of most of the faiths of the world, they are now no longer dependent upon the authority of these works."[39] Moreover, as Anthony Parel points out, Gandhi underscores how the conclusions he has drawn should be open to further consideration by others.[40] It is useful therefore to look beyond Gandhi's own experiments with truth in order to understand the epistemic utility embodied in the techniques of *satyagraha* and *ahimsa*.

An important example of how this is possible can be found in Farah Godrej's reinterpretation of *ahimsa* as a "civic virtue," which can be used "as a public standard for the justification of and arbitration among political views and actions" absent Gandhi's metaphysical convictions.[41] In this reinterpretation, Godrej outlines three requirements, all of which are detached from Gandhi's virtue-based truth seeking, that serve to guide civic *ahimsa*. The first requirement is that of "epistemological humility and self-scrutiny."[42] This position entails the acknowledgement of one's one fallibility and an initial respect for one's interlocutors (until proven otherwise) in order to be open to what they have to say to us.[43] The second requirement is that one engage in moral persuasion through nonviolent *discourse* in our initial attempt to convert an adversary to our own moral position.[44] Being open to our interlocutor, while simultaneously attempting to convert them to our position, may seem to be contradictory requirements. However, these requirements assume that the practitioner understands her political dialogue as *a search for truth,* not as a "struggle for political advantage or victory in arguments."[45] But as we cannot assume our interlocutor embraces this assumption or is open to what we have to say, the final requirement is that the practitioner must also be willing to suffer nonviolently, undergo punishment, and invite legal sanction, if necessary, when the initial dialogue fails to illicit openness.

The strategies that Godrej outlines in civic *ahimsa* focus on the key insight *satyagraha* has for prescriptive hermeneutics – its capacity to alter an interlocutor's affective disposition as means of breaking through their "rational defenses" when political dialogue initially fails. For example, the idea of "motivated rationality," in which individuals ignore information that refutes their political beliefs, allows them to "rationalize" the validity of their original position. In this instance, one's capacity to reason is not the problem, but rather their lack of *openness* to new information. The solution to this intransigence lies not in constructing more reasonable and/or persuasive arguments, but rather in facilitating openness. Moreover, eliciting openness in our interlocutor is insufficient as we must be open ourselves as both Gandhi and Gadamer constantly remind us. Indeed, "[b]eing open to each other's point of view is of course the hallmark of a true *satyagrahi.*"[46] The practice of self-suffering and use of the body while engaged in dialogue serves the dual purpose of preparing the practitioner to be open and evoking openness in her interlocutor.

Because of his focus on linguistic understanding and textual hermeneutics, Gadamer neglects the more corporal and emotive elements involved in understanding. In the following section, I demonstrate how Gandhi provides a corrective to this omission. Specifically, I argue that a Gandhian approach, which puts the body and emotions at the center of truth seeking and understanding, offers a prescriptive complement to the limitations Gadamer outlines in dialogical hermeneutics. I turn now to demonstrating how the logic animating the praxis of *ahimsa* and *satyagraha* helps us move toward a prescriptive mode of hermeneutics.

A GANDHIAN APPROACH TO PRESCRIPTIVE HERMENEUTICS

Gandhi and Gadamer both suggest that what we know, and how we know it, is an infinite process, as we must constantly test our relational truths, or what Gadamer calls horizons. Moreover, an important part of this testing occurs when we encounter horizons and truth claims that are dissimilar to that of our own. Indeed, when engaged in dialogue, "understanding is always the fusion of these horizons supposedly existing by themselves."⁴⁷ Specifically, Gadamer argues that we are able to examine our fore-meanings critically through experience, which is essentially an iterative process (that is, false generalization being continually refuted by new experiences). Thus, the "experienced person" is undogmatic as she is constantly open to new experiences and new points of view (e.g. alterity) that may challenge, not necessarily confirm, her preexisting knowledge. Indeed, Gadamer remarks that "the experienced man knows that all foresight is limited and all plans uncertain," highlighting the finitude of human experience.⁴⁸ In order to arrive at an understanding while engaged in dialogue, the experienced man and the *satyagrahi* must be cognizant of their own fallibility. Again, this does not suggest that their fore-meanings are likely to be wrong, but rather conditional as they are a function of the horizons in which they are bound. This is a delicate balance then, as we must embrace our fore-meanings and truth claims, but at the same time, subject them to constant scrutiny that can either strengthen or weaken our adherence to them.

Gandhi uses the parable of the seven blind men and the elephant to illustrate this point. In this story, each of the blind men touch the elephant at different parts, leading to different descriptions of the elephant. According to Gandhi, these descriptions "were all true from their own points of view and yet each appeared to be untrue from the points of view of the rest. The truth was beyond all the seven."⁴⁹ While Gandhi uses this parable to demonstrate the limited ability to perceive Truth, it is also useful for illustrating the need for a prescriptive hermeneutics. In order for the seven blind men to reach an agreement, a common understanding of what the elephant is, they must move beyond the particularity of their own horizons. However, in moving, they need not abandon their relative truth (i.e. horizons). Just as Gadamer argues that we must evaluate our fore-meanings through conversation, rather than thinking we can abandon them beforehand, Gandhi claims that those seeking truth must hold fast in their convictions, until this seeking leads them to re-evaluate them in light of new experiences.

Indeed, it is only by fusing their relative truth claims that the blind men can arrive at a common agreement, a common understanding, of what the elephant is. However, we can also see the precarious nature of such a situation, as the blind men need to stand by their respective truth while concomitantly exercising epistemic humility and facilitating openness. The problematic nature of this situation leads Gandhi to claim that following the truth is "like walking on a razor's edge" and that it is only through *self-mastery* that one is able to do so.⁵⁰ The practice of hermeneutics and *satyagraha* both underscore a need to attain a certain degree of self-mastery in order to avoid the tendency to be blinded by one's prejudices and motivated rationality. Moreover, it is not enough that only one of the blind men possesses self-mastery if the others are not open to what he has to say. However, Gandhi goes beyond Gadamer by outlining how one is able to achieve such openness in their interlocutors.

Drawing on Hindu scriptures, which suggest a direct correlation between clear vision and self-discipline through suffering, Gandhi argues the process of suffering brings us to the realization of the finite nature of human understanding. Gadamer himself uses *Aeschylus*'s formula for "learning though suffering" (*pathei mathos*) to demonstrate that all foresight and fore-meanings are limited. According to Gadamer, "[w]hat a man has to learn through suffering is not this or that particular thing, but insight into the limitation of humanity, into the absoluteness of the barrier that separates man from the divine."[51] Indeed, self-suffering brings one to the realization of one's own epistemological limitations, yet enhances one's ability to seek truth. However the ability to listen to and scrutinize one's relative truth is a conscientious state and, as Gandhi argues, can only be " acquired by laborious training ... a conscientious man hesitates to assert himself, he is always humble, never boisterous, always compromising, always ready to listen, ever willing, even anxious to admit mistakes."[52] Therefore, one's ability to be open to and seek truth is not a method per se, but a process that positively reinforces itself.

Recall that Gandhi is explicit that one cannot simply follow his path in order to achieve the self-mastery necessary to effectively seek truth, but rather one must suffer in order to find one's own path. However, Gandhi does outline a *guide* for one's conduct that can help hone one's ability to listen and seek truth – what he refers to as disciplined consciousness. In his words, "the etymology of conscious is 'true knowledge' ... [p]ossession of such a faculty is possible only for a trained person, that is, one who has undergone disciple and learned to listen to the inner voice."[53] While a complete discussion of Gandhi's prescriptive program is beyond the scope of this essay, Gandhian ashrams (spiritual community or commune), in which this program was institutionalized, provide a telling example. Although not all ashrams are alike, they typically translate the teachings of Gandhi into a way of life characterized by "constant self-examination and a rigorously disciplined lifestyle geared toward the total cultivation of *ahimsa*" (for example, simple and sustainable living, self-sufficiency, community service, penance, and meditation).[54] The commitments embodied by ashram life are built on the reciprocal relationship between the *practice* of spiritual obligation and self-abnegating asceticism and the inner transformation necessary for the practice of both negative and positive *ahimsa*. Although Gandhi admits that it is impossible for individuals to realize perfect *ahimsa* through such practices, we can become closer to this ideal by ceaselessly striving and meditating on it. Gandhi therefore offers us a practical, albeit demanding, means by which we can come closer to attaining the requisite self-mastery outlined in Gadamer's ideal hermeneutic dialogue.

Specifically, disciplined self-suffering serves a hermeneutic purpose by invoking the sort of openness and humility that is required in Gadamerian hermeneutics. However, this is not the only insight that Gandhi has to offer prescriptive hermeneutics. While engaged in political discourse, it is not enough that a *satyagrahi* has disciplined her conscience, if the goal is to reach a mutual understanding. Although Gadamer understands textual hermeneutics as dialogue, a text need not be open to the interpreter for a fusion of horizons to take place. Indeed, the goal of interpreting text is not to change the mind of the text, but rather overcome one's own limitations and allow the text to speak to oneself. Gadamer's use of dialogue as a metaphor for describing linguistic hermeneutics overlooks how this process becomes much more dynamic, and complicated, between two living beings. Specifically, attention to the affective dispositions that can influence how understanding and dialogue take place becomes essential.

Gandhian thought alternatively demonstrates how emotions and the use of one's body are a crucial means by which we come to know and understand each other and ourselves.[55] Rather than painting emotion as a force that interferes with reason and understanding as the Enlightenment and the natural sciences might suggest, Gandhi recognizes that "political solutions require appeal to the emotive and affect-driven parts of human personality" and that these are a part of, not antithetical to, our capacity to understanding and reason with one another.[56] Specifically, Gandhi claims that humans universally share something, what he called a "divine spark," that one can appeal to through *satyagraha* in order to achieve mutual understanding.[57] To make sure that our interlocutors are with us while engaged in dialogue, we must first break through their "motivated rationality" by evoking affective dispositions through self-suffering. Therefore, while we need not expect that our interlocutors possess the ideal self-mastery necessary for mutual openness, a *satyagrahi* can circumvent their propensity to engage in motivated rationality by appealing to emotions elicited through activities such as fasting, "occupying," "sitting-in," and any related physical punishment and/or legal sanction that accompany such actions. Indeed, self-suffering serves as a sort of "shock treatment" to the potentially defensive position of her interlocutor by dramatizing the *satyagrhai's* moral position vis-à-vis her willingness to suffer for it.[58]

Nevertheless, even the epistemic humility and mutual openness that the practice of *ahimsa* and *satyagraha* engender does not guarantee the political dialogue will end disagreement. Indeed, even though the goal of dialogue for hermeneutics is an agreement on the subject matter, there is no definitive way of maintaining any such agreement as we are always encountering new experiences, and thus new truths. It follows that how we come to know and understand the world is an inexhaustible process, as we not only have different perspectives, but also are constantly working out the validity of our horizons on which our perspectives are predicated. Gandhi concedes that there is no way of permanently ending disagreement. Indeed, the self-suffering of a *satyagrahi* is not only a means of demonstrating her political conviction; it is also an acknowledgement of her own fallibility. Gandhi claims that violence in politics is never justified, "because man is not capable of knowing the absolute truth and therefore not competent to punish."[59] Therefore, *ahimsa* is not only a principled means of pursuing truth; but is in part, a pragmatic response to the limitations of human understanding in the realm of politics.[60] Indeed, Gandhi was concerned with the use not only of physical violence in politics, but also of epistemic violence.[61]

During India's struggle for independence, Gandhi thus claimed that the "constitutional approach" of the Moderates and the violent approach of the Extremists both presented problematic means of achieving social change and an independent India. The latter's use of violence evinced epistemic hubris while the legal mechanisms employed by the Moderates permitted epistemic violence. Although a barrister by training, Gandhi himself came to disapprove of the profession and its associated means as he frequently claimed that lawyers were focused on winning rather than letting the truth prevail. He therefore advocated *satyagraha* as the only acceptable means of realizing Indian independence as it encompassed both *epistemic humility* and an explicit goal of *persuading one's interlocutors*, not dominating them or winning per se. Nonviolent persuasion is invaluable because even if the practitioner's truth claim is questionable, only the person practicing nonviolence suffers, not one's adversary. Moreover, the willingness to suffer by the practitioner elicits openness, demonstrates her conviction to truth, and a willingness to engage in dialogue.

CONCLUSION

As stated, Gandhi cautions against mistaking *satyagraha* for political action based on mere civil resistance because it also indicates a "relentless search for truth and the power that such a search gives to the searcher."[62] Politics is essentially about power; however, instead of trying to change people through force, Gandhi's abhorrence of violence led him to believe that we must begin by changing ourselves first. He sought this change through asceticism and the example he set while engaged in this arduous process endowed him with a unique moral force, allowing him to lead and change a nation. However, the practice of political action achieved through a *satyagrahi's* self-suffering and firmness to the truth is not limited to saints. Gandhi himself claimed to be a "practical idealist" and that the practice of *satyagraha* was meant "for the common people."[63] Indeed, one need not live in an *ashram* to realize the potential embedded in *satyagraha*, but rather adhere to its requirements of epistemic humility, self-examination, and disciplined self-suffering. Although demanding, the model for political dialogue that Gandhi offers provides complementary supplement to Gadamer's description of his hermeneutic ideal, one that is prescriptive.

The criterion for practicing *satyagraha* will not be the way most individuals go about debating truth claims in order to reach a common understanding. However, if genuine political dialogue requires that "each person opens himself to the other, truly accepts his point of view as valid," then Gandhi's ideas of *satyagraha* and *ahimsa* provide a novel way for thinking about how we can go about evoking mutual openness. Gandhian thought underscores how nonviolent means can facilitate an affective stance between interlocutors, thus opening the possibility for genuine change, understanding, and a fusing of horizons. Although the practice of *ahimsa* and *satyagraha* cannot guarantee a fusion of horizons, it does mitigate the likelihood that political dialogue will produce a vicious circle in which we leave a conversation further closed off, rather than open, to what our interlocutor has to say.

NOTES

1. Georgia Warnke, "The Hermeneutic Circle Versus Dialogue," *The Review of Metaphysics* 65, 2011, p. 11.
2. Hans-Georg Gadamer, *Truth and Method*, Second revised edition (New York, Continuum, (1975) 1989), pp. 270, 277.
3. Ibid. p. 276.
4. Ibid. p. 295.

5. Ibid. p. 267.
6. Ibid. p. 311.
7. Ibid. p. 268.
8. Ibid. p. 359; Warnke "The Hermeneutic Circle," p. 11.
9. Gadamer *Truth and Method*, p. 358.
10. Ibid. p. 359.
11. Ibid. p. 361.
12. Ibid. p. 361.
13. Warnke, "The Hermeneutic Circle," p. 13.
14. Brendan Nyhan and Jason Reifler, "When Corrections Fail: The Persistence of Political Misperceptions," *Political Behavior* 32, 2010, pp. 303–30.
15. Saharon Begley, "Why We Believe Lies, Even When We Learn the Truth", Newsweek, available at http://www.newsweek.com/why-we-believe-lies-even-when-we-learn-truth-78775 (last accessed 2009).
16. Ibid.
17. Gadamer, *Truth and Method*, p. 295 (emphasis added).
18. Ibid. p. 269 (emphasis added).
19. Ibid. p. 371.
20. Mohandas K Gandhi, *An Autobiography: The Story of My Experiments with Truth* (Boston: Beacon Press, 1993).
21. Raghavan Iyer, *The Moral and Political Writings of Mahatma Gandhi*, Vol. II (Oxford: Clarendon Press, 1986), p. 126.
22. Ibid. p. 163.
23. Gandhi, *An Autobiography*, xviii.
24. Iyer, *The Moral and Political Writings*, Vol. II, 125.
25. Ibid. p. 177, xxviii.
26. See Farah Godrej, "Nonviolence and Gandhi's Truth: A Method for Moral and Political Arbitration" in *The Review of Politics* 68:2, 2006.
27. Iyer, *The Moral and Political Writings*, Vol. II, 187.
28. Ibid. p. 216.
29. Jane Ardley, *The Tibetan Independence Movement: Political, Religious and Gandhian Perspectives* (New York: Taylor & Francis, 2002), p. 99.
30. Gandhi, *An Autobiography*, p. 58 [emphasis added].
31. Joan Valérie Bondurant, *Conquest of Violence: The Gandhian Philosophy of Conflict* (Princeton: Princeton University Press, 1988), p. 22.
32. Karuna Mantena highlights the conceptual distinct, albeit inextricably interwoven, dynamic between destructive and constructive nonviolence "Another Realism: The Politics of Gandhian Nonviolence," in *American Political Science Review* 106:2, 2012, p. 465. Gandhi is generally known for his use of destructive nonviolence – the primary instrument of political change and action (e.g., civil disobedience and noncooperation). However, constructive nonviolence is his ethical position that animates a need to demonstrate truth to our interlocutors and ourselves.
33. Iyer, *The Moral and Political Writings*, Vol. II, 45.
34. Ibid. p. 45.

35. Iyer *The Moral and Political Writings*, Vol. II, 126.
36. Anthony Parel, *Gandhi: Hind Swaraj and Other Writings* (Cambridge: Cambridge University Press, (1997) 2009), xv.
37. In the Gujarati text the same word is used for self-rule and self-government (Parel, *Gandhi*, lxvi.)
38. See Gandhi–Nehru dialogue in Parel, *Gandhi*.
39. Iyer, *The Moral and Political Writings*, Vol. II, 212.
40. Parel, *Gandhi*, lxiii
41. Farah Godrej, *Cosmopolitan Political Thought: Method, Practice, Discipline* (Oxford: Oxford University Press, 2011), p. 82.
42. Ibid. p. 84.
43. Ibid. p. 84.
44. Ibid. p. 84.
45. Ibid. p. 84.
46. Parel *Gandhi*, lxiii.
47. Ibid. p. 306.
48. Ibid. p. 357.
49. Iyer, *The Moral and Political Writings*, Vol. II, 168.
50. Ibid. p. 171.
51. Gadamer, *Truth and Method*, p. 357.
52. Iyer, *The Moral and Political Writings*, Vol. II, p. 125.
53. Ibid. p. 126.
54. Godrej, *Cosmopolitan Political Thought*, p. 59; Iyer, *The Moral and Political Writings*, Vol. II, pp. 564–9.
55. Indeed, more recent scholarship demonstrates how the incorporation of emotions into an ontological understanding of social reality has opened the door to new insights regarding affect, feeling, and emotion. See Deborah Gould, *Moving Politics: Emotion and ACT UP's Fight against AIDS* (Chicago and London: University of Chicago Press, 2009) and Nancy Whittier, *The Politics of Child Sexual Abuse: Emotion, Social Movement, and the State* (Oxford: Oxford University Press, 2009).
56. Farah Godrej, "Gandhi's Civic *Ahimsa*: A Standard for Public Justification in Multicultural Democracies" (*International Journal of Gandhi Studies*, 2010), p. 19.
57. Iyer, *The Moral and Political Writings*, Vol. II. 162.
58. Godrej, *Cosmopolitan Political Thought*, p. 85.
59. Mohandas K. Gandhi, *Speeches and Writings of Mahatma Gandhi*, 4th ed. (Madras: Natesan, 1934), p. 506.
60. Godrej, "Gandhi's Civic *Ahimsa*," p. 4.
61. See Gayatri Chakravorty Spivak, "Can the subaltern speak?" in C. Nelson and L. Grossberg (eds.), *Marxism and the Interpretation of Culture* (Urbana: University of Illinois Press, 1988).
62. Raghavan Iyer, *The Moral and Political Writings of Mahatma Gandhi*, Vol. III (Oxford: Clarendon Press, 1987), p. 74.
63. Iyer, *The Moral and Political Writings*, Vol. II. p. 299.

6 Philosophical Hermeneutics and the Politics of Memory

GEORGIA WARNKE

Thomas McCarthy suggests an important difference between the former East and West Germanies in their relations to their Nazi pasts.[1] In West Germany, the historians' debate in the 1980s compelled West Germans to engage in national discussions about the Holocaust and to consider the elements of German political culture that may have led to it. East Germany, in contrast, continued to separate itself from the Nazi past, emphasized its victory over Nazi Germany and refused to acknowledge any ties or connection to it. In the 1990s, the East was the center for protests against asylum, immigration and "guest workers" while in the West those protesting did so against anti-foreigner violence and nativist politics. Currently, the East remains less friendly to foreigners and more sympathetic to the right-wing National Democratic Party, the members of which are often accused of lionizing Hitler.[2] Indeed, after the murders of 17 people by terrorists in Paris in early 2015, marchers at anti-immigration rallies in Dresden chanted, "we are the people," a slogan, according to National Public radio correspondent, Soraya Sarhaddi Nelson "very much like the sort of thing one heard during the Nazi era."[3] In Munich, in contrast, protestors sought to stop a rally by an affiliated anti-immigration group.[4]

McCarthy does not suppose that "Germany has fully mastered its Nazi past." The current immigration crisis in Europe and protests against it also suggest the limits of this mastery. Nevertheless, if we turn to the United States what is surprising is the absence of any serious national reflection on its past and, particularly, on the history and experience of Americans of African descent. Well before current reports of shady mortgage instruments sold to African Americans during the financial crisis and before the widespread circulation of videos of police shootings of African American men, observers, historians, and journalists were already painting a damning picture of the treatment that African Americans have received from their government and fellow citizens, not only during slavery and the era of segregation but far into the twentieth century. Yet many of these observations and reports have simply been ignored and, although others received some attention for a time, none has become part of the country's standard public history. To the contrary, a 2015 bill in Oklahoma would bar state funds for Advanced Placement history courses in public schools because the revised framework, the bill's sponsor Dan Fisher said, "trades an emphasis on America's founding principles of Constitutional government in favor of robust analyses of gender and racial oppression and class, ethnicity and the lives of marginalized people."[5]

As in East Germany, the reluctance in the United States to incorporate such "robust analyses" into its standard history arguably has a profound effect on its political culture. As just one example, take discussions of the expansion of health insurance. A 2013 National Journal poll suggests that whites who oppose the Affordable Care Act do so because they do not see it as a universal benefit program such as Social Security or Medicare.[6] Rather, they view it as an income-transfer program similar to food stamps or welfare and benefitting only the poor, whom they regard as generally non-white and generally as freeloaders whose poverty is self-imposed.

Together with the Oklahoma bill, this sort of response seems to provide support for the recent interest in epistemologies of ignorance and in particular for what Charles Mills calls "white ignorance,"[7] a phenomenon that, he says, reflects the way racism has so infected Europeans since their first encounters with people of color that the latter, their cultures and their history are made to disappear. As an antidote to this ignorance, Mills looks to the standpoint theory developed by Marxists and feminists and advocates a synthesis of what he considers the more veridical insights of marginalized and subordinated groups. In contrast, I want to draw on Gadamer's philosophical hermeneutics to explore the basis on which to acknowledge a general and inevitable ignorance, one that can, I think, help to open up a much-needed and prolonged national consideration of the United States' racial history. I begin by recalling some parts of that history as emphasized by just the past 25 years of research. I then turn to Mills's notion of white ignorance and, finally, look to what I see as the contributions of philosophical hermeneutics.

RECENT RESEARCH ON RACIAL DISCRIMINATION

"Torn from the Land" is a 2001 report by the Associated Press that looks at some of the ways generations of post-Civil War African Americans in Southern and border states lost the lands they once owned.[8] Documenting 107 land-takings in 13 states, a figure the AP considered simply the tip of the iceberg, the press found that 57 of the takings were violent; during Jim Crow, prosperous African American farmers were simply lynched and their lands sold off to whites.[9] Other land transfers were the result of terror and intimidation, legal chicanery and the refusal during Second World War by government agencies such as the Navy to recompense African Americans (but not European Americans) for the market value of the land it acquired through eminent domain. Current land-takings involve partition sales that have deprived African Americans of 80 per cent of the 5.5 million acres of farmland they owned in 1969.[10] Many rural African American landowners in the South lack access to legal services and often (up to 83 per cent of them) die without wills. Whenever they do so their heirs inherit the estate, owning the land in common. When those heirs also die without wills, the number of people possessing the land in common multiplies and continues to multiply over generations. Any heir can sell his or her small share in the property and once someone buys it, he or she can then petition a judge to put the entire property up for sale at auction. The remaining family members are usually not in a financial position to buy their properties back and the land is lost. The AP report quotes Thomas Mitchell, a University of Wisconsin law professor: "Imagine buying one share of Coca-Cola, and being able to go to court and demand a sale of the entire company."[11]

In their comprehensive 1993 book, *American Apartheid*, Douglas S. Massey and Nancy A. Denton take up housing discrimination against African Americans, beginning with the early twentieth century hostility of whites in northern cities to the influx of African Americans fleeing Jim Crow.[12] In race riots in various cities such as New York and Chicago, African Americans were beaten, shot and lynched; later, residential color lines made it difficult for even well-to-do African Americans to live outside of designated "black belts" or "darkytowns."[13] Those who tried were encouraged to leave their new neighborhoods, often violently and sometimes with bombs. More organized solutions as the century continued included neighborhood improvement associations and restrictive housing covenants that enforced a residential color line and redlining. Middle class African Americans could rarely escape the ghetto because the color line moved with them: realtors would designate a neighborhood for black expansion, encourage whites to vacate, break up houses to lease to single renters and let the neighborhood decline. To add insult to injury, the Federal Housing Authority established as part of FDR's New Deal provided low-interest loans to white homeowners but refused mortgages to African Americans whose homes, in redlined districts, it saw as less likely to increase in value.

In *When Affirmative Action Was White*, Ira Katznelson details other effects of the New Deal on African American lives.[14] Provisions establishing a minimum wage, Social Security, unemployment insurance and workmen's compensation originally excluded agricultural and domestic work. Yet, in the South, most employed African Americans were engaged in just these occupations. Likewise, the G.I. Bill helped 16 million veterans of the Second World War attend college, receive job training, start businesses and purchase their first homes. However, Southern Congressmen insisted that local rather than federal officials direct the programs. The result was that in the South African American veterans were regularly denied housing and business loans, excluded from job training in emerging fields such as radio, mechanics and commercial photography and shunted into lower paying "black jobs." By October 1946, the employment service in Mississippi had placed 6,500 veterans in non-agricultural jobs: whites held 86 percent of the skilled and semiskilled jobs; African Americans held 92 percent of the unskilled ones.[15] African Americans were, of course, also denied admission to whites-only colleges and universities. If African Americans residing in Southern states wanted to make use of this aspect of the G.I. Bill they had to attend underfinanced, badly equipped black colleges and makeshift professional schools.

Katznelson notes that the discrepancies in implementing the G.I. Bill were not limited to the South. In 1946, the University of Pennsylvania in the North enrolled 46 black students in a student body of 9,000 and most of the other Ivy Leagues universities enrolled fewer. As for home ownership, in New York and northern New Jersey, "fewer than 100 of the 67,000 mortgages insured by the G.I. Bill supported home purchases by nonwhites."[16] Ta-Nehisi Coates adds Chicago to this record. Indeed, African Americans, he says, were largely excluded from the legitimate mortgage market in Chicago well into the 1960s and had to settle for buying their houses on contract.[17] Under the terms of these contracts, they acquired no equity in their homes until the contract was paid in full. Furthermore, one missed payment resulted in their losing the initial payment, all the monthly payments and the house. Those African Americans who were able to make good on their contract mortgages remained subject to redlining and exclusion from neighborhoods where their houses might have increased in value.

Recent research notes a significant difference in the current wealth of African American and white families in the United States. White Americans accumulated wealth both in the post-Second World War homes they were granted loans to buy but that African Americans were not, and in the value of their G.I. funded education and skilled jobs – opportunities that were, again, largely withheld from blacks. Moreover, because the residential segregation created in the twentieth century continues to set a ceiling on home equity for African Americans, their houses do not increase in value as much as houses in whiter neighborhoods. Tracing a set of the same households over 25 years, Thomas Shapiro, Tatjana Meschede and Sam Osoro found that the total wealth gap between white and African American families nearly tripled, from $85,000 in 1984 to $236,500 in 2009.[18] In an earlier article, Shapiro notes that whites are still about one and one half times as likely to come from families with assets than are African Americans.[19]

The point of recalling some of this readily available research on African American history is to ask why it is not a larger part of U.S. public memory. To the contrary, we can compare it to two beliefs on the part large numbers of white Americans. First, they think that since the end of segregation African Americans have possessed the same opportunities as whites. Hence, if African Americans continue to suffer socioeconomic disadvantages, these are largely their fault, products of black cultural pathologies or, as McCarthy puts it, of African Americans "possessing too little of the crucial economic-individualistic virtues – motivation, self-discipline, hard work, and the like – that enabled Irish, German, Italian, Jewish and other minorities to overcome prejudice and work their ways up."[20] Second, as a 2011 study found, there is a growing perception on the part of whites that they are currently more victimized than African Americans and that the latter have made gains at their expense.[21] Insofar as such beliefs seem to fly in the face of the available research, I want to ask how we are to make sense out of them. As one possible explanation, I turn next to Charles Mills's account of "white ignorance."

WHITE IGNORANCE

Appealing to recent social epistemology, Mills begins with what he considers some of the crucial components of social cognition contributing to white ignorance: perception, conception, memory, testimony, and group interest. Perception, he thinks, was already a problem for

European settlers in the Americas insofar as they apparently could not see either the sheer numbers of people that inhabited them or the houses, towns, roads, fields and earthworks they built.[22] Instead, for Europeans, as John Locke put it, the New World was a vast empty land.[23] Later African American writers remarked on a similar invisibility. Mills quotes Ralph Ellison:

> I am an invisible man. I am a man of substance, of flesh and bone, fiber and liquids – and I might even be said to possess a mind . . . I am invisible, understand, simply because people refuse to see me . . . When they approach me they see only my surroundings, themselves, or figments of their imagination – indeed, everything and anything except me."[24]

Ellison's reference to figments of white imagination points to the second dimension of white ignorance for Mills: conception. In the past few decades, he maintains, epistemological research has discredited "the idea of a raw perceptual 'given' unmediated by concepts" and shown, instead, that perception is concept laden.[25] Conceptions, moreover, are not simply individual creations but are rather acquired from one's cultural milieu. What European settlers could and could not see as a town or as evidence of agriculture depended upon the ways they had been socialized within a particular time and place. To the extent that this socialization included the assumption that non-whites were nomadic savages, Mills says, it would have been difficult for Europeans to comprehend Native American activities or to see their products as forms of agriculture or government. He quotes Hilary Kornblith:

> The influence of social factors begins at birth, for language is not reinvented by each individual in social isolation, nor could it be. Because language acquisition is socially mediated, the concepts we acquire are themselves socially mediated from the very beginning.[26]

They are also linked to one another in "complexes of ideation," Mills says. The European attitude to the people of color it encountered in its colonies and empires reflected a notion of human development that situated Europe at the top and was oblivious to the exploitation of other groups that put it there. Military conquest, the labor of others in the gold and silver mines of Mexico and Peru and profits from plantation slavery played no role in the European account of its ascendency. Rather, according to Mills, in societies structured by relations of domination, complexes of ideation are "likely to be shaped and inflected in various ways by the biases of the ruling group(s)."[27] Mills maintains that the explicit racism found in older European views of people of color and in American discrimination against African Americans now takes the form of a belief in the post-racial society in which nonwhites have the same social and economic resources as whites (or, indeed, better resources, as the 2011 report found.) "If originally whiteness was race, now it is racelessness, an equal status and a common history in which all have shared, with white privilege being conceptually erased."[28]

Memory also has a role to play here. Mills explains that because our complexes of ideation issue from our socialization they are related to the memory of those who socialize us. As he also points out, memory is selective and this characteristic extends to the public memory that is articulated in textbooks, expressed in ceremonies and public holidays and embedded in memorials and monuments.[29] In societies structured by domination what is remembered and what is forgotten will have a particular bias. In societies structured by white domination, public memory will have a white bias. A case in point, of course, is the "moonlight and magnolias" myth about American slavery promulgated not only in Hollywood films but also by academic historians well into the 1950s.[30] Thus, Ulrich B. Phillips at Yale University disseminated the idea that slavery was largely benign and had even had a civilizing effect on African slaves while his student, Columbia University professor, William A. Dunning rued the humiliation Reconstruction imposed on the defeated South and even praised the Ku Klux Klan. For his part, Mills looks to "the postbellum decision to rehabilitate Robert E. Lee," which he argues "signified a national white reconciliation that required the repudiation of an alternative black memory."[31]

Given the biased nature of memory, testimony, to take the fourth aspect of white ignorance that Mills examines, is all the more important. Yet if certain groups are denied the right to testify or perceived as non-credible witnesses when they do and if they are silenced or terrorized when it appears that they might speak or write, then the testimony that is taken up as the public record will be partial and skewed. Mills points to the 1921 Tulsa riots which almost disappeared from history because the official Tulsa records mysteriously vanished and African Americans were still, decades later, too traumatized to give evidence. Indeed, when many finally showed researchers their photographs of the event, they did so only under the condition of anonymity.

The last feature of white ignorance that Mills considers stresses the relation of perception, conception, memory and testimony to a group's self-interest. One does not, he says, need Marxism's elaborate account of ideology to uncover a "vested white group interest in the racial status quo."[32] Rather, we can "detach from a class framework, a Marxist 'materialist' claim about the interaction between exploitation, group interest, and social cognition and apply it with far more plausibility within a race framework."³³ Ignorance of continuing racial disparities and their causes serves whites insofar as it allows them to regard racism an experience of the past, to consider any focus on race as a symptom of an unwillingness to move on and to absolve them of any imperative to act against racial injustices or their causes. White ignorance is thus a motivated ignorance, one that affects,

> ... the concepts favored (for example, today's color blindness), the refusal to perceive systemic discrimination, the convenient amnesia about the past and its legacy in the present, and the hostility to black testimony on continuing white privilege and the need to eliminate it to achieve racial justice.³⁴

What is Mills's solution to white ignorance and privilege? Before turning to the way in which philosophical hermeneutics takes up some of the same themes Mills considers, I want to consider the recourse to standpoint theory and notion of "alternative epistemologies" that he first sketched out in 1988 and that he still largely seems to endorse.³⁵

STANDPOINT THEORY

Mills's solution follows standpoint theory as it has developed in Marxism and feminism and argues that because subordinate groups have experiences that diverge from those of the dominant group, they also possess more accurate knowledge of the dynamics of the social system of which they are a part.³⁶ Thus, on a Marxist view, as Mills understands it, the working class possesses a better understanding of the structure of capitalism than the bourgeoisie because the proletariat's experience of capitalist production dissolves the semblance of equality in the buying and selling of labor power. Transferred to women and racially subordinated groups, the same logic means that both also possess a better understanding of the dynamics of their societies than dominant groups. On the basis of their experiences as work, on dates and in public women understand the constancy of the threat of rape and the way it serves as a mechanism of repression. On the basis of their experiences with housing, the job market and the police, people of color understand the persistence of racism despite official claims about its demise. Different experiences produce different epistemic consequences so that, Mills says, we need to draw "internal distinctions between different varieties of social causation, according to their likelihood of producing positive or negative epistemic consequences." Whereas dominant groups "characteristically" have experiences that foster ignorance, he claims that subordinate groups "characteristically" have experiences that "(at least potentially) give rise to more adequate conceptualizations."[37] It follows, in his view, that we can correct for white ignorance by synthesizing the epistemic positions of the latter groups.

This correction has a number of limitations. Mills suggests that positive epistemic consequences are disillusioning and suited to puncturing the myths a society tells about itself. Yet what about the disillusioning experiences white working-class men can have of affirmative action policies that may cause disillusionment about the United States as a meritocratic society but also lead to white working-class racism? How, moreover, are we to synthesize the standpoints of all subordinated groups? Mills is aware of the complications posed by intersections of race, class, gender and the like, complications that require acknowledging the different experiences that different groups of women, of African Americans and so on can have. He knows, for example, that American women of European descent may not experience the same sort of discrimination and marginalization that American women of African descent do, for example. Nevertheless, if not, do the former still have epistemic privilege as women or, as European Americans, are their insights rather marked by white ignorance? What about African American men? Are their insights as African Americans independent of their lack of insight as men or conditioned and even skewed by it?

Mills denies that intersectional considerations justify what he calls a "retreat into a nonjudgmental epistemic neutrality."[38] Rather, he conceives of the perspectives of differently intersected groups as providing consecutive corrections:

> Because the working class Marx studied was not an abstraction but a group composed largely of white males, their subversive insight into the structure of social oppression ... was only partial. Women's perspective was required to uncover the significance of rape as a sustaining mechanism of patriarchal repression. But because the women who developed this analysis were themselves largely white, they in turn tended to miss the particular historical significance of rape accusations made against black men by white women. Again, therefore, a theoretical corrective was necessary, this time in the form of a critique of white, middle-class feminist theory by black women ... In each case a better approximation to the holistic reality of the situation is being achieved.[39]

This conclusion follows, however, only if the corrections offered by consecutive epistemic perspectives are compatible and cumulative. Yet if African American women correct white middle-class feminism by pointing to the historical threats to African American men posed by white women who falsely accuse them of rape, what about the African American women raped by white and African American men? If rape is a mechanism of subordination, is it only white women who feel its threat? Mills's analysis strangely erases African American women. Indeed, the very sensitivity to the subordination of African American men that Mills conceives of as a mark of privileged insight serves to reinforce ignorance about African American women.[40]

Still, perhaps the more severe problem with Mills's recourse to standpoint theory is that it remains unclear how exactly it is meant to correct for white ignorance. It may present perspectives from which the continuing effects and existence of racism become clear. Yet we do not lack for such perspectives: even if we limit our survey of African American experiences to the past 25 years, those years have been replete with reports and discussions of anti-black violence, racial discrimination and disparate treatment. To be sure, twentieth-century violence and discrimination against African Americans forced some into silence; yet others such as W. E. B. Du Bois, the black press in general and others documented and described it. Indeed, white Southern newspapers themselves trumpeted the successes of lynching as a method of subordinating African Americans. The problem is, thus, not that we have lacked accounts and analyses of either our past or the ongoing effects of racial marginalization and discrimination. Nor, moreover, are these effects visible only from the standpoints of those who have suffered. The problem is that these accounts and analyses are either not yet incorporated into the understanding the United States has of itself or, as in the case of the state of Oklahoma, potentially consciously suppressed. In other words, the issue is not establishing the privileged standpoints from which marginalization and discrimination appear but trying to ensure that reports of what already appears from many standpoints become part of the standard history and public memory of the United States.

How might we accomplish this task? In what follows I want to explore a response that dispenses with recourse to standpoint theory and rests, instead, on philosophical hermeneutics and indeed, on what we might call the "unexpected virtue of ignorance."[41] The appeal of standpoint theory for Mills lies in its opposition to theories relativizing ideas of truth and falsity, facts and reality. "The phrase 'white ignorance,'" he writes, "implies the possibility of a contrasting 'knowledge,' a contrast that would be lost if all claims to truth were equally spurious."[42] Yet we do not have to follow Mills in the implication here that our sole epistemic options are either supposing that a synthesis of the alternative epistemologies of marginalized groups offers us superior knowledge or retreating to epistemic neutrality. Rather, we can ask what avenues for historical understanding might become available to us once we adopt the Socratic knowledge of knowing that we do not know. I want to examine this question in connection with the perspective of philosophical hermeneutics on the entwinement of perception, conception, memory, testimony and group interest that Mills emphasizes.

PHILOSOPHICAL HERMENEUTICS

It may be, as Mills claims, that "a central theme in the epistemology of the past few decades has been the discrediting of the idea of a raw perceptual 'given.'" Nevertheless, Anglo–American philosophy is surely a latecomer to this insight, one that, in any case, was central to Heidegger's philosophical hermeneutics in the 1920s and to Gadamer's in the 1960s. For Heidegger, understanding is always understanding as. It is not a matter of encountering objects in a neutral way or as raw perceptual givens and then deciding how to understand or describe them. Rather, we always already understand them in some way or other. To use Heidegger's preferred example, we understand a hammer as a tool for nailing in the course of our engagement with our world and before we abstract from that engagement to conceive of the hammer as an object of a certain weight, shape or atomic make-up. Understanding is a kind of pragmatic know-how in which we anticipate or project meanings as part of a context of relations and significances. What things are for us, they are within activities involving in-order-to's and for-the sakes of's. Gadamer makes the same point about our engagement with texts.[43] As in the case of a hammer, we do not encounter them objectively or in a neutral way and then impose interpretations upon them. Rather, we always already possess a relation to them as a part of our involvement with our world. We understand a play by Shakespeare or Marlowe, for example, as a play by Shakespeare or Marlowe and in doing so already possess anticipations and expectations with regard to its themes, language, quality, importance and so on before we engage in explicit interpretations of it.

At work here is what Mills considers the orientation of perception by conception and what Heidegger and Gadamer call the fore-structure of understanding. Gadamer also stresses the same point that Mills does: that the orientations we possess are not simply our own creations but rather consequences of our cultural milieu. Moreover, just as Mills includes as part of this cultural milieu the memories of those who compose it and the testimonies of those able to be heard in the past, Gadamer looks to historical tradition. The fore-structure of understanding that is part of our encounter with the works of Shakespeare and Marlowe is one we inherit from previous generations. The anticipations and expectations that orient us to that which we are trying to understand reflect the results of their own encounters with the texts and the ways in which they took them up, related them to other texts and events and passed them down to us. The same holds for text-analogues such as actions, institutions, practices and events. We anticipate their meaning on the basis of historical pre-orientations or assumptions that our predecessors bequeath to us by and that contain the interpreted results of their experiences. As an alternative to citing Kornblith's claim that the influence of social factors begins at birth, Mills might therefore as easily have begun with Gadamer: "Understanding is, essentially, a historically effected event."[44]

Yet we can draw very different implications from this insight than Mills does. Four are of particular significance here. First, because we belong to different historical traditions and because historical traditions are internally complex, we anticipate different meanings and are oriented to that which we are trying to understand in different ways. We approach texts and text analogues in terms of different interests, concerns and contexts of relations that open up different vantage points for understanding them. Take Herman Melville's *Benito Cereno*. While interpretations of the 1950s thought Melville played up the blackness of the Africans in order to emphasize their evilness, Mills understands the novella as a depiction of his thesis of white ignorance. Boarding the crippled ship, *San Dominick*, the white Amasa Delano "has all around him the evidence for black insurrection, from the terror in the eyes of the nominal white captain . . . as his black barber Babo puts the razor to his throat to the Africans clashing their hatchets ominously in the background. But so unthinkable is the idea the inferior blacks could have accomplished such a thing that Delano searches for every possible alternative explanation for the seemingly strange behavior of the imprisoned whites."[45] Andrew Delbanco has yet a third interpretation, conceiving of the novella in terms of the events of September 11, 2001: "In our own time of terror and torture, *Benito Cereno* has emerged as the most salient of Melville's works: a tale of desperate men in the grip of a vengeful fury that those whom they hate cannot begin to understand."[46] Thus, while Mills focuses on Delano's inability to grasp the temporary victory of the Africans on the *San Dominick*, Delbanco focuses on the extent of their wrath. Whereas Delbanco emphasizes the Africans' perspective as a way of trying to comprehend the contemporary fury many currently feel towards the United States, Mills emphasizes Delano's perspective in order to provide a graphic case of white non-comprehension.

The second important implication we can draw from the way understanding is historically affected follows. Neither Mills's nor Delbanco's interpretation of *Benito Cereno* is the last word on the book. Not only do their understandings differ both from one another and from other interpretations but, in addition, history continues so that different generations of interpreters understand the same texts and text-analogues differently. Later generations understand them in terms of concerns and interests earlier generations cannot have had and they can relate them to new findings and new or different texts and text-analogues. If critics in the 1950s thought the Africans symbolized evil, more recent readers see the novella as a critique of slavery. If critics could not have understood *Benito Cereno* in terms of the attacks on the World Trade Center towers before they happened, Delbanco takes the attacks as his reference point. The same holds for our understanding of historical events. We can understand the Reagan presidency as a turning point in U.S. history in a way we could not at the time because we could not know what came next. Likewise, those in the future may be able to situate this presidency in a longer arc in which it becomes part of a conservative blip that dissolves towards the middle of the twenty-first century. What we might call the after-history of a text or text-analogue is never-ending. Understanding is part of an ongoing history and as long as that history does not end, texts and text-analogues will always be understood in a new and different ways.

For Mills, of course, these first two implications we can draw from philosophical hermeneutics can reflect only a pernicious relativism. To maintain that we can understand differently given the different contexts of significances and relations in terms of which we understand seems to require that we give up on all possibility of adjudicating between different understandings. If we are to say that Delbanco and Mills are equally insightful in the interpretations of *Benito Cereno*, are we also to say that we should take African American perceptions of inequality no more seriously than we take the perceptions of those whites who claim to be currently more victimized? Worse, perhaps, are we to say that we should take neither seriously but view all claims to truth as "equally spurious?"

To suppose that we need to answer either of these questions in the affirmative presumes that there is an easy way to move from the claim that all understandings of meaning are equally historically effected to the conclusion that all are equally valid or, indeed, equally spurious. It also presumes that there is an easy way to move from the claim that no one group possesses privileged insight into its society to the claim that all views of all groups possess or lack the same level of insight.

Nevertheless, to say that some interpretations are equally valid is not to say that all are. There is a difference between an understanding that allows for the possibility of understanding differently and a failure to understand at all. We can integrate the aspects of *Benito Cereno* and research into discrimination in some different but equally plausible ways, ones that draw different connections and emphasize different figures and actions. Still, we need not allow for any interpretation at all, even those that discount most or all the text or evidence.

In this connection the tradition of hermeneutics has always relied on the hermeneutic circle and conceives of plausible interpretations as those that are able to integrate part and whole. Thus, if what we took to be a white victimhood fails to cohere with research into the legacy and effects of discrimination against people of color, we must assume a problem with either the thesis of white victimhood or the research; if that research coheres with itself, with the facts it discovers, the testimony it hears and so on, then we must give up on the claims to victimhood. Nevertheless, we cannot get outside of our understanding to check how well it maps onto or coheres with text or text-analogues as a "raw, perceptual givens." Rather, because we always already understand *as*, our only basis for determining the reliability or plausibility of our understanding is to check how well it coheres with itself – that is how well it is able to integrate its parts into a coherent whole. At the same time, insofar as both that which we are trying to understand and we are part of a complex history affording different entry points to understanding and insofar as neither history not its complexity ends, even an internally consistent understanding will never be the final word on the matter. For this reason, the hermeneutic circle cannot be considered a method for achieving correct or privileged understanding. Instead, although it serves to cast doubt on certain understandings, it allows for parity between equally legitimate understandings.

The third implication we can draw from the way understanding is historically effected is thus that it is incomplete. We never know all the meanings a text or text-analogue can have. Rather, texts, institutions, practices, actions and the like take up relations to new texts, text-analogues and circumstances; across and within historical time frames, different interpreters situate texts and text-analogues in relation to different issues and concerns; different interpreters emphasize different aspects of texts, institutions, practices and the like and integrate them with one another in different ways.

A fourth implication of effective history follows. We are ignorant and we always have more to learn. We can never know all the meanings a text or text-analogue can have because we cannot know the future;

nor to the extent that tradition relies on testimony and memory, can we assume that we know all the facets of the past. Rather, there are always new and rediscovered voices to which to listen and new meanings we can uncover. Indeed, the only way we can begin to compensate for our ignorance is to acknowledge it and to engage in ongoing investigations and interrogations in which we sift through archives, listen to the testimonies of others and engage in conversations with them in which we discover other ways of understanding from which we may be able to learn.

Gadamer insists that this last compensation is the one of the "greatest insights" we can gain from Plato's account of Socratic questioning. When other characters in the Socratic dialogues ask questions, they usually "come to grief" because they assume that they know the answers in advance. Although they provide comic relief, they fail to advance consideration of the topic at issue. In contrast, Gadamer thinks that Socrates's questions advance consideration of the topic because they issue from a desire to know and that desire to know, for its part, issues from "knowing that one does not know."[47] We may not agree with Gadamer's view of Socrates's sincerity in asking questions or in claiming he knows that he does not know. Nevertheless, Gadamer is surely justified in suggesting that whereas asking questions to which we think we know the answers leaves us with no possibility of ever knowing more than what we already know or think we already know, asking questions of texts, artifacts and others on the basis of a self-acknowledged ignorance affords us the possibility of learning.

Where those of whom we are asking questions also ask questions of us and do so because they recognize their own inevitable ignorance, we engage in a reciprocally educative dialogue. We each set the understandings of the other against our existing understanding of the subject matter and where these do not cohere, we and our conversation partners engage in a mutual process of revising one or the other understanding or both. Because the starting point of this process is a desire to know founded in a recognition that we do not know, the point of questioning is not to show the superiority of our position but to bring out the strength of the positions or interpretations of others. The same holds for the questions our conversation partners ask. This learning will remain a partial one on both sides. Yet this partiality point suggests the value of continuing to engage in dialogue with others about ourselves and our past. "The art of questioning," Gadamer writes, "is the art of questioning ever further – i.e., the art of thinking. It is called dialectic because it is the art of conducting a real dialogue."[48]

CONCLUSION

Of what significance is dialectic or real dialogue to the worry with which we began: that a quarter century of research and reports on African American experiences has failed to alter significant white perceptions or to lead to the incorporation of the racial history of the United States into its standard public history? Mills excoriates white ignorance and seeks to replace it with the truth revealed by a synthesis of the alternative epistemologies of marginalized groups. Here he may be concerned less with the compatibility of their particular claims than in their common reorientation of the trajectory of American history. For Mills and others that history is centrally a history that begins with the decimation of native peoples and runs through the exploitation of slave labor, the passage of the Chinese exclusion act, the internment of Japanese–Americans during the Second World War, Jim Crow, racial terrorism and the current incarceration of masses of African American men. Versions of American history that conceive of these events as deviations, even extended deviations, from its constitutional ideals reverse the proper relation between the main trajectory, which is one of marginalization and subordination, and the deviations, which may be ones of intermittent social justice. To begin with freedom and equality, however, and to conceive of American history as a progressive attempt to meet these ideals is fundamentally to misunderstand it and to do so in a motivated and self-congratulatory way. Rather, one must begin and end with white ignorance and racism.

Philosophical hermeneutics dissents from this claim. To be sure, the refusal of Americans to confront their own past at all continues to distort its politics. To the extent, for example, that white Americans attribute the disadvantages African Americans suffer to cultural factors and think that, as whites, they are unfairly put upon, any policy that promises to assist African Americans is seen as yet another way in which white Americans bear undue costs. Yet to insist on the need to integrate African American history into the standard history of the United States is not to suppose that only one version of American history can be correct. From a historical perspective within a history that is multifaceted and does not end, we cannot know how to write the "true" history of the United States. Rather, we can legitimately understand American history differently than Mills does, stressing, say, the actions of Quakers and abolitionists and the effects of the Civil Rights movement, *Brown v. Board of Education* and Stonewall as well as the decision of countless city clerks in 2014 and 2015 to extend their operating hours in order to issue marriage licenses to same-sex couples, often before the final approval of the courts. We need not pick between this version and an anti-progressivist version; instead, just as we allow for different interpretations of texts, we can allow for some different interpretations of American history that emphasize some different trajectories and align events in different ways.

Indeed, philosophical hermeneutics suggests that while we work against white ignorance, we acknowledge the ignorance to which we all are subject. The concept-laden character of perception and the dependence of conception on the inherited effects of memory, testimony and what is omitted from both are not characteristics only of white ignorance but rather reflect our immersion in history. As much as any particular tradition of interpretation may reveal about particular texts and text-analogues it also obscures. It does not take up all the events and all of the memories and testimonies of the past but only those events that have been recorded and passed on and only the memories and testimonies that have been preserved and heard. If our understanding is oriented by what our ancestors have understood, it is also oriented by what they have ignored, refused to hear and even suppressed. Because we are also uninformed about the future, we are all ignorant.

Acknowledging ignorance may have a certain strategic advantage. Accusing whites of ignorance while attributing superior insight to others or to marginalized and subordinated groups serves only to reinforce white intransigence, as exemplified by the Oklahoma state legislature. In contrast, admitting to a universal ignorance can encourage openness on the part of others. We no longer insist on the superiority of our standpoint but can rather present it as a contribution to an ongoing discussion in which we model for others a commitment to listening. In any case, acknowledging our ignorance aptly reflects our historical situation insofar as we are effected by the past, oriented by our own interests and concerns and unwitting with regard to the future.

Philosophical hermeneutics proposes that the response to this ignorance is not to insist on the superiority of one or another standpoint but rather to engage in dialogue, to commit ourselves to ongoing conversation in which we presume we can always be educated by others, whether living or dead, human or non-human, who know and understand things we do not. The point of this education is not to achieve an approximation to what Mills calls the holistic reality of the situation. Rather, acknowledging our ignorance opens the politics of memory to a continuing and open conversation. We appreciate different interpretations of texts because we think we can learn from them, because we think they deepen our understanding; likewise we can appreciate different interpretations of our history in a similar attempt to go beyond what we already think and think we know. Admitting to our ignorance allows us to see Mills's recourse to privileged standpoints and Oklahoma's attempt to suppress what it admits are robust analyses of marginalized groups as equally dogmatic. The point of admitting that we do not know is to stress the importance of continuing to ask.

NOTES

1. See McCarthy, *Race, Empire and the Idea of Human Development* (Cambridge: Cambridge University Press, 2009), pp. 105–7.
2. Rick Noack, "The Berlin Wall fell 25 years ago, but Germany is still divided," *The Washington Post*, October 31, 2015, available at http://www.washingtonpost.com/blogs/worldviews/wp/2014/10/31/the-berlin-wall-fell-25-years-ago-but-germany-is-still-divided/?tid=sm_fb (last accessed April 10, 2015).
3. Soraya Sarhaddi Nelson, "Anti-Immigrant Rally Draws Thousands In Dresden," *National Public Radio* January 12, 2015, available at http://www.npr.org/2015/01/12/376788787/anti-immigrant-rally-draws-thousands-in-dresden (last accessed April 10, 2015).
4. Melissa Eddyjan, "Big Anti-Immigration Rally in Germany Prompts Counterdemonstrations," *New York Times*, January 12, 2015, available at http://www.nytimes.com/2015/01/13/world/europe/big-anti-immigration-rally-in-germany-prompts-counterdemonstrations.html (last accessed April 10, 2015).
5. See Kevin Conlon, "Oklahoma bill would make AP U.S. History history," available at http://www.cnn.com/2015/02/18/us/oklahoma-ap-history (last accessed April 10, 2015).
6. http://www.nationaljournal.com/next-america/newsdesk/support-for-the-affordable-care-act-breaks-down-along-racial-lines-20150331.
7. See Charles Mills, "White Ignorance," *Race and Epistemologies of Ignorance*, Shannon Sullivan and Nancy Tuana (eds.) (Albany, NY: State University of New York Press, 2007).
8. Dolores Barclay, Todd Lewan "Torn from the Land," available at http://theauthenticvoice.org/mainstories/tornfromtheland (last accessed April 10, 2015).
9. For a count of the numbers of lynchings, see Equal Justice Initiative, "Lynching in America: Confronting the Legacy of Racial Terror", available at http://www.eji.org/files/EJI%20Lynching%20in%20America%20SUMMARY.pdf (last accessed April 10, 2015).
10. "Torn from the Land."
11. http://theauthenticvoice.org/mainstories/tornfromtheland/torn_part5/
12. Douglas S. Massey and Nancy A. Denton, *American Apartheid: Segregation and the Making of the Underclass* (Cambridge, MA: Harvard University Press, 1998).

13. Ibid. p. 32.
14. Ira Katznelson, *When Affirmative Action Was White: An Untold History of Racial Inequality in Twentieth Century America* (New York: W.W. Norton and Company, 2005).
15. Ibid. p. 138.
16. Ibid. p. 140.
17. Ta-Nehesi Coates, "The Case for Reparations," *The Atlantic Monthly* (June 2014), available at http://www.theatlantic.com/features/archive/2014/05/the-case-for-reparations/361631 (last accessed April 10, 2015).
18. Thomas Shapiro, Tatjana Meschede and Sam Osoro, "The Roots of the Widening Racial Wealth Gap: Explaining the Black-White Economic Divide," available at http://iasp.brandeis.edu/pdfs/Author/shapiro-thomas-m/racialwealthgapbrief.pdf (last accessed April 10, 2015).
19. Thomas M. Shapiro, *The Hidden Cost of Being African American: How Wealth Perpetuates Inequality* (New York: Oxford University Press, 2004), p. 62. Charles Mills also cites Shapiro's interviews with whites who admitted the parental largess they had received that helped launch them in their careers but then seemed to forget it in describing themselves as "self-made." See "White Ignorance," p. 31.
20. McCarthy, *Race, Empire and the Idea of Human Development*, p. 119
21. Michael A. Norton and Samuel A. Sommers, "Whites See Racism as a Zero-Sum Game That They Are Now Losing," *Perspectives on Psychological Science* vol. 6 no. 3 (May 2011), pp. 219–21.
22. Charles Mills, *The Racial Contract* (Ithaca, NY: Cornell University Press, 1997), pp. 49–50; see also William M. Denevan, "The Pristine Myth: The Landscape of the Americas in 1492," *Annals of the Association of American Geographers*, Vol. 82, No. 3, *The Americas before and after 1492: Current Geographical Research* (September 1992), pp. 369–85.
23. Subsequent European-Americans tended to see it the same way. Frank Margonis notes that John Dewey called the frontier "free land" and a "wealth of unused territory" where Americans learned to be egalitarian and resourceful. See Frank Margonis "John Dewey, W. E. B. Du Dois and Alain Locke: A Case Study in White Ignorance and Intellectual Segregation," *Epistemologies of Ignorance*, p. 177.
24. Cited in Mills, "White Ignorance," p. 18.
25. Mills, "White Ignorance," p. 24.
26. Ibid. p. 24.
27. Ibid. pp. 24–5.
28. Ibid. p. 28.
29. See also Sam Duran's art installation, "Proposal for White and Indian Dead Monument Transpositions," highlighting the quantity and massiveness of monuments to whites in comparison to the very few monuments to selected, white-identified Native Americans.
30. See Ulrich Bonnell Phillips, *American Negro Slavery* Chapter XV: Plantation Labor. Also see Thomas McCarthy, *Race, Empire and the Idea*

of *Human Development*, pp. 109–10 and David Brion Davis, "A Review of the Conflicting Theories on the Slave Family," *The Journal of Blacks in Higher Education*, No. 16 (Summer, 1997), pp. 100–3.
31. Mills, "White Ignorance," p. 30.
32. Ibid. p. 34.
33. Ibid. p. 34.
34. Ibid. p. 35.
35. "The idea of group-based cognitive handicap is not an alien one to the racial tradition, if not normally couched in terms of 'ignorance.' Indeed, it is, on the contrary, a straightforward corollary of standpoint theory: if one group is privileged, after all, it must be by comparison with another group that is handicapped." See Mills, "White Ignorance," p. 15.
36. Charles Mills, "Alternative Epistemologies," Mills, *Blackness Visible: Essays on Philosophy and Race* (Ithaca, NY: Cornell University Press, 1998), p. 28.
37. Ibid. p. 28.
38. Ibid. p. 38.
39. Ibid. pp. 38–9.
40. See Kimberlé Crenshaw, "Mapping the Margins: Intersectionality, Identity Politics, and Violence against Women of Color." *Stanford Law Review* 43(6) (1991), pp. 1241–99.
41. See the movie, *Birdman* (or The Unexpected Virtue of Ignorance).
42. "White Ignorance," p. 15.
43. *Truth and Method*, p. 267.
44. Ibid. p. 300.
45. "White Ignorance," p. 18.
46. Andrew Delbanco, *Melville: His World and Work* (New York: Vintage Books, 2006), p. 231.
47. *Truth and Method*, pp. 362–3.
48. Ibid. p. 367.

PART III

Place, Play and the Body

7 Place and Hermeneutics: Towards a Topology of Understanding

JEFF MALPAS

The language of understanding is deeply imbued with ideas and images of place and space. To speak of "understanding" is itself to draw upon a sense of "standing in the midst of" or "between" (from the Old English, *understandan*)[1] – one might even say, then, that to understand is "to draw near" or "to be close to".[2] Heidegger points to the character of the German *Verständnis* as having "the original sense of 'standing before' [*Vorstehen*]: residing before, holding oneself at an equal height with what one finds before oneself, and being strong enough to hold out"[3] – and here too there is surely also a sense of standing "near to". The French, *comprendre*, on the other hand, a term which also enters into English as "comprehend", does not draw upon any idea of standing "before" or "near", but the idea on which it draws is no less spatial or topological, namely, of grasping or seizing – even of taking in or bringing together.[4]

The way understanding appears to bring with it such spatial and "topological" associations may be seen as an example of the primacy of *bodily* metaphor, not only in the manner in which we speak and think about understanding, but in all our speaking and thinking, especially in our speaking and thinking about the "inner space" of the mind and its activities.[5] In *Metaphors We Live By*, George Lakoff and Mark Johnson argue that such "metaphors" do indeed underpin our thinking,[6] and in *The Body in the Mind*, Johnson develops this idea specifically in relation to the understanding of the mind and the mental.[7] Part of Lakoff and Johnson's argument concerns the need to pay attention to the metaphors that they claim are at work here (and in other domains) and to their character *as metaphors*. In this respect, one can see Lakoff and Johnson as drawing attention to aspects of our ways of speaking and thinking that might otherwise be said to pass largely unnoticed – and it certainly does seem to be the case that, for the most part, we barely attend to the bodily, the spatial, or the topological character of the language we use and the concepts we employ, especially in our speaking and thinking about the mind and the activities we associate with it.

Yet what is primarily brought to our attention in Lakoff and Johnson's work, and what they claim has otherwise been overlooked, is the supposedly *metaphorical* character of that speaking and thinking. The starting assumption of their work is thus that we can indeed identify certain language and ideas as metaphorical, and, as a consequence, the *content* of the metaphor, and so, in this case, its spatial, topological, its bodily character, seems actually to be secondary. Even Johnson's *The Body in the Mind*, although it shifts to explore the role of image schemata in providing the basic structure that underpins thought and experience in general, still seems largely to focus on the role of the assumed *metaphor* or *image* rather than of its spatial, topological, or even bodily *content*. The question as to whether there is a fundamentally spatial and topological character *to understanding* that is indicated by the prevalence of spatial and topological imagery and idea in the structure of our speaking and thinking *about understanding* never really emerges as even an issue. Indeed, the very assumption that what is at issue is metaphor or image (where image is itself understood as continuous with metaphor) already predisposes Lakoff and Johnson's inquiries in a particular way – space and place do not appear in their work other than as metaphors or as expressed in terms of metaphor or image.

Accepting, as do Lakoff and Johnson, that space and place, as well as the body (although I take the latter as a secondary notion here, since it already depends upon some notion of space and place), but refusing the assumption that the way space and place appear is metaphorically or merely imagistically, the question then arises as to what is the role of space and place in thinking and experience, and so in *understanding*. Might understanding itself be spatially or "topologically" structured? Moreover, given the way language also intrudes here, one might ask what the role of space and place might be in relation to language or to metaphor and image. From the standpoint of contemporary hermeneutics, concerned as it is with both understanding and language, these ought to be viewed as significant questions, even though they are questions upon which hermeneutics has, with some notable exceptions, tended not to reflect. In what follows, my aim is to explore some of the spatial, and especially the topological character of understanding, and so also to explore the connection between hermeneutics and what I have elsewhere referred to as philosophical topology or topography.[8] My argument will be directed at showing that not only is understanding imbued with the spatial and the topological, but that hermeneutics is itself essentially topological in character.

I

Hans-Georg Gadamer is undoubtedly the central figure in twentieth-century hermeneutics. It is Gadamer who draws out and develops, in explicit fashion, the hermeneutical implications of Heidegger's thought, at the same time establishing hermeneutics as a distinctive mode of philosophy and demonstrating (even if it also remains contested) the essentially hermeneutical character of philosophy itself. On the face of it, Gadamer might be thought to have little to say about the topological character of understanding or of the hermeneutical – he nowhere draws attention to hermeneutics as determined by place, and place is not a central term or theme in his writing – moreover, if anything, it might be thought that it is the temporality of understanding that preoccupies him, and not its topology. Part of what I aim to do in the discussion below, however, is to demonstrate the ways in which place and topology are indeed present in Gadamer's work – the topological character of understanding is thus something that emerges in Gadamer no less than in Heidegger, and indeed, is present even in the very temporality of understanding.

Certainly if understanding is topological, then one would expect to find topological modes and figures at work in Gadamer just as they must also be at work in all thinking and all understanding – one of the tasks of a philosophical topological ought, in fact, to be one of retrieving the topology that is inevitably present within the history of philosophy in general and so to make explicit the topological underpinnings that are present even in the work of the most seemingly atopic thinkers. In Gadamer, however, the topological character of his thinking is not merely present as part of the general topology that governs all thinking, but instead appears, if sometimes implicitly, in the very articulation of the hermeneutical as such. One only needs to reflect on the topological character of notions such as horizon and situation to see how this is so. Yet if hermeneutics is itself essentially topological, then not only will the topological character of hermeneutics be evident in key hermeneutical notions, but the very thematization *of the hermeneutical* will itself bring a topological orientation with it even if the topological orientation is not itself thematized. This seems to be very much the case with Gadamer.

It is significant, from a topological perspective, that, when talking about the formative influences on his thinking, especially in regard to

Heidegger, Gadamer turns to Heidegger's lectures on 'The Origin of the Work of Art.'[9] Gadamer comments:

> In these lectures, it was the concept of the 'earth' with which Heidegger dramatically transgressed the limits of German philosophical vocabulary once again ... These three lectures so closely addressed my own questions and my own experience of the proximity of art and philosophy that they awakened an immediate response in me. My philosophical hermeneutics seeks precisely to adhere to the line of questioning in this essay and the later Heidegger, and to make it accessible in a new way.[10]

What appears in the lectures from 1935–36 is a dramatic new orientation in Heidegger's thinking, although an orientation that has strong continuities with his earlier thought, that is not merely focussed on the artwork, but on the artwork as it stands in relation to truth and to "site" (*Stätte*). It is in the explication of the "sitedness" of the artwork – what I would term its "placing" or "being placed" (the sense of "site" at issue here is not the abstract notion associated with the mere projection of a plan, but the "site" as that which "gives room to" through the "clearing of ground for") – that the idea of earth emerges in direct juxtaposition with "world". Often identified with the Dionysian and the Apollonian,[11] these two terms are perhaps best understood as encompassing two fundamental aspects of place and of being in place: Earth is place as that which grounds, supports and shelters; world is place as that which expands and opens up.[12] Both of these are essential elements of place and in 'The Origin of the Work of Art' it is the tension between them – a tension that arises out of their being brought together in the work, that also opens up the space that belongs to the work, and that is the space of appearance, of understanding, and of truth.[13] Even though the lectures that make up 'The Origin of the Work of Art' may be thought of as a *Holzweg*[14] – a path that leads to its own "clearing" but ends there, offering no direct way onwards[15] – still the basic shift to the idea of "site" or "place", continues into Heidegger's work of the 1940s, '50s and '60s. It is thus no "dead-end", but rather constitutes a development central to Heidegger's later thinking (and is explicitly treated as such by Gadamer[16]), as well as to the thinking of place more generally.

As explored by Heidegger in 'The Origin of the Work of Art', the happening of truth is an establishing and opening up of world, and yet it occurs always and only in relation to a singular work – a work that stands in the midst of things at the same time as it draws things into relation and so also into appearance. Without the work, without the thing, there can be no happening of truth, nor any opening up of world. In Gadamer, the work has a similar primacy – it is in and through our relation to the work, whether it be a text or utterance, a performance or painting, a sculpture or a building, it is the work that guides and constrains our interpretive engagement with it – and that also provides the mediative focus (with an emphasis here on the mediative as precisely that which pertains to the 'between' – *das Zwischen*) for our engagement with others. As Gadamer writes in *Truth and Method*, "Understanding belongs to the encounter with the work of art itself", and, he adds, "this belonging can be illuminated only on the basis of the being of the work of art itself".[17] It is thus that 'The Origin of the Work of Art' does indeed take the artwork as central to the happening of truth, and it is precisely in the focus of attention on the being of the work that the importance of place itself becomes evident.

There is no work that does not also bring its own situatedness with it – the work, the thing, is always situated or placed. That situatedness belongs to the work and is that on the basis of which the work can appear as a work. In 'The Origin of the Work of Art', the situatedness of the work is partly captured through Heidegger's emphasis on the way the work stands before us, stands in a certain place, stands there, in the case of the Greek temple, on the rocky plain – stands, one might say, *on the earth*. Earth here appears as that which supports and sustains, but also that which places, as it provides a "site-for" (in the sense of a clearing of ground).

In 'The Origin of the Work of Art', Heidegger's emphasis on the standing character of the work is complicated by a shift in Heidegger's German between *stehen* and *stellen* – a shift he later acknowledges and recognizes as problematic. Both of these terms can be translated as "to stand", but whereas *stehen* is the simple standing of that which stands, *stellen* is standing is the sense of being "set in place" or "positioned" (*stellen* is at work in a range of other terms including *her-stellen*, *vor-stellen*, and also *Ge-stell*).[18] In its own "standing there" *in its place* the work possesses an autonomy (though not an autonomy, as becomes clearer below, that implies independence or separateness) that is the proper ground out of which comes its own determinative role in the happening of truth or of understanding. However, the "placing" of the work associated with this sense of "standing there" can easily be confused with the "placing" that is a "setting in place" of the work – a "placing" that is imposed upon the work and that claims to determine the work rather than allowing the work to be determinative.

Recognizing the centrality of the work, and in a hermeneutical context, of that which is the focus for understanding, whether it be artwork, text, or thing, thus also means recognizing the placed character of the work. The work appears as work through the way in which it stands in its own place, but this does not mean that the work stands alone and apart. Gadamer emphasizes the way the work is no mere "object", but rather, in standing in itself, the work "not only belongs to a world; its world is present in it".[19] The character of the work as belonging to its world in this way is taken up in Heidegger's later thinking through the inquiry into "the thing" – exemplified by a simple jug or, elsewhere, a bridge.[20] Rather than understand the thing as some separate, self-subsisting entity or object, Heidegger takes the thing to be a dynamic nexus that draws together as it also sets apart. The thing gathers, and its gathering is also a gathering of world, but that gathering occurs through the thing's own "standing there" (its *Da-stehen* – or as it might also be put, its own "being there", its own *Da-sein*). In 'The Origin of the Work of Art', the work, for instance, the temple, functions in this same way. In being itself placed, the work opens up and establishes a place for everything else that comes into appearance around it:

> The temple's firm towering makes visible the invisible space of the air. The steadfastness of the work stands out against the surge of the tide, and in its own repose, brings out the raging of the surf. Tree and grass, eagle and bull, snake and cricket first enter into their distinctive shapes [*Gestalt*] and thus come to appearance as what they are.[21]

The "gathering" that occurs in the work or the thing appears as an establishing of identity through differentiation. The work stands "in itself", but in standing so, it also stands in relation to its world, and so also to everything that appears within the world. The work stands, then, within a dense web of relations – through those relations it gives shape and focus to other things, but in doing so it also gives shape and focus to itself.

There is thus a mutuality that exists between the work and world. The world is drawn to appearance in and around the work, even while the work itself appears through its standing within the world. There is, however, a certain priority within the mutuality that obtains here. This priority derives simply from the fact that the relationality at work here is indeed ordered or "gathered", and it is the work or thing that is the focus for that ordering. This means that the relations that appear do not ramify endlessly. The opening up of the world is not the opening up of a homogenous and horizon-less space lacking in orientation or direction (such a space would lack any genuine openness – would not be able to be grasped as a space), but is precisely the opening of an expansive and yet unified whole that is essentially configured in relation to what appears within it. The world is not given in relation to just any *one* thing, nor in just *one* place alone, and yet is configured in relation

Place and Hermeneutics: Towards a Topology of Understanding 149

always to *some* thing and *some* place. It is only in and through things and places (the two being bound together) that the open-ness of the world is possible.

II

The way Gadamer emphasizes the role of the work in his reading of Heidegger is not merely a feature of that reading alone, but also reflects a central element in Gadamer's own hermeneutics. His claim that "understanding belongs to the encounter with the work of art itself" is thus intended as a claim that indicates a key direction in Gadamer's own account. It is to the character of the work, of the thing, of that which is the focus for understanding that is the key to unlocking the nature of understanding. In looking to the work and to the thing, we are also forced to attend to the manner of their being, and so also to the placed character of that being. In discussing Heidegger's 'The Origin of the Work of Art', in a way relevant to his own as well as Heidegger's thinking, Gadamer comments:

> Heidegger speaks of the 'clearing of being' which first represents the realm in which beings are known as disclosed in their hiddenness. This coming forth of beings into the 'there' of their Dasein obviously presupposes a realm of openness in which such a 'there' can occur. And yet it is just as obvious that this realm does not exist without beings manifesting themselves in it, that is, without there being a place of openness that openness occupies.[22]

What appears here is a mutuality between "beings" and the "realm of openness" in which they are disclosed that mirrors the mutuality of work and world. As Gadamer puts it here, the "realm of openness" is distinct from the "there" of beings, since he talks of the "there" presupposing that "realm of openness." I would argue that the "there", understood as designating a certain place or placedness implies an openness that belongs with it rather than an openness that it presupposes,[23] but this does not affect the key point regarding the mutuality between beings and the open, and so the way place, whether understood in terms of the 'there' or openness as such, is indeed implicated here.

The openness that is at issue is an openness into which we also are drawn, and here the character of the openness that is tied to the thing connects directly with the character of the openness that belongs to *play* (which Gadamer takes as a concept central to the ontology of understanding). The latter openness resides in the "in between" character of play (it occurs between players, and also between players and the game itself), but also in the character of play as itself open within the bounds of the 'space' in which the play is defined. Gadamer thus says of play that it "does not have its being in the player's consciousness or attitude, but on the contrary play draws him into its dominion and fills him with its spirit. The player experiences the game as a reality that surpasses him."[24] This "surpassing" of the player is reflected in the character of understanding as also a surpassing that occurs through the focus of understanding on that which is to be understood, and that occurs in the experience of art through our being taken up in the artwork. This "surpassing" is itself a phenomenon that can be understood – and perhaps ought to be understood – topologically, since it involves a surpassing of the interiority of experience or thought in the direction of the exteriority of the thing and the world as that occurs through our being drawn into the space and place before us, into the space and place of the thing, the space and place of the play.

Gadamer's own talk of play, and much of his discussion of understanding, tends to emphasize the character of both as *events*. In his discussions of Heidegger, too, it is often the idea of the event that is to the fore. So, for instance, when Gadamer asks the question as to the nature of the "there" – the *Da* that appears in the term *Dasein* – he answers:

> ... this '*Da*' does not mean something merely being present: rather it *signifies* an event. Every '*Da*, like all things earthly, dwindles, passes away, and is carried off into oblivion – yet it is a '*Da*' precisely because it is finite, that is, aware of its own finitude. What is happening there [*da*], what happens as a '*Da*', is what Heidegger later calls the *clearing of Being* [*Lichtung des Seins*].[25]

Two points emerge here: one is the dynamic character of the *Da*; the other is its finitude. Both might be said to be tied to modes of temporality, and yet that connection can also be a misleading one. Although Gadamer seems, in this passage, to insist on understanding the topological in terms of the temporality of the event, I would argue that only if the temporality of the event is understood topologically, can it be understood aright. I would argue further that such an understanding is implicit in Gadamer, as it is in early Heidegger also, although the fact that it often remains implicit means that its significance is also sometimes overlooked.

To be "there," that is to say, to be in a place, is already to be situated within a complex set of relations that connect to other things, other places – to be "there" is, in this respect, to be situated within the world. But just as the "there", and that which "is there", does not stand apart from things, but as interconnected with them, so the "there" and what "is there", is not some mere "being present", as if its being were just a matter of some static perdurance. To be there is to be bound up in the world, and to be bound up in relation, but that worldly relationality is itself an active and dynamic ordering – an ordering or gathering, as we saw above, that occurs in and through that which is "there", and so in and through the thing or the work. Perhaps the simplest way to see this is to reflect on the character of orientation – understood as both a sense of being in place and of having a sense of relation to place. Such orientation is not a matter of what might be referred to as mere "positionality" – of being at such and such a point or location – but rather of being actively focussed on the place in such a way that enables one to move and also to act within it. This is what orientation is: most literally, to have a sense of the east (the orient), of the position of the sun, and so to have a sense of the ordering of movement that belongs to the place; and then, since one cannot have any sense of such movement unless it is related back to oneself (as Kant emphasizes),[26] also to have a sense of the ordering of one's own movements or capacities for movement in that place.

Neither place nor placedness can be understood other than as already having a dynamic character that belongs essentially to them, and that is itself directly related to their relational character. This may lead us to say that places are events, except that events cannot themselves be understood other than in relation to place – events are, one might say, always happenings of place. That this is so is part of what is indicated by the centrality of the work or thing in the happening of art as well as in the event of understanding. Once again, the work or thing may be said to have an event-character, but equally if not more significant here is the way in which the work or thing provides a unitary focus for the happening that occurs in and around them – the way, in other words, in which they gather. Such gathering cannot be understood as a purely temporal phenomenon (and so "event" itself is not a purely temporal notion either), but is also spatial (and necessarily so), although the spatiality at issue, because it is focussed and ordered (and so, is in an important sense, bounded), can only be made sense of in relation to place. Place is itself the key concept here, and it is the notion of place that is actually invoked by ideas of finitude and the finite. Human being is itself finite, not merely in virtue of its being curtailed in time, but rather through it being turned back towards its own there, towards its own being as given in the there – which, as with the experience of art, or the event of understanding is given content and meaning through being oriented and placed, through being focussed on the *singularity* of its being, a singularity that is precisely a consequence of its *being placed*.[27]

III

The topological is at work in Gadamer no less than Heidegger. It can be discerned in Gadamer's own constant resort to spatial and topographic ideas or to notions that presuppose such ideas – whether in relation to the notion of play, the between, the fusion of horizons, the circularity of understanding, the nature of conversation, or of the worldly character of understanding. The way the topological operates in Gadamer's thinking is particularly evident in his account of language. That this is so is partly a function of the character of language as already "outside" of ourselves, and so as moving in that common realm that exists "between."[28] As is so often the case, the way Gadamer approaches this is initially through a claim about temporality, but the discussion almost immediately moves to draw upon spatial and topological ideas. So Gadamer writes:

> It is man's having language that sets off his form of life from that of certain kinds of herd animals. His communication is not just the expression of a particular condition ... It manages to make manifest what is helpful and what is harmful. That means pointing out things that we want to recommend or warn against even when they do not immediately recommend themselves ... One thinks of bitter medicine, or of the doctor's painful surgery, which requires a distance from what is present and a looking forward to what is coming. One is no longer given over and delivered up to the rush of the moment. This, then, is what we recognise in the essence of language: a distance by means of which, in the breath of our voice, fleeting as it is, we can embody everything that occurs to us, making it audible and communicable to others. Obviously it is this kind of distance with respect to ourselves that opens us up to the other ...[29]

How are we to interpret the language of space and distance by which Gadamer here explicates the opening up that occurs in language? First, it is crucial that, *pace* Lakoff and Johnson, we not immediately resort to the metaphorization of this language. Not only is there nothing to indicate that it is a metaphorical use of distance that is at issue, but it is quite unclear how such a metaphor would work or what it could mean. Indeed, I would go so far so to assert that *in ontology, which is surely what is at issue here, there are no metaphors* – at least not in any straightforward sense (which is not to say, however, that there may not be other tropes at work).[30] Second, one might be inclined to say that what Gadamer describes here is an opening of the temporal, and so the language of the spatial and the topological has to be understood in light of that temporal focus – except that what is at issue is also a freeing from the temporal, or at least from the temporal understood as the "rush of the moment" (or even the succession of moments) in which we might otherwise be thought to be trapped.

Inasmuch as the temporal is invoked here it is both as that *from which* we are freed and as that *into which* we are freed that is achieved through the rethinking of the temporal as itself an open domain. But this "freeing into" is actually a freeing into time understood as an oriented region, as determined in terms of place. The rethinking of time that is at work already occurs in Heidegger's work, particularly in, but not restricted to, *Being and Time* (which suggests a re-reading of that work as *Being and Place*, no less than it is *Being and Time*). In 'The Origin of the Work of Art', this rethinking of the temporal occurs through the thinking of the topological character of the event and that rethought conception carries through into the later Heidegger and is itself at the heart of the idea of the *Ereignis* (literally, the Event, but also translated in various other ways also) as well as the fourfold (*Das Geviert*).[31] At the very end of *Truth and Method*, Gadamer also addresses the character of language in a way that emphasizes this idea of the temporal as topological, and so draws attention, once again, to the topological character of language – but the starting point here is the event of understanding *as linguistic*, and of language as itself a *play*:

> The weight of things we encounter in understanding plays itself out in a linguistic event, a play of words playing around and about what is meant. Language games exist where we, as learners – and when do we cease to be that? – rise to the understanding of the world. Here it is worth recalling what we said about the nature of play, namely that the player's actions should not be considered subjective actions, since it is, rather, the game that plays, for it draws the players into itself and thus itself becomes the actual subjectum of the playing. The analogue in the present case is neither playing with language nor with the contents of the experience of the world or of tradition that speaks to us, but the play of language itself, which addresses us, proposes and withdraws, asks and fulfils itself in the answer.[32]

In the last sentence here, Gadamer evokes a way of thinking about language that draws language into the topological – that lets it appear as topological. Language belongs to the very play of place, and that play itself belongs to language.

The topological character of language that emerges here is an enormous and hugely important, yet also relatively neglected topic. One might argue that, from a certain perspective, the topic ought to be taken to be the most pressing concern of any future hermeneutical inquiry. It is this topic, moreover, that also draws us directly back, as is already evident, to some of the issues that underline the inquiries of Lakoff and Johnson. I noted at the very beginning of this discussion how understanding seems to bring a certain topology with it. Lakoff and Johnson argue for space and the body having a key role in the way we think as well as in our thinking about thinking. Their approach, however, is one that takes the focus on space and the body as part of a larger role played by metaphor in thought and cognition. As soon as we begin to recognize the genuinely topological character of understanding – and so of thought and cognition – then we are also led to recognize the topological character of language itself (something implied by Lakoff and Johnson's approach but not itself directly thematized or taken up). But that ought to render uncertain the very idea of the metaphorical as a notion that can be assumed in any straightforward way. If part of what is at issue is the topological character of language, then the topological has to be recognized as operating at a level that may itself turn out to be presupposed by the very idea of metaphor just inasmuch as metaphor already presupposes the structure of language.

IV

It would seem dubious to suppose that we could use metaphor to understand the topology of language, since it must surely be in the very topology of language that metaphor finds its own ground. The role of topology, then, whether understood as referring to a structure or the inquiry into that structure, is not as a source of metaphor nor does topology work primarily or solely through metaphor. The task that the recognition of the topological character of understanding presents is the task of explicating the topology that belongs to understanding – of explicating the proper *place* of understanding – but this also means explicating what topology itself might mean here. It is this task that must lie at the heart of any genuinely philosophical hermeneutics, moreover that task is also one that involves an explication of the topological character of the hermeneutical, and so might be said to involve the explication of the hermeneutical character of the topological as well, and that does so with an explicitly *ontological* orientation. The task at issue is one of providing an articulation of the ontology of understanding in a way that takes seriously the topological character of understanding as well as of ontology.[33]

The turn towards place that is at issue here is one that follows from the hermeneutical focus on the finitude of understanding and on such finitude as the enabling condition of understanding – an idea that is at the very heart of the philosophical hermeneutics of Heidegger and Gadamer.[34] The turn towards place cannot be characterized as merely temporal or spatial in its orientation, but rather encompasses both – as place itself does.[35] Similarly, it is not a turn towards work or thing taken on its own, nor towards pure relationality, but instead attends to both thing and the relationality within which the thing is embedded. The turn towards place is not a turn towards any form of constructionism, since place is that which determines the very ontology within which any form of construction must itself be understood (constructionism is, in any case, and to use a Heideggerian distinction, an 'ontic' more so than an 'ontological' position, playing a role within certain contemporary theoretical discourses, but inadequate as a grounding concept within or with respect to those discourses). Place cannot itself be understood as either a subjective or an objective phenomenon, being that out of which the very distinction of subjective from objective emerges.

The turn towards place, and so also the topology to which hermeneutics leads and which it embodies, is a turn that is directly relevant to many contemporary intellectual developments: "externalist" conceptions within analytic philosophy converge with elements of topological thinking;[36] topology connects with key ideas at work in so-called "material culture studies";[37] holistic and relationalist conceptions can be seen to themselves draw on an essentially topological mode of thinking; the emphasis on the geographic – whether in psycho-geography or geo-criticism – can be read as implying an emphasis on the placed no less than the spatial.[38] It is partly because of its connection with such a range of developments that the real potential and significance of hermeneutics, and certainly one of the most productive areas for future work, seems likely to lie in the direction of a more explicit engagement with the topological. Such an engagement would also constitute, if my argument here is correct, a more explicit engagement with what the hermeneutical itself *is*.

NOTES

1. See *Chambers Dictionary of Etymology*, ed. Robert K. Barnhart (Edinburgh: Chambers, 2001), p. 1183.
2. So the entry in the *Online Etymology Dictionary* includes a similar derivation to the *Chambers*, but adds: "perhaps the ultimate sense is 'be close to'" – see http://www.etymonline.com/index.php?term=understand (last accessed April 16, 2015).
3. Heidegger, Seminar in Le Thor 1969, *Four Seminars*, trans. Andrew J. Mitchell and François Raffoul (Bloomington: Indiana University Press, 2003), p. 40. The *Chambers Dictionary of Etymology* entry for "understanding" also refers to the German as having the sense of "to stand in front or on top of," and the *Online Etymology Dictionary* notes that "Similar formations are found in Old Frisian (*understonda*), Middle Danish (*understande*), while other Germanic languages use compounds

meaning 'stand before' (German *verstehen*, represented in Old English by *forstanden* 'understand,' also 'oppose, withstand')".

4. The French post-colonial theorist Edouard Glissant takes up precisely this aspect of the etymology of *comprendre* as a reason for being suspicious of the usual language of "comprehension" and "understanding" – see Glissant, *Poetics of Relation*, trans. Betsy Wing (University of Michigan Press, 1997), esp. the 'Translator's Introduction', p. xiv. Glissant pays no attention, however, to the broader topologies that might be at issue here.

5. Of course, the examples adduced here are from European languages alone, and it is an empirical question whether quite the same examples could be found in other languages, especially other non-European languages. Unfortunately, there has been very little exploration of these sorts of conceptual and linguistic issues across languages and cultures outside the European, or even English, context – the work of Lakoff and Johnson, for instance (see below), is restricted to English alone. Chinese offers enormous scope for exploration of the spatial and topological in virtue of its use, in its written form, of both phonological and optical-graphical components (ideograms) – this is evident, for instance, in Tze-wan Kwan's approach to Chinese script as set out in "Phenomenological Interpretation of the 'Six Ways' of Chinese Script Formation," in *Visualizing Knowledge in Signs: Encoding Meanings in Logographic and Logophonetic Writing Systems, Berliner Beiträge zum Vorderen Orient* (BBVO), Vol. 23 (Berlin: Pe-We-Verlag, 2014), pp. 157–202.

6. *Metaphors We Live By* (Chicago: University of Chicago Press, 1980).

7. *The Body in the Mind: The Bodily Basis of Meaning, Imagination, and Reason* (Chicago: University of Chicago Press, 1987).

8. This exploration is one that I have also undertaken (though in different ways) elsewhere, most specifically in 'Place and Situation', in *Routledge Companion to Philosophical Hermeneutics*, edited by Jeff Malpas and Hans-Helmuth Gander (Abingdon: Routledge, 2015), pp. 354–66, and 'The Beginning of Understanding: Event, Place, Truth', in Jeff Malpas and Santiago Zabala (eds.), *Consequences of Hermeneutics* (Chicago: Northwestern University Press, 2010), pp. 261–80. See also "Self, Other, Thing: Triangulation and Topography in Post-Kantian Philosophy," *Philosophy Today*, 59 (2015), pp. 103–26. Although not always addressed in so direct or explicit a fashion, the connection between hermeneutics and topology is a theme that can be said to run throughout my work – it is already present, for instance, even if couched in slightly different terms, in *Donald Davidson and the Mirror of Meaning* (Cambridge: Cambridge University Press, 1992).

9. See Heidegger, "The Origin of the Work of Art," in *Off the Beaten Track*, trans. Julian Young and Kenneth Haynes (Cambridge: Cambridge University Press, 2002), pp. 1–56.

10. See Gadamer, "Reflections on My Philosophical Journey," in Lewis Edwin

Hahn (ed.), *The Philosophy of Hans-Georg Gadamer*, Library of Living Philosophers 24 (Chicago: Open Court, 1997), p. 47.
11. See, for instance, Julian Young, *Heidegger's Philosophy of Art* (Cambridge: Cambridge University Press, 2001), p. 40.
12. See my "Place and Singularity," in Jeff Malpas (ed.), *The Intelligence of Place: Topographies and Poetics* (London: Bloomsbury, 2015), pp. 65–92.
13. Gadamer writes that: "earth is the counterconcept to world insofar as it exemplifies self-concealment and concealing as opposed to self-opening" ('Heidegger's later Philosophy' in *Philosophical Hermeneutics*, trans. and ed. David E. Linge [Berkeley: University of California Press, 1976], p. 222). Although I think the contrast between concealing and opening is indeed present in the contrast between earth and world, I also think that it is important to recognise that neither term can be wholly identified with one or the other, since the event of truth, which arises out of the conflict of earth and world, is itself an event that encompasses both concealing and opening (it is an event of opening out of concealment).
14. The volume in which 'The Origin of the Work of Art' originally appears is *Holzwege*, (*Gesamtausgabe* 5 [Frankfurt: Klostermann, 2003] first published in 1950). The term *Holzweg* (literally: "wood path") is peculiar to German, and usually refers to a path in the woods that leads nowhere in particular, hence the rendition of *Holzwege*, in the French translation of the volume, as "paths to nowhere" – see *Chemins qui ne menent nulle part*, trans. Wolfgang Brokmeier, ed. François Fédier (Paris: Gallimard, 1962).
15. Their character as a *Holzweg* is reinforced by the problematic character of much of Heidegger's thinking during this period – a thinking that often remains compromised by Heidegger's entanglement with Nazism, and that is still searching for a way forward after the impasse of *Being and Time*. See my discussion in "On the reading of Heidegger: Situating the Black Notebooks," in Ingo Farin and Jeff Malpas (ed.), *Reading Heidegger's Black Notebooks 1931–1941* (Cambridge, MA: MIT Press, in press, 2015).
16. The lectures are thus the central focus for Gadamer's discussion in "Heidegger's Later Philosophy."
17. *Truth and Method*, trans. Joel Weinsheimer and Donald Marshall, second revised edition (New York: Crossroad, 1992), p. 100.
18. See my discussion in "Nihilism and the Thinking of Place," in Laurence Paul Hemming and Bogdan Costea (eds.), *The Movement of Nihilism* (London: Continuum, 2011), pp. 110–27.
19. "Heidegger's Later Philosophy," p. 222.
20. See *Poetry, Language, Thought*, trans. Albert Hofstadter (New York: Harper and Row, 1971): "The Thing," pp. 161–84, and "Building Dwelling Thinking," pp. 141–60.
21. "The Origin of the Work of Art," p. 21.
22. "Heidegger's Later Philosophy," p. 225.

23. Place, to which the "there" is surely related in an essential way, is itself best understood as a bounded openness – see my *Place and Experience* (Cambridge: Cambridge University Press, 1999), pp. 21–2.
24. *Truth and Method*, p. 109.
25. "Martin Heidegger – 75 years," in Heidegger's ways, trans. John W. Stanley (Albany, NY: SUNY Press, 1994), p. 23.
26. See Kant "What is Orientation in Thinking?" in *Kant: Political Writings*, trans. H. B. Nisbet Cambridge: Cambridge University Press, rev. edn. 1991), pp. 238–9; Kant, "Concerning the Ultimate Ground of the Differentiation of Directions in Space" [1768], trans. David Walford and Ralph Meerbote, in *Theoretical Philosophy 1755–1770, The Cambridge Edition of the Works of Immanuel Kant* (Cambridge: Cambridge University Press, 1992), pp. 361–72. See also my own discussion of this issue in "Heidegger, Space, and World," in Julian Kiverstein and Michael Wheeler (eds.), *Heidegger and Cognitive Science* (London: Palgrave-Macmillan, 2012), pp. 312–17.
27. On the singularity that belongs to place see my discussion in "Place and Singularity."
28. Heidegger himself writes of "the factical mode of the actualizing of λόγος", which he takes to be at work in hermeneutics, as directed towards "making something accessible as being there out in the open, as public," *Ontology: The Hermeneutics of Facticity*, trans John van Buren (Bloomington: Indiana University Press, 1999), p. 8. See my discussion in "The Beckoning of Language: Heidegger's Hermeneutic Transformation of Thinking," in Ingo Farin and Michael Bowler (eds.), *Hermeneutic Heidegger* (Evanston: Northwestern University Press, forthcoming, 2015).
29. *Praise of Theory: Speeches and Essays*, trans. Chris Dawson (New Haven: Yale University Press, 1998), p. 6.
30. This is a point that becomes very clear in Heidegger, even though it is a point to which attention is seldom given. See my "Poetry, Language, Place."
31. On the topological character of *Ereignis* and Fourfold see esp. my *Heidegger's Topology* (Cambridge, MA: MIT Press, 2006), pp. 221–30.
32. *Truth and Method*, p. 490.
33. See my "The Beckoning of Language" in which I discuss the way in which Heidegger's transformation of ontology through the turn to hermeneutics (and of hermeneutics through the turn to ontology) is also tied to a turn to the topological.
34. My reading of the topological underpinnings to the hermeneutics of both Heidegger and Gadamer puts my account somewhat at odds with that of Günter Figal (as set out, in particular, in Figal, *Objectivity: The Hermeneutical and Philosophy*, trans. T. D. George (Albany, NY: SUNY Press, 2010), pp. 121–53; see also Figal, *Unscheinbarkeit. Der Raum der Phänomenologie* (Tübingen: Mohr Siebeck, 2015)), even though it also draws close to Figal's account on some points. Where Figal and I can be

seen as largely in agreement is in the centrality of some notion of spatiality to the hermeneutical. Where we differ, most significantly, is on the understanding of spatiality itself – Figal takes spatiality as the key notion, with no reference to any developed notion of place, and his concept of spatiality seems essentially that of unbounded extension. My account takes spatiality always to be derivative of place, the latter being the key concept, and so the concept of space at work in my thinking is always a *bounded* spatiality. Where we also differ is in our respective readings of Heidegger and Gadamer – I read a topological account into their thinking, whereas Figal tends to develop his spatialised account of hermeneutics partially in opposition to the sort of account he sees in Heidegger and especially in Gadamer. For a brief discussion of Figal's position, see my "Place and Situation," pp. 362–3.

35. It should also be noted that the topographical hermeneutics envisaged is not necessarily incompatible with the 'eventual hermeneutics' advocated by Claude Romano – see his *Event and World*, trans. Shane Mackinley (New York: Fordham, 2009). I take place to have an essentially "eventual" character (to use Romano's term, although I would argue that event itself cannot be understood independently of place – and something like this connection may be suggested by a comment Romano makes near the very end of *Event and World*. Using his own neologism "advenant" to refer to the human being understood in the light of the event, Romano writes that: "an advenant only advenes to himself if time 'takes place'; he 'is' only the 'place' where time 'takes place' as such" (*Event and World*, p. 211).

36. See (among many other works) my *Donald Davidson and the Mirror of Meaning* (Cambridge: Cambridge University Press, 1992) as well as "Place and Situation." Björn Ramberg attempts to approach the issue of externalism in direct relation to Gadamer's hermeneutics in "The Source of the Subjective," in Lewis Edwin Hahn (ed.), *The Philosophy of Hans-Georg Gadamer*, The Library of Living Philosophers XXIV (Chicago: Open Court, 1997), pp. 459–72, but Gadamer's response (see 'Reply to Björn T. Ramberg', *The Philosophy of Hans-Georg Gadamer*, pp. 472–4) is more one of bafflement than genuine engagement. The exchange reflects the difficulty of this sort of encounter across philosophical traditions – the same difficulty is evident in Davidson's contribution to the volume ("Gadamer and Plato's *Philebus*," *The Philosophy of Hans-Georg Gadamer*, pp. 421–33) as well as Gadamer's reply ("Reply to Davidson," *The Philosophy of Hans-Georg Gadamer*, pp. 433–6), and in Gadamer's reply to the essay by David Hoy (Gadamer, "Reply to David C. Hoy," pp. 129–30, and Hoy, "Post-Cartesian Interpretation: Hand-Georg-Gadamer and Donald Davidson," pp. 111–29, both in *The Philosophy of Hans-Georg Gadamer*).

37. Into which Dan Hicks and Mary C. Beaudry (eds.), *The Oxford Handbook of Material Culture Studies* (Oxford: Oxford University Press,

2010) provides a useful point of entry. The focus on material culture has become an increasingly prominent theme in contemporary archaeology, anthropology, cultural theory, and sociology. For myself, I would prefer to talk, less of a purely "materialist" focus, but instead of a form of "materialist romanticism" or "romantic materialism" (since what is at issue is the embedding of the romantic – memory, belief, desire) in the "material" and of the material in the "romantic," rather than of a pure materiality alone – see, for instance, my "Building Memory," *Interstices: Journal of Architecture and Related Arts* 13 (2012), pp. 11–21.

38. See my "Putting Space in Place: Relational Geography and Philosophical Topography," *Planning and Environment D: Space and Society*, 30 (2012), pp. 226–42.

8 Verbal and Nonverbal Forms of Play: Words and Bodies in the Process of Understanding

MONICA VILHAUER

In Gadamer's magnum opus, *Truth and Method*, Gadamer describes the phenomenon of understanding, in all of its forms, as a play-process in which interlocutors engage in a dance of presenting and recognizing meaning with each other, and come to a shared knowledge about the truths of our world. The same play-process of understanding takes place, Gadamer reveals, whether one is encountering an artwork, a text, a ritual, a festival, any form of tradition, or another person face to face. In fact, Gadamer claims, following Heidegger, that understanding "pervades all human relations to the world"[1] and that understanding is our very way of being-in-the-world. Hermeneutics, thus, "embraces the whole of its [the human being's] experience of the world" (TM, xxx). With such a broad notion of understanding, Gadamer, thus, implies throughout *Truth and Method* that the play-process of understanding can occur both verbally (as when one reads a text, or has a conversation) and non-verbally (as in dance, silent rituals, or a multitude of basic practical tasks) in which communication is body-to-body. Yet, at the end of *Truth and Method*, Gadamer privileges explicit, verbal dialogue-play as the mode in which genuine communication and understanding take place. There he says of the play-process of understanding: "we are to note that *this whole process is verbal*" (TM, 384). Where does this leave non-verbal forms of play, communication, and understanding that take place body-to-body? Is Gadamer's late prioritization of verbal play, as the mode in which genuine dialogue and understanding take place, a valid one? Are there types of understanding that words just cannot clarify or improve, in comparison to physical or practical involvement and repeated experience? Finally, what happens to the role of bodies in communication and understanding in Gadamer's ultimate privileging of verbal dialogue-play?

With this constellation of questions in mind, I argue that Gadamer has a rather ambivalent attitude toward the body and its role in understanding. Though there are many resources within *Truth and Method* that suggest the positive contribution of the body in all understanding, and the possibility of genuine body-to-body understanding, they seem to be abandoned. One can detect a kind of intellectualism and forgetting of the body at the end of *Truth and Method* that ultimately (1) diminishes the body's role in communication and understanding; (2) diminishes those kinds of understanding that are primarily physical or practical, and (3) is at odds with his earlier explication of modes of understanding that occur without any words at all, in particular the understanding of artworks and rituals. It also seems to be at odds with his notion that our primordial mode of "being in the world" is one of understanding and that understanding pervades *all* of our human experience.

UNDERSTANDING AS PLAY-PROCESS

Gadamer begins his description of the play-process of understanding by considering our encounter with a work of art. Against modern science's claim to have a monopoly on knowledge, Gadamer adamantly insists that, in a wide variety of non-methodological experiences, genuine knowledge of genuine truth occurs. In our encounter with art, for instance, "a truth is experienced that we cannot attain in any other way" (TM, xxiii). Such a truth, which is "certainly different from that of science, but just as certainly not inferior to it" (TM, 97), is experienced in a way that is significantly different from the Cartesian subject–object model of knowledge, upon which modern scientific method is built. In contrast to the Cartesian model of knowledge, in which the detached subject independently observes and makes an accurate representation of a passive object, Gadamer's phenomenological account of the play-process of understanding offers a vision of knowledge as a social, collaborative, open-ended engagement with some meaningful subject matter.

A work of art, according to Gadamer, is "not an object... the work of art has its true being in the fact that it becomes an experience that changes the person who experiences it" (TM, 103). How does this experience occur? Gadamer explains that art presents for an audience a meaningful whole that it intends for the audience to recognize. In an artwork some "Thou" makes a "claim to truth" about our world, and aims to share that truth with us. The goal of an artwork, is thus, a joint understanding, which comes to completion when the audience grasps what it is trying to say. Such an understanding occurs in the back and forth movement between artists and spectators, in which meaning is presented and recognized. Art itself, according to Gadamer, only exists in the occurrence in which its meaning is grasped by an audience. So, art is neither a static thing to be sized up and tested through scientific method, nor is it an idea in the mind to be grasped through a psychological analysis. It is an "event" that encompasses both artists and spectators. It is what Gadamer calls an "event" of understanding. Thus "a drama really exists only when it is played, and ultimately music must resound" (TM, 116).

The same is the case not only for the performing arts (drama, music, dance), but for the plastic and literary arts as well. A picture or sculpture really exists only when it is viewed, and a poem or novel only comes to life when it is read. Gadamer extends this point about the literary arts to all texts. All texts communicate meaning for an audience, and their meaning only comes to life in the activity of being read. Texts, thus, also exist only in the back-and-forth play-process of understanding in which meaning is presented and recognized by an audience. Gadamer says:

> Just as we were able to show that the being of the work of art is play and that it must be perceived by the spectator in order to be actualized (*vollendet*), so also it is universally true of texts that only in the process of understanding them is the dead trace of meaning transformed back into living meaning. (TM, 164)

A book "has its original existence in being read ... Thus the reading of a book would still remain an event in which the content comes to presentation" (TM, 160, 161). Gadamer asserts that artworks and texts – as well as festivals, rituals, legends, religions, philosophies, laws, and so on – are all forms of tradition, in which truths are articulated about our world, and meaning is handed down and appropriated by new generations. The passing on of tradition is, thus, like a conversation in which interlocutors attempt to grasp what each other says about the world, and share some truth. A living conversation, too, is for Gadamer a play-process in which human beings share meaning, learn from each other, and cultivate knowledge. So, whether we encounter an artwork, a text, a festival, a ritual, or another in living conversation, the understanding that takes place is a dynamic, communicative, social, play-process in which meaning is shared and our world is disclosed.

To understand better what it means that understanding is a play-process or game, let's take a look at some of the unique aspects of the movement of play. First, play is not a solitary act. It requires someone or something else with which one plays. Play is a movement that takes place "in between" players. This game of understanding, thus, cannot be played privately, but is a joint endeavor. Second, play is bigger than the players and has a life of its own, in which the players become immersed. Gadamer emphasizes that the subject or focus of play is not the players, but the movement itself and the pattern that emerges from it. In the game of understanding, the focus of play is the truth about our world that is beyond both players, and that the players aim to know. What interests Gadamer most about play is the way that it decenters the players, for "all playing is a being played ... the game masters the players" (TM, 106). This means that, third, play is not something one can control but, rather, it is something in which one "loses" oneself (TM, 102). In the game of understanding, the player must give up control, bring herself into an interpretive process whose outcome she does not know in advance, and let the subject matter lead. To be a true participant in play is to give oneself over to the game, to let go of one's preoccupation with oneself, and to let go of the temptation to dominate the other players or control the outcome of the game. If one player dominates the other players to the extent that they no longer have the space to move, the game will stop. In the game of understanding, the player must not try to overpower, manipulate, or silence her partner, but create space for his different point of view. In the game of understanding, the goal is not winning an argument, but finding out the truth. Play is, thus, a unique kind of movement that involves freedom, difference, and surprise, and offers a stark contrast to modern scientific method, which aims for mechanical and repeatable steps, and control over the object of study. We might be tempted to think that a game is something that is not very serious, but Gadamer emphasizes the opposite. He suggests, fourth, that play does not function very well when the players hold back or see it as "just a game." He declares: "Someone who does not take the game seriously is a spoilsport" (TM, 102). In the game of understanding, one must take seriously what the other has to teach us, and approach them with a good will to understand. One must also consider the game of understanding itself to be a worthwhile endeavor, and deserving of one's efforts. Just as in any game, where the player must engage wholeheartedly, risk her talents, and allow herself to be challenged, tried, and transformed, the player who aims to understand must risk her old beliefs, open herself to finding out that her prior understanding was limited or incorrect, and be willing to learn something new.

UNDERSTANDING AS LINGUISTIC: THE BROAD MEANING OF LANGUAGE AND THE CONTRIBUTION OF BODIES

The game of understanding is a kind of conversation between voices that attempts to articulate some subject matter together, whether that conversation takes place through the medium of a painting, a song, a dance, a text, a sacred rite of passage, a law, some other form of tradition, or face to face. The game of understanding is, thus, a *dialogical* play-process. It is a *language* game. Throughout the first and second parts of *Truth and Method,* Gadamer makes repeated suggestions that the play-process of understanding is fundamentally linguistic in nature. But his notion of "language" in these first two divisions is quite broad. Gadamer describes the ways in which art "speaks" to us, even if not in words. Music, dance, pictures, paintings, sculptures are all, for Gadamer, language and "*all encounter with the language of art is an encounter with an unfinished event and is itself part of this event*" (TM, 99). The same is true of rituals, festivals, and all other forms of tradition, which also "speak" to us, whether they are handed down through the explicit "word" (as in texts, spoken legends, laws) or not (as in pictures, sculptures, music, dances, and a variety of cultural practices like clapping, bowing, giving gifts, etc.). These forms of tradition make "statements" to us about our world, whether they are verbal or nonverbal. Gadamer states: "Understanding must be conceived as a part of the event in which meaning occurs, the event in which the meaning of all statements – those of art and all other kinds of tradition – is formed and actualized" (TM, 165). So, we have here, in the earlier sections of *Truth and Method,* a notion of language that surely involves gestures, sounds, rhythm, images, movements, clothing, and any other human expressions that aim to communicate meaning. Though he does not reflect on it as a theme in *Truth and Method,* the implication here is that bodies not only play a crucial role in the play-process of understanding and communication, but that understanding can also take place body-to-body without any words at all. In other words, bodies can speak and recognize meaning non-verbally. Let's consider how bodies do this.

Bodily Perception as a Form of Understanding

Gadamer claims, following Heidegger, that we human beings *exist* as understanders. He asserts: "[U]nderstanding is not just one of the various possible behaviors of the subject but the mode of being of Dasein itself." The entire breadth of our human experience in the world involves understanding. All understanding is itself interpretive, and all interpretation takes place in language, as "language is the form in which understanding is achieved" (TM, xxxiv). This means that we are always already wrapped up in language games. Gadamer claims: "*Language games* exist where we, as learners – and when do we cease to be that? – rise to the understanding of the world" (TM, 490). So, all of our experiences, even our basic bodily perceptions, are themselves forms of understanding, are interpretive, and are linguistic. How so?

Gadamer explains that everything we experience, we experience "as" something ... "as" something distinct (as this and not that) and "as" something meaningful (as good, or bad, or beautiful, or useful). We experience things "as" distinct and meaningful in a wider context – that is, in relation to other things, in relation to our own past, our current interests, and our future projects. Everything we encounter, we encounter by way of taking "as." So, when we see, for instance, we focus on certain aspects and ignore others, we foreground and background what is there, we see relationships, we associate meanings with what we see in relation to a larger context, and we evaluate. For example, it's not that I see at the playground a small human being with turned up mouth corners, a pointy head, and brown paste on his face – I see a kid in a birthday hat eating cake and having fun, and I associate celebration with it. "Thus our perception is never a simple reflection of what is given to the senses" (TM, 90). Seeing is a "seeing-as," which is always already an articulation of what is there, and a way of "understanding-as."

> All understanding-as is an articulation of what is there, in that it looks-away-from, looks-at, sees-together-as ... Thus there is no doubt that, as an articulating reading of what is here, vision disregards much of what is there, so that for sight, it is simply not there anymore. So too expectations lead it to "read in" what is not there at all. (TM, 91)

The same is the case with hearing. In hearing we "listen" to certain parts and ignore others, and again hear relationships and associate meaning. The way we initially perceive something is influenced by the context of our past perceptions. Such a context is made up of our personal past experiences and our historical–cultural situation.[2] Even in perception, there is a play-process of understanding at work – a play-process in which we enter into a relation with things, we let those things reveal themselves to us, and we interpret what is shown to us in terms of our own historical–cultural horizon of meaning. In other words, even in basic perception we *articulate* what is before us. Even before we bring a subject matter into explicit speech, we encounter it linguistically. This enables Gadamer to claim: "[M]an's being in the world is linguistic" (TM, 443). Everything we encounter is already put on the scale of language, even if not yet in explicit words. For us, according to Gadamer, the world itself is linguistically constituted (TM, 444). The implication of this discussion of perception is that we are able to interpret, understand, and articulate body-to-body, without the need of any words at all. Our bodies are able to understand non-verbally.

Body-to-Body Understanding in Non-Verbal Art

Let's consider how this body-to-body understanding works when we encounter non-verbal art. Arguing that art is not mere entertainment, but that it speaks truth, is Gadamer's obsession in the first division of *Truth and Method*. Gadamer spends considerable time discussing the way in which performance arts and pictures bring forth truth when we engage them (TM, 108-159), and yield knowledge. Gadamer's examples of music, dance, theater, painting, sculpture, and architecture all represent what I am calling "non-verbal" art. They are artworks that present meaning through some other medium than words, and our experience with them is body-to-body. Let's consider the way in which human bodies are both the presenters of a story, and the perceivers and recognizers of that story, in an artwork like the ballet *Swan Lake*.

The bold, assertive, snapping movements of the male black-bird figure communicate power, and his mischievous expression communicates bad intentions, deception or harm. The soft graceful movements of the white swan queen communicate innocence and her tentativeness suggests some element of fear or suffering. The interactive movements of the prince, the main character we follow through the whole story, and the swan queen suggest curiosity, attraction and soon – in the way he grows closer to her, touches her, lifts her, dances in unison with her – affection and love. Of all of the white swans, she is the object of his interest, always in the center of the stage or up front. She is the favorite. He follows her around the floor. The entrance of the male black bird while they are together, with the change in musical tempo, and the juxtaposition of his powerful movements and the couple's soft movements and avoidance of him, suggests he is a threat. The confident and sharper movements of the woman in black, offered to catch the prince's attention, reveal a different kind of woman from the white swan queen. Her half smile-half smirk, and her association with the male black-bird figure, suggests she might be a danger. The flurry of movements of the white swan queen watching the prince and the woman in black together suggests anxiety, and the expression on her face suggests sadness and disappointment. The bowed heads and forward contracted positions of the other white swans suggest solidarity in sadness with her. All of this is told through the movements, gestures, and tempo of the dancers, and the music, lighting, costumes, and scenery on stage, without any words at all. The audience members perceive and recognize what is going on silently, as they bear witness and become wrapped up in the music, the movements, and the whole performance. One knows while watching, without any discussion, that it is a love story. One recognizes the way disappointment and pain can tragically intervene in love, and how the foul play of others can be a destructive force on it. One undergoes the truth of love presented on stage through a communicative interaction that takes place between bodies.[3]

The treatment here of dance applies also to the play-process of understanding music, in which the musicians physically perform their song, express a variety of emotions, and tell a story, while the audience listens, recognizes, and undergoes the emotions along with the musicians, sharing in their drama. The same applies also to viewing a painting, a sculpture, or a photograph, in which we recognize the meaning presented to us without the need of words at all, and undergo an experience in which we walk away changed. Gadamer spends quite a lot of time in *Truth and Method* describing the way in which a picture is able to bring forth being and present it to us in such a way that we recognize it, and come to "know more" than we did before. He says "The picture is an event of being – in it being appears, meaningfully and visibly" (TM, 144). No necessity for words is mentioned in this revelation of being. In a later lecture from 1964 entitled "Image and Gesture," Gadamer returns to the theme of art that speaks without words. Here he says of the visible arts that they speak meaning through the language of gesture. He says: "A gesture is something wholly corporeal and wholly spiritual at one and the same time . . . The whole being of the gesture lies in what it says."[4] This confirms the notion that in our encounters with nonverbal art, there is a language of body-to-body in which spirit is able to speak without words, meaning is presented and recognized, and genuine knowledge of genuine truth is experienced. Confirming this again, Gadamer says in the same lecture, of a landscape painting, that its pictorial gestures "speak the silent language of heraldry, a language of symbol that allows us to recognize things that belong together with no need of words" (IG, 80). Of a painting of a hunter, he mentions that the pictorial "primordial gesture of the hunt until the arrow strikes us hardly calls for explicit interpretation" (IG, 80). And, finally, of a challenging painting almost entirely in blue, he says: "Although the picture as a whole seems written in almost undecipherable characters, we can still divine in it a meaning that speaks to us directly" (IG, 81). These statements confirm what is implied, though never treated specifically as a theme, in the early sections of *Truth and Method*: Genuine communication and understanding can occur without any words at all. The play-process of understanding need not be verbal to be fulfilled.

All of the primarily physical modes of communication – gesture, facial expression, movement, posture, tone, rhythm – which are at the center of the performing arts and also of rituals, rites of passage, and festivals, work together to speak meaning and to form culture, which is handed down to us and which we hand down anew. They are a part of tradition, and Gadamer says that tradition "is *language* – i.e., it expresses itself like a Thou. A Thou is not an object; it relates itself to us ... tradition is a genuine partner in dialogue" (TM, 358). We can conclude, thus, from the early divisions of *Truth and Method* that tradition speaks, with or without words, through so many manifestations of language – through art, festival, ritual, and of course also through text and living conversation. We come to understand tradition by engaging in a kind of conversation with it, which may take place in explicit verbal discussion, but may also take place in the silent witnessing and recognition of what it has to say, or in the interactive physical movements that are required for participation. If the domain of language is so broad as to include all of these different verbal and non-verbal modes of articulating, recognizing, and communicating meaning, then so also is the domain of hermeneutics, whose task is to interpret and understand that language. Language consists, not just in what is written or spoken, but in all "spiritual creations" (TM, 165), which articulate and present meaning, and reach out to others to address them.

Everyday Communication Through Body Language

Though Gadamer does not address it in *Truth and Method*, body language is a powerful communicator not only in the arts, but in the way we share meaning with each other in everyday life. The smile, the hug, the outreached hand are all gestures that communicate welcome and affection. The crossed arms and averted eyes communicate discomfort. Fidgeting, playing with a paper clip, twirling one's hair all suggest nervousness, tentativeness, lack of confidence. The limp handshake, slouching in one's seat, and looking at the floor all suggest disinterest. Dating and job advice websites are filled with reminders of what we communicate with our bodies, which they claim we ought to be more aware of so that we don't give a bad impression, and so that we better interpret what the other's understanding of the situation is.[5] The implication is that our bodies speak volumes on their own about whom we understand ourselves to be, and how we interpret the situation we're in. In fact, the claim is repeatedly made that our bodies often speak more loudly and directly than our words. They tell the "real" story that our words won't always tell. One thing is certain. We realize how much bodies contribute to the whole communicative scenario when we are denied access to them. We find ourselves at a major disadvantage in a phone interview when we cannot see the boss's facial expression and gestures. We find ourselves even worse off in email correspondence, in which we are constantly questioning the tone of the comment made – was it a criticism, or a joke? Was she being serious or sarcastic? Gesture, tone, and facial expressions tell us volumes about the meaning of the words delivered – whether what is being said is questionable, tentative, declarative, urgent, dangerous, sarcastic, strange, secretive, or funny. The bodily interactions that occur during dialogue are not some unnecessary appendage or distraction from what is being said. They actually inform and help to designate the meaning of what is being spoken.[6]

Feminist philosophers, most notably Judith Butler, have done a tremendous amount of work elaborating the ways in which bodies perform, and thus communicate meaning, in particular cultural gender roles. For Butler, inspired by Simone de Beauvoir, acting out gender norms actually constitutes one's socially recognized gender identity. This means, in Beauvoir's terms, that "one is not born, but rather becomes, a woman,"[7] and in Butler's terms "what is called gender identity is a performative accomplishment."[8] The designation and communication of gender is, thus, something we "do" through bodily acts. The way one sways one's hips, the tone of one's voice, the clothes one wears, and the way one wears them, all communicate gender-meaning.[9] The communication that occurs – the presentation and recognition of gender-meaning – is body to body. Butler calls this gender-communication "a corporeal field of cultural play."[10]

Bodies as crucial contributors to the articulation and interpretation of verbal language, and body language itself as a species of language in its own right, may not be a theme of discussion for Gadamer, but it follows from his discussions of the ways in which art and ritual speak, the ways in which audiences or inductees participate in that meaning, and, finally, the ways in which understanding is our very mode of being in the world. Gadamer's ontological claim about understanding – that it is our very mode of being in the world – stretches the breadth of the domain of language, and of the task of hermeneutics that aims to understand that language, to the universal. Such a broad scope of understanding and language must certainly include body-to-body communications, whether in art, ritual, or everyday encounters.

The Role of the Body in Practical Understanding

There is one more type of understanding that Gadamer focuses on that suggests the positive role of the body in understanding, as well as the ability of the body to understand on its own without the need for words: Practical understanding. For Gadamer, understanding connotes not just something theoretical, but also a practical ability. Understanding involves "being well versed in something" (TM, 260), and is a way of knowing one's way around, or of being able to "do" something competently. Gadamer spends a good amount of time in *Truth and Method* considering how application is a key component of all understanding and interpretation, which puts practical understanding at the center of his hermeneutic theory. When we understand something, Gadamer says, we apply its meaning to our concrete situation. "[A]pplication is neither a subsequent nor merely an occasional part of the phenomenon of understanding, but codetermines it as a whole from the beginning" (TM, 324). Gadamer mentions three models of the way understanding involves application: to understand a law means to be able to apply it to the concrete case at hand; to know the meaning of a song or drama is to be able to play it in a way that brings its meaning to life in the present historical–cultural context; and to understand a certain code of ethics is to be able to put it into action in one's behaviors and habits. These are all forms of practical understanding that involve physical know-how, in which the body plays an important role. They are all ways of "knowing one's way around" some field or situation. Of course this knowing involves interpretation – seeing-as, taking in context, relating with, comparing, evaluating, sizing up, and gauging meaning – and so articulating what is there, which we've already mentioned in our discussion on perception can be done by the body without the use of words. But it also involves knowing *what to do* with one's own body. In practical know-how, one must not only size up the concrete situation, and interpret embodied beings and their relationships to one another; one must also figure out what is demanded of oneself as an embodied being in that situation. One must figure out how to fulfill that demand successfully. Such a "figuring" requires physical trial, error, revision, and repetition. It requires the body's practice.

There are many more examples of practical understanding in its broad sense (of concrete "know-how") that illuminate not only the central role of the body in understanding, and the body's ability to understand on its own without words, but furthermore the insignificance of words in learning such knowledge. Consider learning how to hammer a nail without hitting one's thumb, learning how to do a flip on a trampoline, learning how to do it with a twist without getting lost in the air, learning how to hit a tennis ball, ride a bike, sing harmony, keep a beat, or dance. Consider learning what amount of salt is needed in the soup, learning how to brown and not burn the butter, learning how not to overcook the noodles. Consider learning that when she crosses her arms, she is uncomfortable and one should back off; learning that that smirk means trouble and one should be on guard; learning that if his eyes dart around the room, he's not interested and one should move on; learning that a deep sigh and an eye-roll means boredom and one should step up the conversation. Most of the time this learning occurs without the use of words at all. But, furthermore, words offer little help in our education of this practical knowledge in comparison to trial, error, revision, repetition, and perhaps imitation. Even when some level of speech is included, or some verbal instruction or guidance is offered, the role of physical practice supersedes that of words. (Consider whether your Dad's instructions about how to ride a bike are very useful, in comparison to your own physical experiments peddling, falling, and trying again.) No amount of description or verbal instruction is going to be enough to teach one "how" to act and act well. In the kind of knowing that involves "doing," the body must do the learning, and the test of whether one has achieved knowledge is not saying the right words but competent action.

If a human being is a "being in the world," as Gadamer says, then the body, of course, is the precondition for the ability to experience and understand anything. Our embodiment is what places us, or "throws" us, into some time and place in the world, and is the starting place or the standpoint from which our horizon of understanding is formed. We cannot properly understand "understanding" or the "human being" unless we recognize the finitude that is central to our way of being, and we cannot understand this finitude unless we consider the body.[11] But the body is not just a conditioning factor in the sense of a limitation. It is a positive force, as I've tried to show, in our ability to interpret anything. It does not just limit where and how we are in the world. It is what connects us to the world, reaches out, makes contact with, and interprets that world. Even when understanding is verbal to the extreme – as in a phone conversation or an email – still the ears and eyes are at work, interpreting emphasis and tone. The body is always at work in interpretation. Furthermore, as I've tried to emphasize, there are some forms of understanding in which the body can fulfill the task of understanding without any words at all, as in basic perception, understanding non-verbal artworks, everyday body-language, and in practical knowledge. And, finally, there are forms of understanding in which words neither improve nor complete the tasks of understanding, as is the case in many forms of practical understanding. A closer look at what the body can do, and how it understands, is an important project for philosophical hermeneutics, which aims to account for the way in which *all* understanding works. It is a project toward which many resources in Gadamer's work point, but it is never pursued.[12] Gadamer's reflections on understanding art, ritual, and festival, his discussions of the hermeneutic dimensions of perception and experience in general, his emphasis on our primordial "being in the world," his discussions of finitude, situation, and horizon, and his development of application as a part of all understanding, all offer resources for the recognition of the importance of the body in understanding and in language, but the topic is not only skipped over as a theme – it is, I'm afraid, abandoned by Gadamer. The body seems to be treated more and more by Gadamer, at the end of *Truth and Method*, as merely a condition for the more important activity of verbal dialogue, and even a limitation to be superseded.

UNDERSTANDING AS VERBAL AND THE DIMINISHED ROLE OF BODIES

Throughout most of *Truth and Method*, Gadamer appears, as I've shown, to have a rather broad notion of language – which frankly he must have if he is to say that all understanding is linguistic, and include in the "events" of understanding our encounters with artworks, festivals, rituals, the practical activities of getting around in the world, of perception, and our very way of "being" in the world. In the third part of *Truth and Method*, however, in which the linguistic nature of understanding and the universal breadth of the domain of hermeneutics is most adamantly asserted, a strange thing occurs: Gadamer begins to use the term language to refer to what is verbal. Right at the moment in which he attempts to expand hermeneutics to its fullest possible extent, and to show that language is both everything we can possibly experience and know, and the way in which we know it, he narrows language to the form of words. Now he declares, of the linguistic play-process that is understanding, that "we are to note that *this whole process is verbal*" (TM, 384). He says: "All understanding is interpretation, and all interpretation takes place in the medium of a language that allows the object to come into words" (TM, 389). He goes on to argue that the hermeneutic object (what it is we try to understand), and the hermeneutic act (the medium of the process of understanding), are both verbal.

First, Gadamer argues that words are the proper object of understanding. Taking up different kinds of tradition again he says: "the essence of tradition is to exist in the medium of language, so that the preferred object of interpretation is a verbal one" (TM, 389). He argues that when meaning is communicated in the form of words, either orally or in writing, it speaks to us directly (TM, 391). This leads us to wonder, then, what is the status of those forms of tradition that do not speak in words – dance, music, painting, sculpture, silent ritual? Do they not communicate with us as well? Do they not teach us truths about the world as well? Are they less than genuine forms of tradition? I fear that Gadamer is saying just that when, at the end of *Truth and Method*, he refers to plastic arts as "dumb monuments" (TM, 390) which "cannot be understood of themselves" (TM, 391) – a strange phrase from the man who taught us earlier that our encounters with art yield nothing less than genuine knowledge of genuine truth. Gadamer explains:

> The understanding of verbal tradition retains special priority over all other tradition ... What has come down to us by the way of verbal tradition is not left over but given to us, told to us – whether through direct retelling, in which myth, legend, and custom have their life, or through written tradition, whose signs are, as it were, immediately clear to every reader who can read them. (TM 389–90)

Gadamer goes on to narrow even further which kind of hermeneutic object has priority. The written word, he claims, has a special privilege over all other forms of tradition. Why is writing so special? First of all, it is able to detach itself from all the contingencies of life that would limit access to it. It is detached from its author, and can go on to address new audiences after the author's death. It, thus, has "a life of its own" (TM, 392). It does not depend on an oral presentation, so is available for the widest audience – regardless of when and where that audience lives. "What is fixed in writing has raised itself into a public sphere of meaning in which everyone who can read has an equal share" (TM, 392). It is the most permanent form of tradition, as it does not wear and tear like works of art. It is detached from the emotional forms inherent in living speech – tone, volume, facial expression, etc. – which Gadamer believes deliver merely psychological information about the author, and can distract from the content of what is said. "In writing, the meaning of what is spoken exists purely for itself, completely detached from all emotional elements of expression and communication" (TM, 392). One can't help but notice that what makes writing a preferable object of interpretation is that it is, of all of the modes of communication, the most detached and abstract. It is detached from the author, and his facial expression and tone (TM, 392). It is detached from its physical form, of "the finitude and transience that characterize other remnants of past existence" (TM, 390), and from its historical situation, or "the mere continuance of the vestiges of past life" (TM, 391). It has reached a state of pure ideality (TM, 390–4). In other words, writing is privileged most because it is the most disembodied object of interpretation. It is the least "dependent" on something that Gadamer is now implying is too vague and too temporary for genuine understanding. Apparently embodiment is now, at the end of *Truth and Method*, a hindrance to understanding, and to be overcome. Whereas Gadamer's treatment of art and tradition suggested earlier that bodies contribute positively to understanding, and that they are able to communicate meaning on their own without any need of words, now the claim seems to be that bodies must be transformed or translated into words to be understood.

Gadamer claims at the end of *Truth and Method* that not only is the object of understanding verbal, but also that the medium in which interpretive understanding occurs is verbal. Interpretive understanding itself is something that happens in words. "Interpretation ... is the act of understanding itself, which is realized – not just for the one for whom one is interpreting but also for the interpreter himself – in the explicitness of verbal interpretation" (TM, 397). Gadamer emphasizes that it is not as if understanding might first occur silently, and then later be put into words (TM, 378), as if words were tools that we use to give expression to our thoughts. Thinking itself is only possible with words. Thinking is a kind of internal dialogue. "We must recognize that all understanding is interwoven with concepts and reject any theory that does not accept the intimate unity of word and subject matter" (TM, 403). This leads us to wonder what the status is of the artist's interpretation of a song she has heard, or a dance she has seen, in her own performance of it. Has she not yet really understood the meaning of the music or dance if she has not yet discussed it (with herself or others), or written about it? And what about the interpretation that occurs when an audience watches a ballet, views a painting, experiences a jazz festival, or takes part in an ancient tea ritual? Are we to think that understanding has not yet occurred, if the audience or participants have not yet spoken about these experiences with others or written about them?

Though there was no mention of a need for discussion for one to genuinely understand the music she was listening to or playing, or to grasp the truth of a picture she was painting or viewing earlier in *Truth and Method*, Gadamer now suggests that non-verbal understanding is really, in a sense, pre-verbal and immature in comparison to the final fulfillment of understanding that takes place in words. With regard to performing artists, he says that in cases "when there is immediate understanding and no explicit interpretation is undertaken ... interpretation {in words} must be possible. But this means that interpretation is contained potentially within the understanding process. It simply makes the understanding explicit" (TM, 398). Furthermore, he asserts: "A performing artist may feel that justifying his interpretation in words is very secondary, rejecting it as inartistic, but he cannot want to deny that such an account can be given of his reproductive interpretation" (TM, 399). So, although some level of "immediate" understanding may be possible without words, Gadamer now does not think it is sufficient for understanding to reach completion. Any such immediate understanding must be speak-able, and bringing such an understanding into words is the way in which the meaning that is understood is concretized (TM, 397). This suggests that the same is the case when a spectator experiences a non-verbal artwork, or a participant experiences a ritual. There may be some level of immediate understanding, but it must be speak-able, and bringing understanding into explicit language makes it determinate. Gadamer says: "Verbal interpretation is the form of all interpretation, even when what is to be interpreted is not linguistic in nature – i.e., is not a text but a statue or a musical composition. We must not let ourselves be confused by forms of interpretation that are not verbal but in fact presuppose language" (TM, 398). Gadamer seems to be claiming here, at the end of *Truth and Method*, that interpretation has as its own internal telos of verbal articulation, in which it may become explicit and determinate. The nature or essence of language is verbal.

The notions that the nature of language is verbal, and that understanding can only occur in words, conflict with his earlier insistence that genuine understanding occurs in our encounters with art (including the non-verbal arts) and in all of our practical activities in the world (including the non-verbal ones). It seems that the best way to try to reconcile Gadamer's conflicting claims about what counts as understanding and language, is to picture understanding and language on a spectrum from most provisional, vague, and implicit to most cultivated, definitive, and explicit. Understanding and language reach their highest form in the verbal. Verbalness is the "nature" of understanding and language in the Greek sense. Just as the Greeks used the term "nature" in a teleological sense to mark a thing's highest form and greatest fulfillment, verbalness, for Gadamer, is the nature of understanding and language. Just as the acorn realizes its nature and fulfillment when it becomes a great oak tree, the initial ability that humans have to recognize the universal[13] are those first sprouts of understanding and language that realize their nature and fulfillment in their most explicit, definitive, concrete, and communicable form – in words. "[T]he word is that in which knowledge is consummated" (TM, 426). More precisely, language reaches its fulfillment in dialogue, or the living language-game, for "language has its true being only in dialogue" (TM, 446). So, when Gadamer says that all language is verbal, he means that language in its highest fulfillment is verbal, not that we are walking around narrating everything that happens in words. Only in this way can we make sense of some further claims at the end of *Truth and Method* that man's relation to the world is verbal (TM, 476), and that all "human experience of the world is verbal in nature" (TM, 447), without trying to make ourselves believe – contrary to everyday experience – that we can only relate to anything if we talk about it out loud. The real clue to Gadamer's understanding of the verbal nature of all experience is in his point that experience "always seeks to find the right word" (TM, 417), and that "putting an experience into words helps us cope with it" (TM, 453). It helps us to make the best sense of it that we can. Understanding reaches fruition when we bring it into words with each other.

But this attempt to reconcile Gadamer's conflicting claims about what counts as understanding and language doesn't reconcile everything. This attempt to reconcile things still places the body-to-body understanding that can happen in art, in ritual, in basic everyday practices, low on the scale of understanding, in comparison to verbal philosophical accounts, in a way that counteracts the wonderfully radical spirit of Gadamer's defense of art as an event that yields truth in its own unique way. It leaves us in an intellectualist stance that devalues the power of bodies to communicate, interpret, apply, and understand meaning.

CONCLUSION

There remains a deep tension in Gadamer's work regarding the power of the body in understanding. The tension exists between his early championing of the experience of art as a model for what happens when we understand, and an example of genuine knowledge of genuine truth, and his later notion that artworks do not speak as directly as writing, and that our interpretation of them must be brought to words for the experience to be one of true understanding. Gadamer's work also presents us with a question about whether the privileging of verbal understanding, as he does at the end of *Truth and Method*, is really valid. His earlier impressive discussions of art and ritual, his treatment of practical understanding, and his notion that understanding is our very mode of being-in-the-world suggest that non-verbal understanding is not only possible, but yields knowledge that cannot be learned in any other (verbal) way. It is clear, especially in many forms of practical understanding, that words neither improve learning (in comparison to practice) nor consummate it (in comparison to competent action). Gadamer's ultimate privileging of verbal understanding seems to reveal an intellectualism that values theory over practice, and words over bodies. In the end Gadamer has a rather ambivalent attitude toward the body's role in understanding, at one moment implicitly recognizing its power in his most radical discussions of art, and at the next moment treating it as merely a limitation on understanding to be superseded by verbal conversation.

NOTES

1. Hans-Georg Gadamer, *Truth and Method*, trans. Joel Weinsheimer and Donald Marshall (New York: Continuum, 2000), xxii. Hereafter cited in text as TM, page number.
2. Even perception is not exactly a solitary or individual experience, because we carry with us all of the voices of our culture with us that inform the ways in which we perceive. That doesn't mean that perception is just a projection of our own cultural notions. The subject matter is our guide. When we "see wrong," we undergo a process of revision. Illusions and false interpretations are revealed to us when the things we sense show us they do not line up with what we initially thought of them.
3. Of course, I am not implying that there is no thinking going on, or that we are dealing with "pure bodies," or sensations without thinking and evaluating. Such "pure bodies" are a strange abstraction. What I am trying to highlight, is the way in which our thinking and evaluating and experiencing in general are embodied, and the way in which this embodiment plays a positive role – and sometimes the primary role – in our communications and understanding of meaning.
4. Hans-Georg Gadamer, "Image and Gesture" in *The Relevance of the Beautiful and Other Essays*, ed. Robert Bernasconi (Cambridge: Cambridge University Press, 1986), p. 79. Hereafter cited in text as IG, page number.
5. Of course body languages, just like any languages, are context and culture specific.
6. David Vessey rightly argues, in his essay "Gadamer and the Body Across Dialogical Contexts" (*Philosophy Today*, SPEP Supplement, 2000, pp. 70–6), that the body plays a special role in the verbal dialogue that occurs

with another person. He emphasizes that verbal dialogue is itself informed by embodied interactions, through gesture, posture, and facial expression, in a way that creates a richness of communication that is lost without such face-to-face interaction. He urges us to see the relationship between linguistic expression and the lived body, and the way "the linguistic expression arises out of and is always co-implicated in bodily comportment" (72). Embodiment is "the condition for the spoken dialogue and the way in which we exist as beings in the world" (72). I take Vessey's point to be that such a recognition about our embodiment, or our way of "being in the world" as Gadamer would say it, should open up an analysis of the way in which the body is always intertwined with verbal language as a positive contributor to the articulation and communication of meaning. Unfortunately, Gadamer tends to see the body merely as a condition for the possibility of dialogue, rather than as such a positive contributor that is able to speak for itself as a "dialogical body". In these points I agree with Vessey. Vessey argues further that the bodily interaction that takes place in living dialogue distinguishes it from other kinds of dialogue, in particular the kind of dialogue that occurs with a work of art, and has a richness that goes beyond what can occur between an artwork and spectator. On this point, I think that, at least in the performing arts, we can find the same importance and central role of the body, and of interactive bodily communication, as we might in live discussion.

7. Simone de Beauvoir, *The Second Sex*, trans. H.M. Parshley (New York: Vintage Books, 1989), p. 267.
8. Judith Butler, "Performative Acts and Gender Constitution: An Essay in Phenomenology and Feminist Theory," in *Theatre Journal*, Vol. 40, No. 4 (December 1988), p. 520.
9. As Beauvoir and Butler both make clear, the body may be a site of external pressures to conform, by performing prescribed meanings, or it may be a site of creativity and the subversion of those prescribed meanings. Of course, subversion can then lead to punishment and violence – yet another body-to-body communication.
10. Butler, "Performative Acts and Gender Constitution," p. 531.
11. It is remarkable that, when discussing our finitude, our situation, and our horizon in *Truth and Method*, Gadamer never mentions the body or embodiment (see *Truth and Method*, pp. 244–9, 302–7, 356–7).
12. Even in the collection of essays published in *The Enigma of Health*, where Gadamer is concerned with how the body should be understood in the patient–physician relation, Gadamer quickly skips over the way in which the doctor might diagnose and treat a patient manually. He makes only a passing comment about the root of the word "treatment" in German (*Behandlung*), and its connotation that all "treatment begins with the hand, with the *palpus*, by means of which the doctor physically examines the patient's body and feels the body tissue" (Hans-Georg Gadamer, *The Enigma of Health*, trans. Jason Gaiger and Nicholas Walker (Stanford:

Stanford University Press, 1996), p. 126). He does not consider how there might be a body-to-body understanding that takes place in many types of medical treatment (consider today's popular field "body-work"), and instead moves on to focus on the importance of the doctor's dialogical relationship with the patient. Gadamer insists that the body must not be objectified as a thing in the medical setting, but taken as an inseparable part of a larger, living, experiencing, human life. Understanding the body and its health can only be achieved by seeing it in its wider context of the patient's experience, habits, and social setting – in other words, the patient's whole life. This can only occur if the doctor enters into dialogue with the patient, in which the patient has a chance to articulate his own embodied experience, and is respected as offering important knowledge to the conversation. Though dialogue is important, Gadamer seems to underestimate all that is learned through body-to-body communications between patient and doctor. There is a reason that doctors don't diagnose and treat over the phone, but require a visit in person. The closest Gadamer gets to recognizing the positive role of the body in diagnostic and therapeutic understanding is when he mentions that treatment involves "the skilled and practiced hand that can recognize problems simply through feeling and touching the affected parts of the patient's body" (Gadamer, *The Enigma of Health*, p. 99). But, as in *Truth and Method*, such hints of body-to-body understanding are not pursued, and he focuses on the communicative superiority of speech.

13. In Gadamer's essay "Man and Language," he takes up Aristotle's explanation of the way in which we begin to recognize common attributes in our sensory field, and grasp a universal from so many fleeting particulars. Gadamer sees this knowledge of the universal as a kind of "entrance into language." Hans-Georg Gadamer, "Man and Language" in *Philosophical Hermeneutics*, trans. David E. Linge (Berkeley: University of California Press, 1976), p. 64.

PART IV

Science, Medicine and Biotechnology

9 On the Integration of Scientific Knowledge into Self-Understanding

PETER FRISTEDT

An old impulse in hermeneutics is to draw a distinction between scientific and everyday ways of knowing. Often, this impulse is accompanied by a skepticism about the philosophical relevance of scientific discovery. And yet, in our world fields like genetics and neurophysiology are increasingly taken as providing thorough accounts of human behavior and thought. Those everyday ways of knowing, far from remaining on one side of a stark conceptual divide, have in fact become permeated by scientific concepts and theories. Not only is there wide acceptance of yet other fields – evolutionary biology, cosmology, and particle physics, to name but a few – as accurately describing the basic furniture of the world; everyday language frequently invokes scientific concepts by way of expressing even the most mundane of sentiments ("my brain really lights up when I see a beer"). There is, perhaps, reason to be doubtful about the extent to which such theories and concepts are really understood, i.e. the extent to which genuine scientific *knowledge* has permeated the everyday perspective on things. And there is also reason to adhere to a hermeneutic skepticism about the epistemological status of scientific claims – to insist, that is, that science itself is irreducibly interpretive. But even in the face of such skepticism, a question remains: just what *is* the place of natural–scientific accounts of human activity in our understanding of ourselves? Should we view them as offering fundamentally true descriptions of our desires, our bodies, our thinking? Do they constitute bona fide self-knowledge or self-understanding? And what, in the end, are we to do with these descriptions as we think about how we are to live?

There are a number of different answers to these questions one might recommend. There is the naturalistic view, held by (many, not all) scientists and Anglo–American philosophers: this is the view that natural science is best placed to answer questions about ourselves, since we are natural entities in a natural world. Among continental philosophers, Nietzsche is perhaps the historically most salient representative of a view like this. Nietzsche takes human thought and action to be an expression or surface effect of deeper, natural forces at play in and through the individual. A Nietzschean answer to the question we posed above about what we are to do with scientific information might be to say that our task is to reconcile ourselves to, and ultimately affirm, the naturalistic truth. Another view is what I take to be the classical position in Continental philosophy, which holds that information about ourselves gained from scientific discovery does *not* constitute genuine self-knowledge. Stemming from Kant's transcendental turn, this view resists viewing humans as natural beings in a physical universe. Genuine philosophical self-knowledge comes from recognizing the constitutive role of the subject or history or language or the body in any understanding of worldly entities scientifically described. Some version of this view is held by thinkers from Husserl to Heidegger to Merleau-Ponty. If one accepts it, scientific discovery does not pose any special existential challenges, and the questions we asked above lose their force. (And indeed, for some such thinkers embracing scientific discovery constitutes a kind of dangerous leading astray.)

There is a third view that has gained traction among both Continental and Anglo–American philosophers in recent decades: since the self is constituted rather than discovered, some thinkers argue, the question of "placement" again loses force. What matters is not what we learn about ourselves, whatever the source, but whether we take such information and incorporate it into the *project* that is the self we are constantly making. Among recent Continental philosophers, Foucault stands out as representative of this view; among Anglo–American thinkers, Korsgaard leads the charge.

None of these alternatives is, it seems to me, satisfactory. The first view dogmatically makes the naturalistic perspective primary; the second and third sidestep the robustness and durability of scientific knowledge as a source of truth about ourselves. This paper will suggest a fourth path. I will argue that the philosophical hermeneutics of Gadamer offers us the best means to address the question of the place of scientific knowledge in our thinking about ourselves. To establish this claim, I will read with Gadamer, taking into consideration his views on the integration of new truths into our view of the world. But I will also read, if not against him, at least in tension with his text: like many European thinkers since Kant, he is wary of the claims of science and allows them at best a highly restricted place at the conversational table. I will argue that he nevertheless provides us with the tools to take

Integration of Scientific Knowledge into Self-Understanding 185

scientific claims seriously – even if we have to move to some extent beyond him in outlining a position that treats science with the seriousness it demands.

I will begin with a clarification of the problem at hand – the question of the status of scientific knowledge in our view of the world and of ourselves. I will then move on to consider arguments that challenge the possibility of integration from the perspective of thinkers who emphasize a strong distinction between the natural and the normative: Laszlo Tengelyi and Christine Korsgaard. I will finish by exploring the hermeneutic alternative, and will offer some hermeneutically-guided thoughts on the possibilities for – and limitations on – the integration of science into self-understanding.

THE PLACEMENT PROBLEM

In recent discussions among analytic philosophers about the philosophical implications of naturalism, the question we have been asking arises less often than does a related one: the concern is not so much about the place of scientific knowledge in our understanding of things as it is about the place of the human perspective – consisting as it does of reasons, meanings, norms, and values – in the natural world as described by science. That world consists of a material order governed by causes, and so appears to leave little room for phenomena that on their face are not material and thus do not interact with things at the level of physical causality. What room is there for these apparently nonmaterial entities in the broader natural world? How *can it be* that in a world of quarks, clouds, and digestion there is also injustice or friendship? David MacArthur call this question "the placement problem,"[1] and he argues that it arises when one accepts scientific naturalism as the right way to look at the world. To someone not already committed to a material–causal conception of things, it is not odd that there are friends – i.e. people who not only receive my love and respect, but who are (at least potentially) *worthy* of it. That worthiness cannot easily be accounted for in the world scientifically understood. Scientific naturalism, argues MacArthur, is committed to two claims that make the placement problem especially acute: there is the "ontological" position that "the only things that there are in the world are those things that are presupposed or posited by the successful sciences"; and there is the "methodological" position that "the only genuine and irreducible form of knowledge or understanding is that resulting from the methods of inquiry of the successful sciences."[2] The world of values and meanings – the world closest to us – would seem to fail on both counts: a boring sunset is posited by no successful science, nor is there knowledge of it resulting from the application of some scientific method.

So why am I proposing to address not the placement problem, but what is effectively the reverse of the placement problem? MacArthur goes on to argue that the placement problem is no problem at all if one does not opt for the unduly restrictive version of naturalism that is *scientific* naturalism, and subscribes instead to what he calls "liberal" naturalism. Such a view maintains that the human sciences – fields like sociology and economics that study the normative phenomena of the human world – are naturalistic and "earn their right to the title of 'science' on the grounds that they do not involve supernatural posits, admit empirical evidence, and provide fruitful explanatory generalizations."[3] If this is right and there is no placement problem, it would seem that there ought to be no tension between a natural–scientific view of the world and a view that accepts normative phenomena as a basic part of the universe. But that there is indeed a tension is hard to deny, and MacArthur allows as much when he says that such a tension "is related to the widely recognized hermeneutic insight that our understanding of normative phenomena is not the same as, and is not exhausted by, the kinds of understanding provided by *any* of the sciences, natural or human, insofar as these are concerned with various kinds of non-normative explanations, for example, nomological, causal, or statistical."[4] That is to say, to think about norms as norms is to understand what justifies them; it is to be caught up in the normative perspective of asking for and giving reasons. The scientific perspective (human or natural) does not help one understand a norm *as* a norm. But that means that the scientific and normative perspectives are genuinely different, and it becomes a question of how they are related – even if there is no placement problem.

A proponent of a particularly strong distinction between the normative and scientific points of view is Christine Korsgaard. She holds that there are effectively two points of view human beings can take on things, namely the first-person and third-person perspectives. Values and reasons are visible from the former, which she also calls the perspective of "reflective consciousness," and not the latter, which is also the perspective of scientific theory and observation. A scientific naturalist might argue against the existence of values and reasons by saying they are explanatorily superfluous: they are unnecessary in understanding why people do what they do. But, argues Korsgaard, we don't primarily posit reasons and values to *explain* anything; we posit them because we need them to make decisions. From the first-person perspective on the world, we are faced with alternatives, and we need to decide what to do. We decide what to do by reflecting on those alternatives and determining which one is justified, which one we have reason to do (which for Korsgaard means which one expresses our "practical identity," "the description under which you find your life to be worth living and your actions to be worth undertaking"[5]). That reflective process is available only from the first-person perspective; the third-person perspective can tell us perhaps what reasons an agent took herself to be acting on, but it cannot reveal, as we might say, the *reasonableness* of those reasons.

Korsgaard develops the idea of this distinction between perspectives further by saying that the world of the perspective of the agent is fundamentally teleological, composed as it is of "tools and obstacles."[6] The world for us as agents has that form because we must act, and to act we have to put objects in the world to use to achieve our ends. We have to view objects as subsumed under our purposes. But the view of things revealed by science not only denudes the world of purposes; it at the same time and for the same reason also denudes it of independently existing objects, as they are given to us in our action-oriented experience. Korsgaard asks: "Why do we say that the stone broke the window, rather than that the state of the world at Time T1 produced the state of the world at Time T2, which included a broken window? Because we can *use* a stone to break a window."[7] In nature, one might say, there are no *stones* – stones reveal themselves to us against a backdrop of usability. The world scientifically described – "a system of neutral laws and forces whose impact on our own fates and interests is largely accidental" – is *quite* distinct from the world we inhabit as agents, and it "requires the *detachment* of perception from the rich normative significance that naturally inhabits it."[8]

Another way to draw a strong distinction of the kind we are considering is to do so not between the everyday and the scientific or between the first and third-person perspectives, but between broad *philosophical* conceptions of the world as a whole. Along these lines, Laszlo Tengelyi distinguishes sharply between naturalism (or what he calls "naturalistic autarkism") and transcendentalism – whether of the Kantian kind or the "metontological transcendentalism of phenomenology." More than differing perspectives on things, these are "agonistic world projects": opposed, irreconcilable, radically distinct. The former posits nature as a "closed and homogenous totality characterized by self-sufficiency"[9] – nature does not depend for its existence on mind or subjectivity. The latter posits nature as something mind or subjectivity rises above in the form of a "world-forming being ... that does not remain captured in its surrounding world but is capable of surmounting the things of its immediate environment in order to relate to the world as a whole."[10]

The difference between these world projects lies in the role of context: for naturalism, the things of the natural world are not dependent for their being on the context in which they are understood, whereas for transcendentalism, natural things can be taken up into different cultural contexts and gain new characteristics in being so taken up.

Now, Tengelyi argues that science and philosophy are perfectly reconcilable, as are scientific information and the everyday perspective of the lifeworld. He notes that through the process Husserl calls *Einströmung*, scientific knowledge "streams into" the lifeworld: "scientific discoveries are indeed often integrated into everyday practice."[11] Nevertheless, the philosophical "world projects" of naturalism and transcendentalism are not thus reconcilable: "the conflict takes the form of a veritable antimony only because the realm of postulated entities [of naturalism] is conceived of as a closed and homogenous totality that, as such, is opposed to the reality of life in our everyday practice."[12] Still, it is hard to see how it can both be the case that scientific discovery streams into the lifeworld, and that nature is a closed and homogenous totality. If the lifeworld is characterized by its phenomenal character – a character that a natural system "closed to mind" lacks – then anything *in* that natural system would in turn lack the characteristics necessary for integration into the lifeworld. So the picture of an antimony between world pictures runs into trouble if one also wants to say that scientific discovery finds its way into the lifeworld. And in spite of the strong distinctions drawn by Tengelyi and Korsgaard, there is a case to be made for the possibility and actuality of this integration of perspectives – testified to by the apparent fact that people incorporate beliefs about the scientifically described natural world into their general view of the world. And, if it is true that something like a "streaming in" of scientific discovery into the lifeworld does take place, then we may want to steer away from the notion that the world described by science and the everyday normative perspective are radically distinct – whether at the metaphilosophical level or at the more mundane level of scientific practice and everyday life.

Still, even if we wish to avoid talk of antinomies, we are nevertheless faced with perspectives that are different – indeed, that appear *very* different. And that means we are faced with the problem of how these two very different perspectives on the world fit together. My claim is that this hermeneutic distinction among ways in which the world is understood ought to incline us not just to ask how they fit together, but specifically to ask how the scientific perspective fits into the normative one. After all, the normative perspective is arguably the one we occupy *most if not all of the time*. We make choices, give reasons, assess the relative value of people and things. As Virginia Held asks in her own attempt to dismiss the placement problem,

> Why should consciousness and moral choice be assigned the burden of showing how they are compatible with the view that scientific explanation can handle all the issues, rather than burdening the sciences with showing how they are compatible with the everyday experiences we know we have?[13]

She answers her question by saying we "cannot, without deceiving ourselves, live our lives from other than [the] point of view" of conscious moral agency. Korsgaard points in the same direction when she argues that the scientific perspective involves an active detachment from the everyday normative one; Kant too makes a related point when he says in the *Groundwork* that:

> To every rational being possessed of a will we must also lend the idea of Freedom as the only one under which he can act ... we cannot possibly conceive of reason as being consciously directed from the outside in regard to its judgments; for in that case the subject would attribute the determination of his power of judgment, not to his reason, but to an impulsion. Reason must look on itself as the author of its own principles independently of alien influences.[14]

Kant's point here is that when I act, I act for reasons, but insofar as I act for reasons I cannot take those reasons to be *caused* by something outside of my ability to reason (for example by my hormones). If I did take them to be so caused, rather than being arrived at through a chain of justification, they would lose their hold on me *as reasons*. The normative perspective for Kant cannot – when one is in its midst – be folded into the third person perspective. Finally, Lorenzo Simpson makes a hermeneutically informed argument along these lines when he speaks of "the inadequacy of science to the project of critical self-understanding."[15] From a hermeneutic perspective, in order for us to come to have a better grasp of ourselves we need to have our prejudices in play. Only so can these prejudices be revealed and possibly overturned. But my prejudices are precisely what scientific theorizing aims to suspend in the search for objective knowledge. So science puts out of play the very beliefs and attitudes necessary for a deepened self-understanding to take place. If we try to take up a thoroughgoing scientific perspective on things we will leave ourselves behind.

Now, it might be objected that while we spend most of our time looking at the world from the normative point of view, it does not follow that the third person observational perspective is not primary or more fundamental or true than the normative. There is no shortage of debunking arguments that aim to show that some value we have or reason we act on is really a function of our empirically describable desires or impulses. I would contend that it is possible to accept arguments like this on a case by case basis, and it is even possible to entertain the idea of the global irreality of the normative point of view. But because it is the everyday perspective of, as we might put it, our being-in-the-world, we cannot overcome it in some permanent way. Again, the reality of the normative perspective asserts itself when one is in the midst of that perspective, and one is almost always in the midst of that perspective. And most important, because it is the perspective we mostly occupy, any attempt at integration in the opposite direction – of the normative into the scientific – will of necessity have to in turn be integrated *back* into the everyday normative perspective. I will have to *live* with all of these scientifically informed conclusions I draw.

Another sort of objection to the claim I am making is that the very project of integrating scientific knowledge into self-understanding is misguided, since, the argument might go, the self is made rather than discovered. If that is the case, then anything we learn about ourselves through scientific discovery would, contrary to what I have been arguing, *not* call out for integration into our understanding of ourselves. We could perhaps take or leave such information, depending on what we choose to make of ourselves. Foucault makes an argument to this effect in "About the Beginning of the Hermeneutics of the Subject":

> Do we really need this hermeneutics of the self which we have inherited from the first centuries of Christianity? Do we need a positive man who serves as the foundation of this hermeneutics of the self? Maybe the problem of the self is not to discover what it is in its positivity; maybe the problem is not to discover a positive self or the positive foundation for the self.[16]

Elsewhere he says: "Maybe the target nowadays is not to discover what we are but to refuse what we are."[17] It is important that we address a view like this, because the argument I am making here is that scientific knowledge makes a *claim* on us: it calls out for integration into our understanding of ourselves. That claim is robbed of its normative force if we don't *have* to respond to it with the labor of integration and interpretation, if we can, in Foucault's words, "refuse what we are."

Korsgaard's argument for the self as constituted rather than discovered is that we *become* agents, become unified selves, through action. We are not first, or from the beginning, unified selves, acting only subsequently and as the result of a process of deliberation and decision. As human beings we are self-conscious, which means we distinguish in ourselves between our desires on the one hand and the principles on which we act on the other. We are in a kind of originary state of disunity. Faced with a desire, we are at the same time faced with the burden of choosing whether to act on it. In acting on it, we unify ourselves:

we bring together desire and principle. But that means that learning about my desires and impulses cannot strictly speaking count as *self-knowledge*. I don't have a unified self at all until I act.

How is it that I am unified through action? Actions are performed by agents, but for an action to be attributable to an agent, that action cannot be the result of something "in" the agent – it must come from the agent *herself*.[18] If *my arm*, for example, spasms and knocks over a priceless vase, then no action has occurred; on the other hand, had *I* picked up the vase and thrown it across the room, an action would have taken place. However, while mere bodily movements are actions only when they stem from me as an agent, agents as we said above do not pre-date actions: it is actions themselves (defined by Korsgaard as an "act done for the sake of an end"[19]), that achieve the task of the constitution of agents, of unified selves. This constitution takes place because in acting, I become *autonomous* and *efficacious*: through my action I myself become the cause of something happening in the world.

Korsgaard does not quite say this, but what I think we should take from her view of the constitution of agency and the self is that the kinds of thing I might *learn* about my impulses and desires – that they are the result of a surge of dopamine, for example – is not material to choices I make in the project of self-unification. For Korsgaard, from the perspective of someone facing a choice what matters is not what causes her desires and impulses, but whether acting on them has the effect of constituting her as a unified self or agent. I do not *have* to choose to act on these impulses and desires, and so learning their biochemical origin cannot tell me anything about the self I am in the process of becoming. Even if I do choose to act on a particular desire, its having been caused by some neurochemical will not count as the reason I chose to act on it. For Korsgaard, my reason for acting on it will ultimately stem from my *conception* of myself, my practical identity. Perhaps, one might counter, that conception can itself be empirically accounted for as biologically adaptive or socially mandated. Even so, from my perspective as someone making a choice, if the identity does not at the same time appear to be *worth* living by, it will not be one I will be motivated to choose.

If all of this is true, then scientific knowledge of my brain or body cannot make normative demands on me in my choice of self. Nor can it demand that I take it seriously as a source of truth about myself. If I did try to form a self-conception as, say, a biological organism, it is unclear what a practical identity informed in part or in whole by such a conception would look like. Practical identities, in Korsgaard's view, have normative implications: to identify myself as *a brother* is to embrace a set of norms that come along with the concept of *being a brother*, and not merely, if I am biologically related to my sibling, to think of myself as sharing a large amount of genetic material with another human being. The concept of being a brother may of course vary from culture to culture or time period to time period, but there will always be some attendant norms implied by this (or any other) practical identity. As an agent I exist in normative space – but from a conception of myself as a biological organism, it appears no norms follow. Organisms survive and reproduce, but I can choose to do neither, and in doing so I have not *necessarily* done something wrong or bad.

So what is wrong with this picture? I want to argue that scientific knowledge *does* make normative demands on us in our conceptions of ourselves. The normative demands it makes are not moral demands, but, we might say, alethic ones: they are demands to be taken seriously as a source of truth about who we are. In addition to having a normatively loaded practical identity, I also have a conception of myself informed by scientific discovery. I am a member of a species descended from other species, I live on a planet orbiting a star on a spiral arm of one of billions of galaxies, and so on. While these identities do not carry the sort of robust norms that practical identities like *citizen*, *teacher*, *supervisor*, or *spouse* do, they are not free of normative implication. Learning that I am a member of a species descended from other species, for example, I may conclude that I ought not think of myself as a divinely ordained master of the natural world. I am not saying that a conclusion like this is required by the Darwinian revelation. Rather, my claim is that people *do* draw these sorts of normative conclusions – justified or not – as part of a process of coming to terms with scientific discovery. The normativity, then, is on two sides: scientific knowledge makes claims on me to integrate it into my self-understanding, and such knowledge is often taken to carry with it normative implications for that very self-understanding. The claims on the first side are stronger than they are on the second: Darwinism may or may not lead me to a greater solicitude for my fellow animals, but it does demand that I see myself in its terms, as a member of a species descended from other species. Because it places this demand on me, we need an account of what I am to do with it in my understanding of myself – what kinds of normative conclusions I should draw, how much weight I should assign it, etc. Such an account is to be found, I will argue, not in the theory of self-constitution (which downplays the place of discovery and knowledge about oneself in the project of choosing a self), nor in a view that draws a strong distinction between the naturalistic and normative perspectives (which cannot account for the degree to which scientific knowledge does appear to inform our self-understanding) but in philosophical hermeneutics.

INTEGRATION AND HERMENEUTICS

There is perhaps a certain perversity in enlisting Gadamer in showing how scientific knowledge is to be integrated into self-understanding. He is the great thinker of truth beyond method, and his entire philosophical project is predicated on the belief that there is knowledge even where there is not science (either human or natural). Not only that: in many of his writings, Gadamer offers a strident critique of modern science and what he takes to be its constricted view of the world. Still, Gadamer does argue for the need for scientific knowledge to be integrated into our understanding of ourselves. And even more important, he gives us a way of thinking about science, understanding, and the interpretive process whereby new knowledge is integrated into old that will allow us to answer the questions we have posed here about the place of scientific knowledge in that understanding. In this section, I will begin by considering Gadamer's critique of science, then move on to look at what he says about the need to integrate it into our broader view of things. I will finish with a number of thoughts on the integration of science from a hermeneutic perspective.

Modern science for Gadamer has a number of problematic (and related) characteristics: it is objectivist, it is monological, and its aim is control and domination. Modern science is objectivist in the sense that it "abstracts and isolates the object from the researcher ... it gives up the anthropomorphism with which the Greeks had viewed the world."[20] Science seeks objective knowledge, which means knowledge of "objects as things standing over against us."[21] In a similar vein, science "invokes the ideal of the non-participating observer"[22] who, because she abstracts from the meanings of the everyday world, is able to grasp the domain of objects as they are in themselves. That grasp in turn allows her to control the domain of objects in question.[23] Gadamer carries with him a fundamental skepticism before this attempt to dominate and control things: at the heart of his hermeneutics is an appeal to the *passivity* of understanding. Understanding is something, he says again and again, that happens *to* me. It is not something I can control through the application of a method. Furthermore, the objectivism of science, its claim to know being-in-itself, is belied by what Gadamer calls science's "concrete existential relativity": the "being-in-itself toward which research, whether in physics or biology, is directed, is relative to the way being is posited in its manner of inquiry."[24] The scientific endeavor is thus a perspective on things, and cannot be said to be the whole.

Science fails to grasp the whole in another way as well: its epistemico–linguistic mode is monological rather than dialogical: "Scientific sign systems ... are exhaustively determined by the research area being designated in any given case."[25] Scientific communication does not involve the mediation of multiple perspectives on a thing, as everyday conversation does, but rather working out the details of a single perspective.[26] It is only in the dialogical form of taken by the natural languages that one has an "orientation toward the whole."[27]

All of this points to the difficulty one would expect scientific knowledge as understood by Gadamer to face in any attempt to integrate it into one's understanding of oneself and the world. To grasp an object objectively or monologically is to subtract its veneer of meanings and values and behold it as it is "in itself" – but then it is hard to see how one could integrate that objective knowledge with the very realm of meanings and values one has subtracted to get at the object in its objectivity. And if the interest motivating objectivism in science is domination, it would seem that such an interest would not sit well beside the presumably less malignant interests motivating understanding – which for Gadamer involves an essential openness to the other, not a desire to dominate and control him. Indeed, Gadamer sometimes draws a very sharp distinction between the scientific and everyday perspective, similar to the strong distinctions we saw in Korsgaard and Tengelyi. In these moods, Gadamer not only erects a high barrier to any possible integration, but he also runs the risk of positing what amounts to a false dichotomy between the two perspectives. Consider the following two passages:

> In reality, the concepts of objectivity and object are so alien to the immediate understanding in which the human seeks to make himself at home in the world, that the Greeks characteristically had no such concepts.[28]
>
> For people today it is the world to be understood – a world in which man is indigenous and a world in which he feels at home – that remains our last court of appeals in the alien world of modern industry wherein it can now only claim a secondary, ancillary function.[29]

The false dichotomy here is between the home world of praxis and interpretation and the alien world of objects disclosed by science and controlled by technology. This dichotomy is false because it is arguably possible to "feel at home" in the technological world of "modern industry"; it is also arguably the case that one way in which human beings "make ourselves at home in the world" is through the objectivizing theories of modern science. It is not at all obvious that riding in

Integration of Scientific Knowledge into Self-Understanding 195

an airplane or understanding the land one inhabits in geological terms is necessarily alienating, or that someone who does not experience it as alienating is failing to be a good human being in some way.

In spite of all of this, Gadamer nevertheless holds that science can and should be integrated into the broader "human" perspective:

> The claim to universality on the part of hermeneutics rests on being able to integrate all of the sciences into it, of perceiving the opportunities for knowledge on the part of every scientific method wherever it may be applicable to given objects, and of deploying it in all its possibilities ... Hermeneutics has to bring everything knowable by the sciences into the context of the mutual agreement in which we ourselves exist. Because it brings the contribution of the sciences into this context of mutual agreement, a context that links us with the tradition that has come down to us in a unity that is efficacious in our lives, it is not just a repertory of methods ... but rather philosophy.[30]

Science actively seeks to understand the world by subtracting the values, biases, and judgments of the observer, but we, the observers, continue to exist in a linguistically constituted tradition, a collective "agreement" about how things are and what we should do. Scientific knowledge has to be "brought back" to that context because it is the context of our existence. Given Gadamer's far-reaching criticism of modern science, there would appear to be a tension between that criticism and his claim that science needs to be integrated. What accounts for Gadamer's adoption of the latter view? It is I think his recognition that science is motivated not only by the desire to dominate and control, but by *questions* – and the kinds of questions that motivate philosophical discourse as well as scientific:

> Hermeneutics not only accounts for the procedures applied by science, but also gives an account of the questions that are prior to the application of every science ... These are the questions that are determinative of all human knowing and doing, the greatest of questions, questions that are decisive for all human beings in their choice of the good.[31]

This integration of science into self-understanding is itself motivated by what Gadamer calls the "exigence of reason for unity,"[32] which he sees at work in the unending process of self-understanding. For Gadamer, science has to be integrated because it ultimately makes claims about *our world* – the totality of beings in whose midst we find ourselves. But integration is a task, something that requires the labor of interpretation, because between the interpreter and the scientific claim there is a *distance* – and hermeneutics as a practice arises wherever there is a gap in understanding between the interpreter and the thing to be understood. Scientific knowledge perhaps stands at a further distance from everyday understanding than other forms of knowing, but insofar as it can be said to be about our world, that distance is not unbridgeable.

So: how can the distance be bridged? What will the integration of scientific knowledge look like – what are its limits, how will it proceed? Taking our lead from Gadamerian hermeneutics, such integration will have a number of characteristics.

Integration is Primarily One-way

Scientific knowledge will be integrated into the linguistically mediated world of our experience, instead of our experience conforming to scientific knowledge. As we have already pointed out, the everyday or normative perspective is the one we occupy most of the time; it is the perspective from which we first learn about scientific discoveries. To be sure, science does sometimes force us to change in a fundamental way the way we look at things – sometimes, integration will not exactly be smooth. So we abandon the view that the earth is at the center of the universe, but that old view does not give in without a fight. But as Gadamer says, after Galileo we don't give up our perspective on the sun as "setting" – it just comes to live alongside the heliocentric view. It does so because we cannot abandon our linguistically mediated view of the world for an exclusively or even predominantly scientific one.

Objectivism Gives Way to Perspectivism

For Gadamer, the everyday world of meanings and values is a world built up in and from conversation. That means that the things understood within that world-orientation – which Gadamer calls *Sachen*, or subject matters – are always understood from multiple perspectives, and have an essentially open structure. The sciences, on the other hand, have object domains, which as we saw means they view their subject matters monologically, from a single, all-encompassing perspective. Objects are essentially closed in a way that *Sachen* are not. The consequences of this for integration are that a scientific account of some everyday phenomenon cannot from the everyday perspective be taken as complete. The everyday perspective for Gadamer is in addition constituted by interpretation, so if science is welcomed into it, it will be *as* an interpretation, as one more linguistically constituted perspective on things. The scientific claim to truth will be respected – to call scientific knowledge a perspective or an interpretation is not to say is in some sense "untrue" or "merely subjective" – but the claim to objective completeness will not be. The moon is a physical thing with a certain geology, but it also reminds me of bygone times, places, and people.

We said above that scientific theories are about our world; to be more precise: *Integration is possible because scientific theories are about things in the linguistically mediated world.* If science disclosed entities that were radically distinct from anything in our experience, it would not need to be integrated into that experience – because it *could* not be integrated into it. But that is not what happens: science discloses truths about things in our world. Bacteriology is not merely the study of really small organisms; it is the study of really small organisms that live in our gut and help us digest food or that enter our bodies and make us sick. But –

Integration is challenging because the perspective offered by science is sometimes very different from the linguistically mediated perspective. Here we come back to the distinction we've considered from the beginning of this essay between the normative or first-person and the natural or third-person perspectives. It can sometimes seem that the picture we get of ourselves through scientific discovery bears little resemblance to the picture we already have of ourselves. We are told the love we have for our children is an adaptive trait that allows our genes to perpetuate themselves into future generations. Just what are we to do with this sort of a claim? Hermeneutics cannot prescribe how information like this will be integrated, just as it cannot prescribe how a text should be understood. Depending on historical, cultural, or personal context, people will integrate scientific knowledge differently. Certainly disruptive scientific theories (evolution, the dating of the earth as more than a few thousand years old) do come to be widely (if not universally!) accepted as telling us the truth about our world. Still, even if we don't want to prescribe how a scientific theory gets interpreted, we may want to ask if there are limits on integration – are there certain theories that resist integration because of the structure of self-understanding or the nature of integration itself?

It may not be the case that any particular scientific theory is strictly speaking immune to integration. But, different scientific theories have features that throw up barriers to integration. First, as we have already seen, a scientific theory will have trouble being integrated into self-understanding if it is actively in tension with the first-person perspective of values and meanings. A theory that posits a one-way causal pathway between neurochemical activity and the first-person perspective – such that the latter is conceived as in some sense a "product" of the former – will fall afoul of our first-person conception of ourselves as free and worthy of respect. Second, a scientific theory will face barriers to integration if it runs contrary to the open structure of the *Sache*, the subject matter of understanding. That which is understood, for Gadamer, has a kind of open essence: in understanding it, I understand it to be graspable as the thing it is from multiple perspectives. A theory that closes the thing in question, that asserts the completeness of its conception of the thing to the exclusion of other perspectives, will fail to live up to the essence of understanding – orientation toward open subject matters – and so will not easily find a place *within* understanding.

Finally, and most important, a scientific theory will have trouble being integrated if it undermines the unity that integration strives for in first place. For a particular view to be integrated into one's general view of the world is for it to be brought into the unity of self-understanding. For hermeneutics, such a unity is also a unity of understanding and *application*. A scientific theory that undermines that unity – that cannot in effect be applied to one's hermeneutic *situation* – will have difficulty being integrated. My hermeneutic situation is constituted by the questions motivating my beliefs as answers, and the "hermeneutic interest" motivating those questions.[33] Hermeneutics recognizes the unity of theory and practice in the understanding that transforms those conversing with each other: "Discussion bears fruit when a common language is found. Then the participants part from one another as changed beings. The individual perspectives with which they entered upon the discussion have been transformed, and so they have been transformed themselves."[34] Because my understanding has broadened, so has my self-understanding: I come to see my prejudices as prejudices, I come (at least in part) to know myself. But that means that I have changed, and that in turn means that understanding is a *unifying practice of myself*. The question then is, which scientific theories preserve this transformative practice of myself? Which undermine it?

Some scientific theories not only preserve this practice, but participate in it. The obsessive-compulsive who thinks she is mad but then learns that she has a "disorder" caused by a deficiency of serotonin in her brain has a prejudice overturned – the belief she is mad – and as a result has been transformed in her understanding of herself. She may then come to live a different sort of life as a result. Or if I come to see, say, my ability to use language as an evolutionary development, then my self-conception changes: perhaps I used not to think of my linguistic ability in biological terms, perhaps I even held language use to be uniquely human, as marking the human difference, rather than as existing on a continuum with animal communication. As a result of my new conception of myself, my practical orientation to humans and animals changes as well. On the other hand, consider a view like the following, as described by Patricia Churchland:

> In all social animals, shunning and isolation are a form of punishment. That is basically because in shunning, oxytocin levels fall and stress hormone levels rise. Inclusion and touching are, by contrast, sources of pleasure and sources of ease. The insula area of the cortex, known to monitor the physiological state of the body, also helps create the "emotional safety" feelings.[35]

The trouble with a view like this one is this. Imagine that I have been shunned by someone or some group of people, and as a result I feel distress; and, as a result of this distress I seek reconciliation with those who shun me. If I engage in a hermeneutic practice, I may come to see that I ought not to seek reconciliation with them, that it matters more to keep doing whatever it was that earned the shunning. That is, some belief I have about my place among the shunners may come into question, and so my actions in relation to them may change as well. The worry is that accepting a theory like the one above could *prevent* me from engaging in this hermeneutic practice in the first place – it could undermine the transformative practice of understanding. I might think that being shunned *just is* this experience that physiologically causes me distress, or that the cause of my distress *just is* physiological. In so doing, I close myself off from putting the very phenomenon of shunning into question. In particular, I won't be able to see it in *normative* terms – whether shunning is a morally problematic communal practice, or merited in some circumstances, or even to be actively encouraged as social policy. Not only that, I stop seeing myself *as* a member of a community (with all of the normative commitments that entails), and instead see myself as a biological organism. That one-sided view of myself indicates, I would argue, that a failure of integration has taken place.

Could one accept a view like the one discussed here without it undermining the transformative practice of myself? Yes: everything hangs on the "because" in the second sentence quoted above. If we read "because" to mean that the fall and rise of the levels of certain neurochemicals (and the resulting feelings) is what *constitutes* the punishment, then we are moving away from integration. We have then identified a phenomenon in normative space – shunning as punishment – with a neuronal mechanism outside of normative space. In a word, we are being reductionists. Integration has failed because with the reduction of the normative to the physiological, there is no normative realm for the physiological to be integrated *into*. If, on the other hand, we read the "because" as saying something like the bad feelings produced by neurochemicals are a necessary but not sufficient condition of punishment, then a theory like this does open itself up to integration.

Punishment, after all, is not punishment unless the punished person in some way recognizes that he is being punished. It may be that this recognition, in animals like us, takes place in the form of a particular emotional reaction, and that this emotional reaction (since we are, let's face it, biological organisms) is possible only because of a particular arrangement of our brains. But to say all of this is to leave open the possibility that punishment by shunning must *also* be understood in normative terms. Punishment by shunning is not punishment by shunning unless the punished person *understands* the precariousness of his position in the social world – understands himself as a social being.

Because I have an understanding of myself as a social being, my prejudices about shunning are open to being overturned. Because I am a living organism, I am subject to certain physiologically describable events that allow me to experience the distress of being shunned. I integrate my knowledge of such events into my understanding of myself as a social being when I see them as taking place *in* me, I who respond to and make decisions in this social world.

One final note on what happens when integration fails, as I have been describing it. Someone might respond to what I have been saying by pointing out that in cases of integration failure, it is not as though people abandon the scientific beliefs in question. It is in fact increasingly common to see views like that offered by Churchland in everyday discourse about ourselves, and those who hold such views appear to do so without a sense of internal conflict. But if what I am saying is right, there *is* a conflict; and if what Gadamer says is right, there is in us an exigence for unity. We see ourselves as single entities, as, if you will, *Sachen*. As *Sachen*, we can be grasped from multiple perspectives. One of those perspectives is through the objectifying lens of the sciences; another is through the normative lens of values and meanings. Human beings are, to get right down to it, both biological organisms and worthy of respect. If two such perspectives on *the same thing* are in tension, then there is an *imperative internal to the thing itself* for integration of perspectives on it. Even if one does not recognize that tension, it does not follow that it does not exist, or that we are not faced with the task, being single entities whose basic orientation to the world is interpretive, of overcoming it.[36]

NOTES

1. "Taking the Human Sciences Seriously" in *Naturalism and Normativity*, Marion De Caro and David MacArthur, eds. (New York: Columbia University Press, 2010), p. 123.

2. Ibid. p. 125.
3. Ibid. pp. 132–3.
4. Ibid. p. 124.
5. Christine M. Korsgaard, *The Sources of Normativity* (New York: Cambridge University Press, 1996), p. 101.
6. Christine M. Korsgaard, *Self-Constitution: Agency, Identity, and Integrity* (New York: Oxford University Press, 2009), p. 40.
7. Ibid. p. 114.
8. Ibid.
9. "Agonistic World Projects: Transcendentalism versus Naturalism," *Journal of Speculative Philosophy* 27 (3) (2013), p. 244.
10. Ibid. p. 246.
11. Ibid. p. 245.
12. Ibid.
13. "Moral Subjects: The Natural and the Normative," in *Proceedings and Addresses of the American Philosophical Association*, Vol. 76, No. 2 (November 2002), p. 12.
14. *Groundwork of the Metaphysic of Morals*, trans. Paul Paton (New York: Harper and Row, 1964), p. 116 (4:448).
15. See "Science, Language, and Experience: Reflections on the Nature of Self-Understanding." *Man and World* 16 (1983), p. 32. Martinus Nijhoff Publishers.
16. Foucault, "About the Beginning of the Hermeneutics of the Self," in *The Politics of Truth* (Los Angeles: Semiotext(e), 1997), pp. 189–90.
17. Foucault, "The Subject and Power," in *Power* (New York: The New Press, 2000), p. 336.
18. Korsgaard, *Self-Constitution: Agency, Identity, and Integrity*, pp. 18–19.
19. Ibid. p. 11.
20. Hans-Georg Gadamer "Greek Philosophy and Modern Thinking," trans. Richard E. Palmer, in *The Gadamer Reader*, ed. Richard E. Palmer (Evanston: Northwestern University Press, 2007), p. 269.
21. Ibid. p. 270.
22. Hans-Georg Gadamer, "Hermeneutics as a Theoretical and Practical Task," trans. Frederick G. Lawrence, in *The Gadamer Reader*, p. 263.
23. *Truth and Method*, trans. Joel Weinsheimer and Donald G. Marshall (New York: Continuum, 2000), p. 450.
24. Ibid. pp. 451–2.
25. Hans-Georg Gadamer, "On the Philosophic Element in the Sciences and the Scientific Character of Philosophy," in *Reason in the Age of Science*, trans. Frederick G. Lawrence (Cambridge, MA: MIT Press, 1981), p. 4.
26. Though as Gadamer says later in this essay, science conducted within its own field of inquiry "is removed from every dogmatic use" it only goes astray when it engages in "speculative dogmatizing" – i.e. when it attempts to make absolute claims about all that is (*Reason in the Age of Science*, pp. 10–11).

27. Ibid. p. 4.
28. "Greek Philosophy and Modern Thinking," p. 270.
29. Ibid. p. 273.
30. "Hermeneutics as a Theoretical and Practical Task," p. 264.
31. Ibid. pp. 264–5.
32. "On the Philosophic Element in the Sciences and the Scientific Character of Philosophy," p. 19.
33. Hans-Georg Gadamer, "Hermeneutics as Practical Philosophy," *The Gadamer Reader*, pp. 242–3.
34. Ibid. p. 244.
35. *Touching a Nerve: The Self as Brain* (New York: Norton, 2013), p. 102.
36. The views expressed here are those of the author and do not represent those of the National Endowment for the Humanities.

10 A Dialogic Approach to Narrative Medicine

LEAH McCLIMANS

In Ann Jurecic's *Illness As Narrative* she asks how we should listen to and indeed understand illness narratives.[1] Specifically, how should we respond to stories of pain and suffering? In asking this question she is particularly interested in finding an alternative to the hermeneutics of suspicion that she argues characterize literature's critical response to these narratives. A ready alternative is what we find in narrative medicine. Here readers are taught to hear illness narratives from the narrator's standpoint. As Arthur Frank has put it, the appropriate response to an illness narrative is not "what can you tell me" but rather, "let me be with you."[2]

In this paper I too am interested in how we should understand narratives of pain and suffering. But while Jurecic admires the "unfashionable earnestness" of narrative medicine[3] and seeks to move literary criticism closer to it, I am less convinced that such an approach does justice to these stories. In what follows I explore two different approaches to narrative medicine and drawing on Gadamer argue that both of them fail to understand illness narratives as offering us the truth about illness. Indeed I will argue that despite attempts to the contrary narrative medicine actually increases the hermeneutic marginalization of those who are ill.

ILLNESS NARRATIVES AND NARRATIVE MEDICINE

Illness narratives were almost non-existent until the mid-twentieth century. With few exceptions – Virginia Woolf among them – the body and what it suffers was not discussed publicly until the 1950s. At this time victims of the polio epidemic begin to break this silence and in the following decades we see those suffering from other illnesses such as cancer begin to tell their tale. But illness narratives do not truly come into their own until the AIDS epidemic of the 1980s. With this disease comes a proliferation of writing: personal experiences, educational pamphlets, plays, poems, and so on. In the twenty-first century we continue to see autobiographical accounts flourish, e.g. *Memoir of a Debunked Woman: Enduring Ovarian Cancer*, *Brain on Fire: My Month of Madness*, *New Life, No Instructions* to name only a few. We even see Jean-Dominique Bauby's story about life with locked-in syndrome made into a successful movie, *The Diving Bell and the Butterfly*.

What accounts for this change? No doubt there are many factors, but one important cause is the changing face of medicine after the Second World War. Post-war saw the institutionalization of medicine, the marriage of clinical medicine and medical research as well as increasing technological advances. These changes affected not only the doctor–patient relationship, but also the material reality of patient care. For those born after the 1950s it may be difficult to understand the ways that medicine has changed, but take the following as an example: in the 1930s house calls were a standard practice for physicians, but by the 1950s only 10 percent of patient encounters were in the home and by the 1960s they represented less than 1 percent of physician–patient contacts.[4] Why the change? Office visits are a more efficient use of the clinician's time and they enable medical technology to service more patients. But efficiency has costs: it is now less likely that patients will know their doctor personally or share similar values and background. Physicians are no longer friends and neighbors, but strangers.

Although moving patient encounters into the clinic in principle increases access to new medical technologies, these technologies themselves are problematic. Firstly, they increase medical costs exponentially, which introduces questions of resource allocation and one's economic ability to avail of them. Thus issues of scarcity and cost become a silent member of the physician–patient relationship, determining in many cases what expertise your doctor can offer. Secondly, although not solely responsible for specialization new technologies contribute to new medical specialties. As a result patients are increasingly treated by a team of clinicians each one attending to the "part" of the patient that they know best. Specialization tends to distort the concept of a physician–patient *relationship* – patients and their clinicians often hardly know one another at all. Thirdly, new technologies often tell doctors more interesting information about their patients than the patients can tell about themselves. Technology has a way of silencing patients.

Perhaps not surprisingly these changes contributed (and continue to contribute) toward a decline in physician–patient communication and trust. By the 1970s patients' health outcomes had improved, but patients were less satisfied in their care. Arthur Frank conceptualizes this move into the clinic and the changes it renders to patient care as a shift to a modern experience of illness. In the modern experience of illness knowledge of what is happening comes from expert others rather than from the patient. This characteristic of modern illness is striking even if familiar. Modern medicine consigns patients and their loved ones to waiting rooms and hospital beds whilst specialists and test results tell them the truth. The results and specialist judgments are then written in the patient's chart documenting that experience. The patient and her voice are lost; she is hermeneutically marginalized.[5] Even modern initiatives to draw attention to the patient as a person, for example patient-centered care, often exaggerate rather than alleviate the problem.

In this modern experience the patient is more of a prop than an agent. The story of her illness is unfamiliar, told by strangers using technical language, to be recorded in a chart the patient rarely reads. And this story – as foreign as it may be to the patient – is precisely the story against which all others are judged as true or false, helpful or not. For Frank, the proliferation of illness narratives represent the recognition that more is involved in the experience of illness than the medical story can tell. At the same time the expression of what *is* involved increasingly cannot be expressed in traditional folk or religious narratives. Frank thus characterizes autobiographical illness narratives as post-modern.[6]

What is the point of post-modern illness narratives? We might think of them as attempts to overcome hermeneutic marginalization. Indeed Frank seems to conceptualize them along these lines. He argues that these narratives have three goals. First, as patients tell their stories and become an agent in their illness they remake the map that orients them in their everyday lives. In doing this patients reject the understanding that the modern illness experience provides them and they begin to find their own. Secondly, such map-making serves as guidance to others who are also ill. Here what patients – whom Franks refers in this context as witnesses – have to offer is less the particular orientations that they have carved from their experience than the demonstration of map-making itself. In other words, witnesses show fellow patients that it is possible to carve out an alternative understanding of their experience. Finally, witnesses offer to health care providers and "normals" – those who are not (yet) ill – an alternative understanding of the ill experience, one that is situated in the body of the witness.[7] If this offer is taken up, then patients may overcome their hermeneutic marginalization.

As witnesses to suffering illness narratives are a form of testimony. The suffering body is the evidence of that testimony. Frank suggests that we conceptualize this testimony as a form of pedagogy that reveals the lessons to be learnt from suffering. He argues that if we can understand illness narratives in this way, then we will find an antidote to the problems of communication and distrust that have followed in the wake of institutionalized medicine. Thus the pedagogy of suffering is Frank's remedy to a form of medicine and indeed a society that is not responsive to the experience of the sick body. As we become aware of that experience he believes a new social ethic will emerge in which clinicians – doctors, nurses, physical therapists, etc. – come to see what they lack and what their patients can offer. Describing the relationships that result from such an ethic he writes:

> If people could believe that each of us lacks something that only an other can fill – if we could be communicative bodies – then empathy would no longer be spoken of as something one person "has for" another. Instead, empathy is what a person "is with" another: a relationship in which each understands herself as requiring completion by the other.[8]

Frank's approach to narrative medicine is focused on how it can aid patients. Given that modern medicine marginalizes patients from understanding their experience he conceives of illness narratives as a tool to reconnect patients to themselves and others. Even in their role as witness he focuses on how their testimony results in reconnecting them to, for instance, health care providers. We can see this move in the quote above: if we can all recognize what we lack, i.e. patients lack health, clinicians lack an understanding of illness, then empathy is less a capacity or skill that clinicians use to reach isolated patients, but rather a relationship in which we get as much as we give. Understanding that the ill have something to give through their testimony – that their testimony is in fact pedagogical – is precisely how, according to Frank, their agency is restored through the illness narrative.

Taking a different approach, Rita Charon considers illness narratives from the perspective of the clinician.[9] Learning to listen closely to patients will improve doctors' ability to care for them. More to the point narrative competence has the potential to improve clinical effectiveness. How can it do so? Charon uses the metaphor of a divide. Patients and families, she argues, are isolated from clinicians by their fear of disease; similarly doctors are isolated from patients by their knowledge of it. Divides such as this one, "prevent them all from doing their best."[10]

Charon invites us to acknowledge that doctors do not understand how fundamentally everything changes when one's child or partner is sick, i.e. doctors do not understand the experience of illness. They do not understand what becomes unimportant, such as bills, politics, weather, nor do they understand what becomes overwhelmingly important, i.e. a test result, a doctor's mood, reliable transportation. Charon's prose is so apt that it is worth a long quote:

> ... the cardiologist makes his rounds in the CCU and tells the wife, "He's got a severe blockage in two of his coronary arteries, and we feel we need to do an emergency bypass operation right away." What does this mean? Will he live? Will he die? They will open her husband's heart like a bruised fruit; he will bleed into the gloved hands of strangers. But will he be well? ... Pale and tired-looking, the wife tightens her grasp on her husband's wrist – she better not dislodge that intravenous line, thinks the cardiologist, the nurses had trouble getting it started. The patient's wife stutters something about her husband's allergy to anesthesia and getting a second opinion at Cornell. Doesn't she realize how sick her husband is? Sending him across town for a second opinion is too risky. He might not survive the ambulance ride. She doesn't trust me to be her husband's doctor, the cardiologist thinks with a sinking heart. How can I do the right thing in the face of her suspicion?[11]

As this passage makes clear it is also the case that patients do not understand the experience of their doctors, but this is not Charon's concern. It is a doctor's job to care for his patient and to do so effectively, e.g. the cardiologist must reach the patient's wife. He must find a way to understand her experience or his patient will die as he and the wife argue about appropriate treatment.

But how do illness narratives help to bridge this divide? Charon argues that by acquiring a competence reading narrative doctors also acquire the ability to imagine what it is like to live in another's shoes. Thus reading illness narratives, even of patients not one's own, prepare doctors for the encounter with the Other. This is not to say that Charon does not also advocate for the practice of listening to one's own patients' stories – she does – but it is the competencies that come from knowing how to read a story that will bridge the patient–doctor divide and improve clinical effectiveness.

Although Charon discusses other aspects of what is acquired when one learns to read closely, she emphasizes the clinical benefits of imagination. She argues that to be an effective clinician one need not empathize with a patient, one need not like her or even feel sorry for her. But if one is to help a patient, then one does need to "*see* the world from the vantage point of the patient and to *experience*, vicariously, events from that stance."[12] Imagination is a faculty that when developed aids clinicians in trading, periodically, their own conceptual map for another's.

But a well-developed imagination is not sufficient for the kind of "seeing" and "experiencing" that Charon takes to be so important.

To inhabit the world of another, be it the world of an illness memoir or one's patient's it is also necessary to pay attention: to read, to listen closely. Imagination can take us to faraway places and unfamiliar experiences, but for those experiences to be accurate, for them to be the experiences of the characters in a book or the patient sitting in front of you, then you also need to pay attention. In describing what she means by attention Charon deploys metaphors of emptying and donating. For example:

> By emptying the self and by accepting the patient's perspectives and stance, the clinician can allow himself or herself to be filled with the patient's own particular suffering, thereby getting to glimpse the sufferer's needs and desires, as it were, from the inside.[13]

Nonetheless, she is quick to point out that paying attention to a story does not entail that one leaves behind one's critical faculties. Indeed since patients themselves are often unable to tell a coherent narrative – their story may stop, start and falter – part of what narratively competent clinicians should do is help make these stories meaningful. For Charon meaning making is akin to donation, "... we donate ourselves – our cognitive machinery, our affective responsiveness, our powers of interpretation, our memories of other texts – to the demands of form and plot."[14]

II

Frank's suggestion that we understand illness narratives as pedagogy of suffering provides insight into how we ought to respond to and understand these narratives. We need to recognize the ill as experts and their testimony as expertise. Such recognition requires a reorientation that allows all of us to see our own lack of knowledge in this area.

That patients might have something to teach clinicians is not by itself a new idea. In Ashley Graham Kennedy's recent paper "Differential Diagnosis and the Suspension of Judgment"[15] she argues that in cases where doctors are skeptical of the veracity of a patient's complaints and a diagnosis is not immediately available, they should charitably suspend their judgment rather than assume their patient is imagining her problems. Why should physicians do so? Firstly, because there are limits to clinical knowledge and what technology can tell us. Sometimes patient experience can reach beyond these limits providing pieces of evidence that would otherwise be unavailable. Second, because the inference from "I don't know what is wrong with you" to "Your problems are in your head" overreaches the evidence available to the physician. The way she puts this point is that to be a good doctor you need to practice good science and taking patients reports seriously as possibly true is what is required to practice good science. In a similar vein Charon argues that to be a more effective doctor one needs to acquire the competence of listening closely to patients.

For Graham Kennedy and Charon striving to understand patient stories is justified in terms of enhanced medical epistemology. For Frank, however, the knowledge one gleans from illness narratives is almost entirely understood as being in service to morality. Thus for Frank recognizing what one does not know is a crucial step in becoming a moral person. When we recognize that witnesses to suffering have expertise that we lack, then we do not listen to them simply because we need something from them, i.e. knowledge to enhance our clinical practice, but because they have something to tell us. Respecting one's capacity to give knowledge to others is as, Miranda Fricker writes, "one side of the many-sided capacity so significant to human beings: the capacity to reason."[16] Honoring that capacity is part of what it is to be a morally virtuous person.

Frank's proposal that we understand illness narratives as pedagogy of suffering is far-reaching and it intimates a genuine paradigm shift. For instance, on his view witnesses to suffering are empowered because they have expert knowledge and as such we should seek them out. Contrast this to the standard view of empowerment, the view that Graham Kennedy and Charon seem to support: patients are empowered when we make special efforts to listen closely to them. Take another example. On Frank's view patient-centered care is what happens after – and only after – we recognize patients *as* witnesses, i.e. as persons with knowledge. On the traditional view patient-centered care is defined as "providing care that is respectful of and responsive to individual patient preferences, needs and values, and ensuring that patient values guide all clinical decisions."[17] What is missing in this definition, and indeed often in practice, is that patients are more than a mere source of knowledge: they are informants. Respecting a patient as a knower requires more than the elicitation of her needs, values and preferences. Why does this difference in orientation to illness narratives matter? The subtle, but profound nature of Frank's proposal suggests that patients suffer from more than their illness; they also suffer from hermeneutical injustice.

In *Epistemic Injustice* Miranda Fricker argues that hermeneutical injustice represents the injustice of having a significant part of one's experience obscured from the collective understanding due to hermeneutical marginalization. Earlier I discussed the ways in which patients are hermeneutically marginalized by the modern illness experience.

Autobiographical illness narratives, however, were understood as attempts to overcome this marginalization. Both Frank and Charon seem to understand their role in this way. For Frank these narratives help patients actively participate in the experience of their illness by helping them create an understanding of this experience, which is different from the one perpetuated by modern medicine. Charon too seems to think of illness narratives as decreasing hermeneutical marginalization. Recall that she conceptualizes illness narratives as bridging the divide between doctors and patients by helping doctors to understand the experience of patients and their family.

Hermeneutical injustice is harmful because it excludes patients from contributing meaningfully to the horizon of understanding. In his discussion of hermeneutical experience Gadamer clarifies the nature of this harm.[18] He discusses three possible relationships one might have when trying to understand the experience of another person, the relationship characteristic of the modern medical experience is what he calls knowledge of human nature. Within this relationship the person one is trying to understand is objectified and the point of this understanding is to discover empirical regularities. Recall my earlier discussion of the hermeneutic marginalization of patients: they are often treated more like props than people. As such patients are reduced to their bodies and clinicians probe those bodies hoping to understand empirical regularities and irregularities in order to make a diagnosis and a prognosis. For Gadamer the moral harm of such a relationship is to render the patient a means to medicine's ends.

But how is Gadamer's summation accurate when medicine aims to improve the health of patients? We can see his point if we remind ourselves of how patients are hermeneutically marginalized in the first place. Recall that the problem here is that the patient's point of view, or epistemic subjectivity as Fricker calls it, is systematically eliminated in the definition and determination of their illness. The diagnosis, the prognosis, the treatment that follows, all of these features of modern medicine are defined and determined independently of the patient's standpoint. No matter how foreign or incomprehensible the story that medicine tells this is the story that silences all others. In this composition the patient's body is merely a means in the effort to achieve these ends, i.e. make a diagnosis, determine the prognosis, develop a treatment protocol.

In Fricker's account of epistemic injustice she discusses the way that this form of injustice is linked to objectification and in doing so she adds to Gadamer's point. According to Fricker treating a person as an object and using that person to obtain some end is not always morally wrong. It is morally wrong only when so treating someone also denies that she is also a subject. She draws on Martha Nussbaum's example: using your lover's stomach as a pillow in the context of a relationship in which he/she is generally treated as more than a pillow is not morally wrong, yet it is an example of instrumentalization.[19] What is crucial to morally pugnacious objectification is the relationship between the parties involved in it. If there is something about the relationship that undermines the objectified person's standpoint or epistemic subjectivity, then the objectification is morally wrong. When objectification is morally wrong the objectified person's point of view is undermined because she is no longer treated as an active epistemic agent, i.e. someone with whom one will enter into the cooperative give and take of reasons that constitutes knowledge formation. In this circumstance a person is treated as a source of information, i.e. a passive body from which knowledge can be collected.

What of the relationship between a doctor and patient? Is there something in this relationship that undermines the patient's epistemic subjectivity? For Gadamer the answer is clearly yes. When we engage in understanding others so we can predict the progress of their disease, then we objectify them in order to apply a methodology. This objectification continues as long as the clinician is trying to understand the progress of the patient's disease. I take it that part of the reason why we must constantly remind doctors that patients are in fact persons – why we have something called "patient-centered care" – is precisely because this objectification is so thorough-going. But there are also other reasons to suspect that doctor–patient relationships are geared toward undermining the patient's epistemic subjectivity. For example, Talcott Parsons influential medical sociology understands the sick role as predominantly a passive one in which the doctor acts as gatekeeper, i.e. who is and is not legitimately ill.[20] Patients as well as the rest of us are expected to accept doctors' determinations.

Excluding patients from contributing meaningfully to the horizon of understanding involves both a moral and epistemic harm. As we have seen patients are morally harmed in being objectified and thus treated as passive bodies containing information, which will aid in the diagnostic/prognostic process. The epistemic harm is twinned with the moral one. When patients' epistemic subjectivity is effectively silenced, we limit what we can come to know about illness. Setting limitations on what we learn about illness is a mistake both in practice and in principle. Charon and Graham Kennedy make the practical point when they argue that listening to patients can further clinical goals. Gadamer makes this same point when he argues that there is no end to our understanding a subject matter; the facts are never all in. We can always understand something differently and more inclusively. That which we try to understand is always indeterminate, our knowledge is always partial. To limit the questions we take seriously, i.e. to limit patients' epistemic subjectivity, is to limit what we might come to know. In medicine if nowhere else such a limitation is counterproductive.

Gadamer's work is particularly helpful in seeing how this epistemic harm is twinned with the moral one. For Gadamer it is through questioning that we gain knowledge. But there are at least two kinds of questions that we can ask or take others to be asking: authentic and inauthentic ones. We ask inauthentic questions when we believe that we already know the answer and wish to prove ourselves correct. We ask authentic questions when we are seeking insight into a subject matter. In this latter situation we are open to learning something new and it is only here that we can gain knowledge. Similarly in our orientation to others we can relate to them such that we are open to learning something from them or we can presuppose that we know them or the subject matter at hand better than they do. Typically when patients ask questions or make comments these questions are not taken as revealing a new route of inquiry into the subject at hand. Instead their questions are either treated as addressing some aspect of a known quantity or they are treated as rhetorical and thus irrelevant to the task at hand.

For Gadamer the only way to understand a patient as a person – to achieve patient-centered care – is to accept the claim she makes as possibly true. It turns out that accepting that claim is equally important to furthering our knowledge. Translated into everyday practice, this means that doctors ought to be open to their patients' questions and comments, they should be ready for them to reveal a new understanding of the subject matter at hand. This openness is not easily achieved. One of the maxims in medicine is "when you hear hoof beets, don't think zebras". This maxim although geared toward diagnosis illustrates a generally conservative attitude toward inquiry. We see here why Charon's work is important: doctors are trained to hear hoof beats, but for epistemic and moral reasons they also need to learn to be ready to hear more than that.

III

Recognizing patients in their capacity as knowers is how we overcome hermeneutic injustice, but do either Charon or Frank manage this? I suggest not. Jointly they recognize the moral and epistemic harm of hermeneutic injustice and equally they recognize that listening to patients is fundamental to overcoming these harms, but as I shall argue neither succeeds at treating patient narratives as possibly true.

In the previous section I discussed one of the relationships we can have with another person when attempting to understand them. I suggested that the kind of relationship doctors typically have with their patients is reminiscent of the kind of relationship that Gadamer categorizes as acquiring knowledge of human nature. I now want to consider another kind of relationship, one that recognizes patients as persons, but nonetheless falls short of relating to them openly. I suggest that it is this kind of relationship that Frank and Charon's work exemplifies.

Gadamer's discussion of this second kind of relationship is ambiguous. In some places he seems to understand it along the lines of a parent–child relationship: a parent may always think she knows her child better than her child knows herself. In such a relationship a child may say and do things to contradict the parent's understanding, but these acts do nothing to change the parent's "knowledge." The parent knows the child as it were in advance of these sayings and doings and as such keeps, "the other person's claim at a distance."[21] In this kind of relationship the parent is not open to her child's questions and conduct; as far as the parent is concerned the subject matter of inquiry – in this case her child – is closed. Gadamer sees this kind of relationship as a form of dominance, i.e. the parent asserts her power by determining who her child is. At the same time the understanding that the parent conveys says more about the parent than it does the child. Thus not only is this relationship a form of dominance, but also it is "reflective", i.e. it reflects the parents' concerns, fears, hopes, etc. more than it does the subject matter.

This way of thinking about the kind of relationship one has with another is not the same as the kind of relationships that Frank and Charon advocate. Clearly neither one of them suggests that doctors can or should understand patients better than they can understand themselves. On the contrary they both emphasize that doctors cannot understand patients *a priori* and that coming to understand them requires some kind of shift. For Frank this shift is to recognize that patients have something to teach us, for Charon doctors must learn to use their imagination and listen carefully. For both authors doctors must be prepared to learn something new.

But when Gadamer translates the experience of the parent–child relationship into the "hermeneutical sphere", i.e. the sphere of textual understanding, he comes closer to describing the kind of relationship Frank and Charon promote. In the hermeneutical sphere he refers to the understanding he is trying to describe as historical consciousness.[22]

He argues that the reader comes to understand a text "in its otherness" and although he likens this experience to the way that the parent in the above example might come to understand her child, I think the two are relevantly different. In his discussion of historical consciousness Gadamer emphasizes not that the reader knows the text in advance, but rather that the reader imagines herself free from her own past, free from prejudices, free from tradition. The reader thus deludes herself into believing that she can understand the text as it was understood when it was written: unbiased, unprejudiced, free from contamination.

For Gadamer this is only an illusion and a dangerous one at that. Those who do not acknowledge the prejudices at work in their own understanding are still dominated by them. By not recognizing these prejudices they in fact perpetuate them and moreover, mislead others by calling the understanding that results unbiased. The lesson here is that we cannot reflect ourselves out of the tradition in which we find ourselves. Indeed as Gadamer famously writes, "It is the tyranny of hidden prejudices that makes us deaf to what speaks to us in tradition."[23]

Both Frank and Charon describe relationships with patients that are susceptible to this criticism. In his discussion of the testimony of those who are ill Frank argues that the appropriate response when listening to an illness narrative is not "What do you have to tell me?" but rather "Let me be with you." He develops this idea into the concept of thinking with stories. Thinking with stories means that when we are listening to an illness narrative we ought to empty our mind and allow it to adopt the logic of the story and *be with* the story. Being with a story means feeling and seeing what the author is describing so that one can ultimately resonate with the story. The point of thinking with stories is to learn something and allow what is learned to change you. Similarly Charon writes about bearing witness when she hears illness narratives. As I discussed earlier this kind of witnessing entails a suspension of the self where the clinician can come to see and experience the world from the patients' point of view. Indeed Charon goes so far as to write that the fruits of acquiring a narrative competence unfold precisely through, "the surrender of oneself to be used as a creative instrument for the representation of the other."[24]

What is wrong with this way of understanding another? To be sure, Gadamer also acknowledges that to understand another we must imagine their situation. He even writes that to understand another we must, in a certain way "transpose" ourselves into another's shoes. But at the same time he is keen to emphasize that this transposition is not a disregarding of the self, it is not an emptying or suspension of the self. On the contrary transposing oneself into another's shoes is a wide-eyed acknowledgment of oneself in juxtaposition with the other. It is only by acknowledging the tension in the differences between myself and another – between the past and present, between a text and tradition – that I can foreground possible prejudices, question them and ultimately understand what the other is saying. Thus the problem with attempting to understand another by emptying and surrendering the self is that one can never empty and surrender oneself to another. We are always lurking in the shadows influencing understanding by proxy. But in the shadows we are safely unattainable and we although can come to discover another's point of view, we cannot find in it a truth that is valid for ourselves. To do that – to take another's claim as possibly true – we must *apply* our own point of view to theirs.

In fairness there are times when Frank and Charon might be read as endorsing Gadamer's claim that we must bring our whole selves to the hermeneutic encounter. I say this because although they emphasize the need to understand patients in their otherness, they also approvingly notice the way that understanding patients changes the listener, allowing in many cases for the listener to find new meaning for herself in their stories. Frank writes, "The first lesson of thinking with stories is . . . to continue to live in the story, becoming in it, reflecting on who one is becoming, and gradually modifying the story."[25] And Charon writes that those who practice narrative medicine become different people because of the experiences they live through with their patients. Yet there is something importantly missing from Frank and Charon's account that is essential to Gadamer's: questioning.

As I already discussed to be morally and epistemically virtuous in the hermeneutic encounter we must be open to that which we are trying to understand. Being open means that we must accept the claims that are made as possibly true. But this does not mean that we simply take these claims to be true without further consideration. Indeed to do so for Gadamer is to suspend their claim to truth, for example a doctor listens closely and attentively to her patient and thinks "this is what it is like to be you." The truth of this patient's story is suspended insofar as the doctor does not apply this claim to her own understanding. But the doctor cannot apply this story unless she is willing to acknowledge and thus challenge her own prejudices; in other words, unless the doctor is willing to bring her whole self to this encounter with the patient. Unless and until she does so the patient's story remains disconnected from the doctor's life, her practice – her knowledge. We are all familiar with this phenomenon, we read a disturbing item in the newspaper, we are surprised to see a friend's position on a topic on facebook, a child tells us a convoluted story, in each case we may bracket our understanding of these things. We may fail to reshuffle the jigsaw of our own understanding to see how these items might fit.

To accept a claim as possibly true means that we have to apply it to ourselves and see what it says to us. In doing so we have to be prepared that it will say things with which we do not agree. We play with the jigsaw pieces of our understanding. What does the jigsaw look like if we move the pieces this way? What if we jettison this or that corner? Or perhaps we have been looking at this new piece upside-down all along and when we turn it a different way we see that it's a duplicate to a piece we already have. We stand back to assess what we have done. Is the new picture more complete than the previous one? Do we understand more? Have we done justice to the new information we were given, i.e. did we do our best to find it a place? Perhaps there are still pieces left over, questions unanswered. Maybe we leave them for a time. This is a picture that is never wholly complete.

Questioning illness narratives is a feature that is often left out of accounts of them. It seems that we only have room to ignore them completely or accept them unconditionally. Perhaps questioning these narratives is mistaken for questioning patients themselves, i.e. throwing doubt on their motivations for telling these stories. It is important to separate these two issues: attempting to understand the truth in the stories that patients tell is not the same thing as attempting to understand the psychology of these patients. Nonetheless, we do patients a disservice when we do not question their stories. This is not to say that the clinical encounter is always the time to hash out the truth of a patient's narrative – we should not leave behind common sense as we strive to be morally and epistemically just. But when we accept illness narratives as true without question we exacerbate patients' hermeneutic marginalization.

I began this essay asking how we should understand stories of pain and suffering suggesting that learning to hear these stories from the narrator's standpoint is not sufficient to do them or their authors' justice. If we seek to dispense hermeneutic justice to witnesses of suffering then we can neither ignore nor acquiesce to their tale. To overcome hermeneutic marginalization we must bring our entire selves to the encounter and allow our prejudices and assumptions – as burly and misshapen as they may be – a voice to question and challenge. This voice need not be out loud, although sometimes it will and indeed it should be so, but my point is that suppressing these questions only furthers marginalization.

To be marginalized is to be on the periphery: to be unimportant, forgettable. To bring an illness narrative and those who suffer to the center we must see it and them as relevant. We must find the truth of their tale within our own narrative. To do so we need to accommodate the piece of the jigsaw that the story represents and this often means questioning the position of other pieces.

NOTES

1. Ann Jurecic, *Illness As Narrative* (Pittsburgh: University of Pittsburgh Press, 2012).
2. Arthur Frank, *The Wounded Storyteller: Body, Illness, and Ethics* (Chicago: University of Chicago Press, 1997), p. 144.
3. Jurecic, *Illness As Narrative*, p. 15.
4. David J. Rothman, *Strangers at the Bedside: A History of How Law and Bioethics Transformed Medical Decision Making* (New York: Basic Books, 1992).
5. See Miranda Fricker, *Epistemic Injustice: Power and the Ethics of Knowing* (Oxford: Oxford University Press, 2009).
6. Frank, *The Wounded Storyteller*, p. 6.
7. Ibid. p. 175.
8. Ibid. p. 150.
9. Rita Charon, *Narrative Medicine: Honoring the Stories of Illness* (Oxford: Oxford University Press, 2008).
10. Ibid. p. 19.
11. Ibid. p. 20.
12. Ibid. p. 112.
13. Ibid. p. 134.
14. Ibid. p. 135.
15. Ashley Graham Kennedy, "Differential diagnosis and the suspension of judgment," *The Journal of Medicine and Philosophy* 38 (October 2013) pp. 487–500. doi:10.1093/jmp/jht043.
16. *Epistemic Injustice*, p. 44.
17. Institute of Medicine, *Crossing the Quality Chasm: A New Health System for the 21st Century.* (Washington, DC: National Academy Press; 2001), p. 6.
18. Hans-Georg Gadamer, *Truth and Method* Second Revised edition (New York: Continuum Impacts, 2004).
19. Fricker, *Epistemic Injustice*, p. 133.
20. Talcott Parsons (with introduction by Neil J. Smelser), *The Social System* (New Orleans: Quid Pro, LLC, 2012).
21. *Truth and Method*, p. 360.
22. Ibid.
23. *Truth and Method*, p. 270.
24. Charon, *Narrative Medicine*, pp. 134 and 149.
25. *The Wounded Storyteller*, p. 159.

11 If Enhancement is the Answer, What is the Question?

LAUREN SWAYNE BARTHOLD

> Now medical ethics is more like a religion, with positions based on faith not argument, and imperiously imposed in a simple-minded way, often by committees or groups of people with no training in ethics ... What medical ethics needs is more and better philosophy.
>
> Julian Savulescu

> The concern with things which are not understood, the attempt to grasp the unpredictable character of the spiritual and mental life of human beings, is the task of the art of understanding which we call hermeneutics ... Understanding plays a role wherever rules cannot simply be applied, and this includes the entire sphere of collective human life.
>
> Hans-Georg Gadamer

I am pretty confident that when the foremost medical ethicist today, Julian Savulescu, recently penned the above words, he did not have in mind hermeneutic philosophy! Nonetheless, this chapter draws on philosophical hermeneutics to deepen the philosophical exploration of a particular branch of medical ethics. I shall defend the relevance of four themes central to Gadamer's hermeneutics, namely, prejudice, finitude, equilibrium, and dialogue for the debates over biomedical enhancement.

ATTENDING TO QUESTIONS, EXAMINING PREJUDICES

In refuting the excesses of Enlightenment thought that promoted a "prejudice against prejudice," Gadamer's hermeneutics defends the saliency of prejudices for knowledge. Gadamer demonstrates how all understanding is motivated by implicit and explicit questions that emerge out of a sociohistorical context and argues that the prejudices stemming from our historically-effected consciousness serve as gateways to knowledge insofar as they 1) motivate, condition, and direct all knowledge and 2) require exposure that invites subsequent reflection leading to either their strengthening or rejection. Hermeneutics therefore maintains that true understanding occurs insofar as we pay attention to the hidden assumptions and pre-judgments underlying our claims. In this section, I will expose some of the hidden assumptions and prejudices motivating certain discussions of biomedical enhancement in order to avoid platitudes and thus engage a more rigorous philosophical approach.

First, what are our prejudices about the very term "enhancement?" What sorts of assumptions are operative in its use? Bio-ethicists broadly agree in distinguishing "enhancement" from "treatment."[1] "Enhancement" generally refers to self-improvement where there is no medical need, illness or impairment; in instances where the latter does exist one refers to intervention as "treatment." DeGrazia cautions that this distinction is neither watertight nor adequate for all scenarios or discussions. Nonetheless, he maintains that "'treatment' and 'enhancement' are meaningful, contrasting terms"[2] insofar as they help distinguish between what may be seen as a medical necessity requiring treatment and an opportunity for personal betterment as a result of enhancement. This difference gains further plausibility insofar as it helps explain that while there may be disagreement over the best means of treatment there generally is not debate over whether (some sort of) treatment is required. When it comes to enhancement, however, debates focus around whether any specific intervention is appropriate at all.[3]

Allen Buchanan adds further nuance to the definition of enhancement by distinguishing between enhancement in general and biomedical enhancement in particular. He defines the former as: "an intervention – a human action of any kind – that improves some capacity (or characteristic) that normal human beings ordinarily have or, more radically, that produces a new one."[4] According to this definition, the printing press, agriculture, and astronomy, and so on, are all forms of enhancement. He then goes on to clarify *biomedical* enhancement as "a deliberate intervention, applying biomedical science, which aims to improve an existing capacity that most or all normal human beings typically have, or to create a new capacity, by acting directly on the body or brain."[5] Accordingly, the taking of pharmaceuticals, the implantation of various forms of technology into the body, and the manipulation of genes would count as biomedical enhancement; education, meditation, and going to the gym would not.[6] While I concur with the general distinction between treatment and enhancement as well as Buchanan's refinement of it, I worry about the tendency resulting from this definition to all too easily call "enhancement" any biomedical intervention that is not treatment. To avoid such a false conclusion that assumes that all non-treatment interventions are necessarily enhancement, we need to attend to some of the assumptions latent in our current usage. In other words, bringing hermeneutics' emphasis on the role of prejudices to bear on the discussion of enhancement reveals some problematic assumptions that are frequently overlooked.

For example, that the use of the term "enhancement" may conceal an unexamined prejudice that the proposed intervention will in fact make one "better" can be seen in John Harris's proclamation that: "If it wasn't good for you it wouldn't be enhancement." As his first sentence of his essay "Enhancements Are a Moral Obligation"[7] indicates, this assertion advances the false assumption – because question begging – that calling an intervention an enhancement does actually make it one. This false assumption again appears a page later where Harris writes, "Enhancements are so obviously good for us (if they weren't they wouldn't be enhancements) that it is odd that the idea of enhancement has caused and still occasions so much suspicion, fear, and outright hostility."[8] These two sentences reveal his assumption that anything named as an enhancement is necessarily and literally so. Such a prejudice renders him unable to realize that one cause of the suspicion, fear, and hostility directed at "enhancements" is the fact that not everyone agrees that everything referred to as "enhancement" is truly worthy of that term. Controversy drives debates over whether, for example, a cochlear implant, breast augmentation surgery, genetic manipulation to prolong one's life, or genetically engineering one's future children indeed enhances one's life.

Since the *OED* instructs us that "enhancement" means "to lift" or "to raise," then there is some legitimacy to assuming that the use of this term indicates that a human life will be raised to a higher level of existence. However, using the dictionary definition of enhancement to justify one's application of it leads to two problems. First, appealing to this general definition of enhancement as sufficient to settle the debate makes it almost impossible to find anyone who would, in fact, be against enhancement per se. For, it would be very hard to imagine anyone who is not engaged in (and/or who argues against) the bettering of her or his life whether through education, health, love, religion, or pleasure. In other words, while the definition of a term may be uncontroversial, this fact does not mean its application to phenomena is also uncontroversial. Thus Harris's blithe quip misses the real reason some people are reticent about enhancement: namely, not because they are against improvement per se (i.e., as specified in the dictionary definition), but because they do not agree that everything called "enhancement" is truly worthy of that name.

The second problem with Harris's pronouncement is that even if we all accept the general project of enhancement (i.e., that it is a good thing to raise human life to a higher level), we lack a specific definition of what exactly constitutes our conception of "higher level." What does a higher level of humanity look like? Does it necessarily include hearing, bigger breasts, a longer life, and perfect children? Sufficient attention to the definition of "higher level" is what arguments like those proffered by Harris leave out. We need to take more care to examine what we are implicitly assuming about what such a higher-level existence entails. Without an explicit account, how can we tell whether either an individual's life or humanity as a whole will actually be raised to a higher level as a result of such intervention? There must be more work done to establish the criteria for what counts as a good life.

My point is that using the term "enhancement" to refer to all interventions that are not treatment occludes conversation about what sorts of interventions and activities lead to the genuine betterment of human life.[9] Attending to the prejudices operative behind the debates, we are better able to see that one pressing question that requires an answer is: when we use enhancement to speak of "raising up," what, exactly, do we believe is being elevated? Again, Buchanan is helpful here in noting the difference between the speaking of enhancing a *capacity* versus enhancing a *human life* and urges us to pay attention to the intended object of enhancement: i.e., a capacity, an individual, and/or a community. Since bio-technologies are always directed at a specific capacity, Buchanan argues that debates must be limited to evaluating whether or not a specific capacity is enhanced; language about enhancing people or human nature remains too vague and imprecise to be of use. He is amongst those who seek to avoid introducing the problematic language of "human nature" into the debate.[10] However, as Buchanan himself is aware, even where an intervention may enhance one's capacity for a specific behavior, this fact does not necessarily mean that one will have a better life overall. Furthermore, he underscores the fact that even if an intervention did improve an individual's life overall that fact alone would not entitle one to undergo that enhancement since there is the good of others that also must be taken into account. Extending the life of a portion of humans on earth might be desirable for those individuals, but extending the life of every human might threaten natural and medical resources and thus impair life overall. However, while I find some legitimacy to his insistence that an enhancement must be thought of as aimed at improving a specific human capacity (rather than thinking that when one uses the term enhancement it refers necessarily to (a) human life in general), his delineation raises some problems of its own.

I am not convinced that these two foci, i.e., specific capacities versus a life overall, are as separable as Buchanan seems to believe. For example, if one is debating whether or not to take Ritalin before a test in order to "enhance" one's mental capacity, then one is nevertheless making the following assumptions about an overall good: a) passing or doing better on this test will improve one's overall life happiness, b) doing better on the test even if one suffers possible side-effects from the medication is preferable to underperforming without side effects, c) taking a drug as a quick fix is better than the slower process of improving one's capacities in a more organic way, etc. Furthermore, there is the question of whether the practice of using pharmaceuticals to improve test scores contributes to the good of society. What I want to suggest is that even when one narrows the debate down to focus on the (alleged) enhancement of a specific capacity, one is still making assumptions about what one takes to be the good life in terms of one's psychological, physiological, and communal state. Focusing solely on a capacity tends to endorse a compartmentalization of capacities as well as to exacerbate the highly subjectivistic rendering that assumes that what one chooses as an individual has no bearing on one's community – one is truly an isolated individual in such situations. I do not think, therefore, that Buchanan's distinction has sufficiently helped us address these often hidden assumptions we make about the human good in general when attending to specific capacities.

What needs further consideration is the question of precisely how we understand an "enhanced" capacity figuring into the good life. To focus too narrowly on the enhancement of a capacity contributes to an instrumentalized approach insofar as we specify what the capacity is for and then see if an enhancement will help achieve that end. But such a piecemeal approach to human life is problematic since it causes us to forget our connections to the greater web of life and to lose sight of the good of the whole – whether the whole individual, society, or eco-sphere. As Gadamer reminds us: "The equilibrium which we call mental health is precisely a condition of the person as a whole being who is not simply a bundle of capacities; such equilibrium concerns the totality of a person's whole relation to the world."[11] If the hermeneutic circle reveals that meaning is only accessible insofar as we are able to integrate the parts with the whole, then we can understand a hermeneutic approach to biomedical enhancements as requiring the integration of the particulars (medical interventions directed at capacities) with the whole (both the individual's and society's good). My point is that while focusing the debate on whether a particular capacity is indeed enhanced can provide some degree of technical clarity and specificity, we nonetheless neglect paying sufficient heed to the meaning and significance of the alleged enhancement for one's life, indeed human life, overall.

I have been trying to complicate the assumption that providing an uncontroversial descriptive definition of enhancement leads to a similarly uncontroversial practical understanding and application of that term. If we agree that the end of human life is flourishing and happiness,[12] and if we can agree with Aristotle that such an end entails activating the highest part of humans to achieve it, then discussions about enhancement must always have in mind what sorts of interventions-as-means will help us achieve this end. Unfortunately, while all philosophers can agree on this end generally stated, fleshing out specifics as to what exactly a happy life is remains contested. I take this as an indication that we must be all the more scrupulous about debating not just means (empirical studies that demonstrate that a biomedical enhancement really augments a capacity) but ends. The hermeneutic approach here is helpful for alerting us to the prejudices we all carry and that inform our beliefs about the good life. Unless we explicate and ponder such questions, our debates about enhancement will remain shallow, inadequate, and reactionary. Thus while I can agree with Buchanan that we ought to refrain from asking the overly general and thus misleading question of whether "enhancement is good," I do not think it is satisfactory to focus on capacities alone. We must strive to articulate what is the ideal of "better humans" that we are implicitly endorsing and whether it is a viable one. We cannot engage debates about the pros and cons of enhancement until we can make explicit the ideal of humanity that we are implicitly endorsing so as to be more reflective about who we want to be. This point leads to the next question: what can a hermeneutic approach contribute to an understanding of the human condition and its good?

FINITE BEINGS DESIRING THE INFINITE

Are there any general features to the human condition that can be articulated and that prove pertinent to the debate over biomedical enhancements? Here I draw on a brief history of hermeneutics, which derives its names from Hermes, the messenger bridging the distance between gods and humans, to suggest a feature crucial to the human condition that proves salient for discussions about enhancement. Initially, disciplines dealing with temporally distant texts, like law and theology, required a "hermeneutic" to provide a bridge of understanding from a contemporary perspective to ancient legal and religious texts. Then, in the eighteenth century, Schleiermacher sought to apply hermeneutics not only to temporally foreign texts, but to any text made opaque by various forms of otherness, e.g., different cultures, languages, and ideas that serve to make the text feel foreign to the reader. Two centuries later, Heidegger ushered in the final expansion of hermeneutics, broadening the scope of hermeneutics from opaque texts to human existence writ large – hence, Gadamer's words in the epitaph to this chapter that describe how hermeneutics is relevant for all experiences where an immediate meaning remains elusive.

Following this trajectory, I believe we are warranted in reading the work of the hermeneuts coming in the wake of Heidegger, namely, Hans-Georg Gadamer, Luigi Pareyson, and Paul Ricoeur, as deepening and clarifying the sense in which the human condition, as ubiquitously marked by efforts to understand what proves baffling in its unpredicatbility, consists in the effort to forge a connection to that which is distant and other. For example, the theme of being open to another – particularly in terms of the listening required by true dialogue – is present in all these three thinkers whose work has implicitly or explicitly called for increased solidarity with the "other." While generalizing to affirm what is similar amongst thinkers always risks oversimplification, I think it is fair to say that these three hermeneutic thinkers affirm the original motif that to be human is to attempt to transcend one's limitations in order to achieve connection with what lies beyond. The transcendent, the inexhaustible, or the excess of Being functioned in the work of Ricoeur, Pareyson, and Gadamer, respectively, to signify that which the finite human strives towards but can never fully achieve.[13]

In other words, the hermeneutic impulse of the twentieth century was to contend with the human tendency towards transcendence (of various sorts) that required an acknowledgement that no attempt to connect with the other can be achieved without acknowledging our fallible frailty, the mark of our finitude. Indeed, the fact that Hermes was also known as a trickster should make us wary about definitive claims to have understood: thinking that one has understood is no guarantee that one actually has. Although the very effort to transcend one's limitations is part of the human condition, humans qua mortals can never fully achieve such transcendence. *Ideologie Kritik* warned us that in spite of good intentions to connect with the other, domination and oppression can still pervade. Does Hermes thus now signify the false hope of a bridge that can never be crossed? Rejecting such a Sisyphean interpretation, I believe that the relevance of this hermeneutic history for our present investigation is that it demonstrates that a better way of understanding the human condition is in terms of our perpetual, because erotic, motion, as described by Diotima in Plato's *Symposium*. In Diotima's tale, all humans are driven by the desire for immortality (which she defines as possessing the good forever). Yet if we pay attention to her account of the ascent we learn that although the highest step on the erotic ladder is beholding the form of Beauty itself, if we want immortality we cannot rest there. To behold is not yet to birth. The beholding of Beauty in itself becomes the means by which, in which, to reproduce, give birth to, true virtue, which Diotima had defined earlier as immortality. The point is that immortality requires both an ascent to the transcendent realm as well as a descent to practice pedagogy in the finite realm. I believe that this tale of human ascent and descent is suggestive of our human condition as seen through a hermeneutic lens. For, if our striving for immortality can be seen as indicative of a drive toward enhancement, then the very desire for enhancement is part of our human condition.

This view challenges those who worry that biomedical enhancement threatens something essential about human nature. Some of the leading enhancement skeptics, Francis Fukuyama, Jürgen Habermas, Leon Kass, Jean Bethke Elshtain and Michael Sandel, all base their criticism on the fact that there is something called "human nature" that human intervention should not breach. Sandel, for example, insists on the "moral status of nature" and defends "the proper stance of human beings towards the given world" as a way of challenging the enhancement project.[14] Elshtain, too, makes assumptions about a stable entity called "nature" and goes on to warn against efforts to override or control such nature.[15] And Habermas laments challenges to the "given": "What hitherto was 'given' as organic nature, and could at most be 'bred,' now shifts to the realm of artifacts and their production."[16] Worries put forth by those skeptical of enhancement often accuse their opponents of "playing God" or reaching for "perfection" and/or "total control." Elshtain, for instance, describes how some "contemporary projects of self-overcoming...promise an escape from the vagaries of the human condition into a realm of near mastery."[17] Habermas laments:

> Due to the spectacular advances of molecular genetics, more and more of what we are "by nature" is coming within the reach of biotechnical intervention. From the perspective of experimental science, this technological control of human nature is but another manifestation of our tendency to extend continuously the range of what we can control within our natural environment.[18]

And both Elshtain and Sandel decry the way in which such projects aim at perfection.[19] However, the question of just what "nature" is and what is properly "given" is not uncontroversial. Buchanan, for instance, refuses to endow "nature" with any argumentative value in these debates. He details why it is philosophically problematic to attempt to establish what is sacred, stable, and identifiable about "human nature."[20] While I will not rehearse Buchanan's fine arguments here, suffice it to say that even a cursory glance at the history of science reveals that such an assumption about the need to control and intervene into the "given" applies to pre-modern conceptions of medicine as well. Without a more adequate definition of the terms "nature" and "given" it becomes difficult to maintain that there is something distinctively malevolent about contemporary biomedical interventions. Defenders of the nature-as-given position fail to explain why we are not justified in taking enhancement as the logical consequence of the western scientific trajectory. The point here is not to argue that being part of the trajectory is automatic justification of its worth or goodness; rather my point is that we cannot use the criteria of "control" or "playing God" as themselves instructive of a dubious intervention at some points in time and not others without specifying the difference between them. Furthermore, esteeming nature as the desirable and inviolable end becomes problematic in light of Alkmaion's statement that "Death itself is simply a return into the cycle of nature."[21] If death is natural, wouldn't any attempt to stave it off count as "playing God"? What entitles us to work against some parts of nature but not all?

Yet in refusing to summon the concept of "human nature" to thwart biomedical enhancement, the question now becomes: if humans are finite yet ever desiring to become infinite, are there, and should there be, any sorts of restraints on this urge? The desire to control and to transcend our environment – an attitude that presumably makes us like God – can hardly be seen as illicit in its own right; in fact, looking at human history one could claim such desires as part of our very "nature" – indeed, one could even argue that "playing God" itself can be seen as part of our "nature." The history of humanity, insofar as we read any progress into it at all, can be read as continuing efforts to increase our ability to transcend our environment, and hence the physical and bodily limitations marking human life. Thus, according to this hermeneutic perspective, it does not make sense to fear or spurn the desire we have to transcend our human condition writ large. What we need, then, is an ethic of enhancement that both affirms our finitude and also takes seriously the human urge for transcendence. And lest my proposal for the acknowledgement of our finite-yet-desiring-infinite conditions seem obvious to some, in fact neither finitude nor our desire to transcend it are included amongst DeGrazia's list of seven inviolable traits that he names as possible criteria that should be considered off limits when it comes to biomedical enhancements.[22] Similarly, Savulescu and Bostom's list of several traits differentiating homo sapiens from other animals also fails to include our urge to transcend.[23] My point is that any conception, or list of core traits, of the human condition should include our ambivalent status between finite and infinite. The question that now follows is: what might serve as the evaluative criterion for assessing the worth of an intervention that takes into account both of these dimensions of human existence?

"HUMAN NATURE" VERSUS EQUILIBRIUM

I want to summon a concept Gadamer develops specifically in his writings on health, namely, equilibrium. Equilibrium, as that state of balance between two opposing forces, is an apt way to describe the human condition of mortals who strive after immortality. I want to appeal to equilibrium as a metaphor that indicates the balance that occurs as a result of recognizing the competing natures comprising humanity. It helps us avoid referencing finitude as a way to decry efforts to improve our current condition (as Elshtain does) or to avoid the significance of finitude altogether. Acknowledging the importance of equilibrium focuses the question on what sorts of limits, if any, should be placed on the effort to overcome human finitude. Are there any theoretical limitations that might differentiate legitimate from illegitimate overcomings? I want to appeal to equilibrium as a criterion for helping to discern beneficial from detrimental enhancements.

Gadamer defines equilibrium as "a condition of experienced weightlessness in which different forces balance each other out" and he describes what this looks like for the human being: it is "a condition of being involved, of being in the world, of being together with one's fellow human being, of active and rewarding engagement in one's everyday tasks."[24] He further talks about the way in which such involvement entails forgetting or losing oneself while remaining open to new possibilities. This description of equilibrium sounds a lot like what Gadamer means by "play" – one of the most central concepts of his hermeneutics. Gadamer's emphasis on the way in which play occurs in all understanding aims to articulate how the understander is caught up in, drawn into, something larger than herself. It describes the state in which one's involvement in the game is directed at continuing the playing rather than winning (whereby the game would cease).

Equilibrium is similarly suggestive of the way in which humans are part of something larger which they cannot fully control but does not render them powerless. Successful play, like the state of equilibrium, requires a balance between the individual's efforts and the force of the game. Gadamer even refers to equilibrium as manifesting the "rhythmic function" necessary to health and life; we could thus say that in a state of equilibrium rhythm takes over. Gadamer turned to the concept of "play" to challenge the subjectivism in which the understander was believed to possess full control over the process. Insofar as "equilibrium," like "play," suggests Gadamer's antisubjectivism that nonetheless affirms the dynamism of the human subject caught up in that which transcends it, it proves helpful for challenging the assumption that the insertion of the human will into natural processes is not always and necessarily a beneficial move. Yet at the same time, some effort and initiative is required – players cannot just remain passive.

Where equilibrium is occluded, the play of human life is thwarted; there is cessation rather than continual movement and openness aimed at forging connections with others, ourselves, and our world. Given the organic nature of such equilibrium – as that which persists above and beyond the will of any individual, Gadamer describes how medical interventions must bear in mind that they are a *techne* rather than a *mechane*. As such, they must take care not to disturb the balance by exerting too much force or trying to build or construct something.[25] As Gadamer warns: "equilibrium can be lost through being forced, through too powerful an intervention."[26] The aim of intervention is not to willfully *produce* an equilibrium – i.e., to manufacture what was not previously there, but to allow the equilibrium to maintain itself: "medical practice is not concerned with actually producing equilibrium, that is, with building up a new state of equilibrium from nothing, but rather is always concerned with arresting and assisting the fluctuating equilibrium of health."[27] The implication of these claims for a discussion of enhancement is that we should evaluate potential enhancements in terms of their excess of power that would disturb the equilibrium, pushing us too far towards either finitude or infinitude. A guiding dictum would be: an enhancement must not impinge upon these necessary functions, must not promote disequilibrium but contribute to equilibrium. In order to appreciate the importance of equilibrium for debates about medical enhancements, I will detail two benefits of appealing to equilibrium as a way of thinking about the limits of human biomedical intervention without having to essentialize nature.

The first advantage of focusing on equilibrium is that it avoids the problematic assumptions about "nature" that either tend to take it as akin to a Divine-like Subject with its own wisdom and will or else objectify "nature" as that which is manipulable due to its passivity. In other words, on the one hand, appealing to equilibrium opens up the possibility of articulating a crucial facet of our human condition without the vague deifications of "nature" that assume nature-as-subject. On the other hand, it bids us take seriously an organic component to nature that should be respected in order to avoid dominating nature-as-object. I want to argue that the appeal to equilibrium as a process akin to play aids us in moving beyond the Nature-as-God versus Nature-as-object dichotomy that seems to characterize most writing on enhancement. To defend an aliveness at play in nature does not require a deification of nature; at the same time, such a defense does protect against reifying nature and treating it as merely a means to human-defined ends.

Since above I have discussed efforts by anti-enhancement theorists who fall into the first of these camps with their tendency to deify nature (e.g., Elshtain, Fukuyama, Kass, Sandel) let me now turn to the others who, in their rejection of the idea of human nature as given and thus inviolable, tend to objectify it. Harris, for instance, who criticizes efforts to treat "human nature" as a subject, nevertheless seems to go too far in the opposite direction by objectifying nature. He defines medicine as "the comprehensive attempt to frustrate the course of nature"[28] and thus assumes that sickness is natural and that medicine is a direct challenge to nature in the attempt to heal. While some sickness indeed occurs in nature and is not the effect of human intervention, his definition seems to deny the way in which medicine frequently enlists nature's own energy to heal itself. Harris's claim obfuscates any sense of nature as itself possessing a *dynamis* that, left to its own, can actively produce balance or equilibrium. One does not need to take nature as a Divine subject in order to accept the fact that the human organism can be robbed of a certain power by any number of human interventions (from pharmaceuticals to physical exercise) that results in disequilibrium. Common practice indicates that we do operate from the position that a healthy, flourishing person is in balance: for example, neither eating too much nor starving oneself, neither exercising too much nor abstaining from exercising, taking only those medications that are necessary to stabilize one part of one's organism, which may require attention to another part that is destabilized by such intervention. I want to note that the assumption here is that such equilibrium is an organism's "natural" state where "natural" refers to what we take as ideal and not simply "given." After all, death and sickness are also "given" in nature. Thus the appeal is not to what is "given" per se but to what our reason and experience project as an ideal, i.e., "natural," state.

Harris's account of medicine is what Gadamer warns about when he describes the dangers of a reductionistic science that is applied to dominate and control nature and that has wreaked havoc in our world. He calls on us to refuse to "see in every object a form of resistance, something to be broken down and mastered through acquiring knowledge about it."[29] For, the goal of an enhancement is to promote equilibrium rather than suppress it by domination. Attending to the importance of equilibrium helps clarify that what is to be avoided is not mastery per se but the attempt to project an accomplishment that fails to take into account a broader view of the whole. Mastery can be a legitimate aim in some circumstances yet it will always have its costs and these must be counted in terms of the whole.

Gadamer captures well our ambivalent relation with nature: "Precisely this is our 'nature' that we must assert ourselves over and against nature as far as we can. But it is also and especially in the nature of human being, in all they know and do, to sustain a relation of harmony with nature."[30] There is no doubt that humans can utilize knowledge in a way to override deficiencies in nature; yet no amount of reason can allow us to transcend nature entirely. This tension recalls the lesson about human nature from the myth of Hermes: our desire for transcendence encourages us to exercise some power over nature, yet we remain always bound by nature. Thus the question becomes: what is the descriptive meaning of being bound by nature that may inflect a prescriptive criterion of a border we dare not cross? This question invites a deeper reflection on humanity's relation to nature.

An emphasis on equilibrium, secondly, also prevents the assumption that "nature" exists independently from human, social, and historical existence. Humans just are the integration of "nature" and "society," where the latter is an offshoot of reason. Any talk of equilibrium must look beyond the physical human organism: "sickness and loss of equilibrium do not merely represent a medical-biological state of affairs, but also a life-historical and social process."[31] Indicating the benefits of an enhancement must take into consideration the equilibrium of not just the human organism in itself but also in relation to the social–natural world. The evaluation of an enhancement must take into account not only the equilibrium of the whole person but also of the integration of human life with the rest of nature. Understanding humans as part of nature and of a system larger than individual organisms means that when we reflect upon equilibrium we must focus not just on our bodies but on the whole web of socio-natural existence. To focus on equilibrium is to bring the discussion back to where we started, with an emphasis on the importance of the pursuit of connection with what is other. Thus a helpful way of putting the question is: does a specific enhancement upset the balance of the whole or disturb a fundamental connectedness as manifest in equilibrium?

Attending to the importance of equilibrium serves as a check on proceeding with enhancements without counting the larger costs as connected to the greater good. In other words, while, as Buchanan demonstrates, human nature is not a fixed entity – since human traits and genes change over time – this fact does not preclude the reality that humans can negatively impact and damage nature in a way that proves detrimental to humans and other life – e.g. global warming. One does not have to argue that there is something definitive and unchanging called "nature" in order to worry that human interventions may cause unpredictable and massive damage. What if some change were to be made that destroyed a key component of what we value about human life right now? Given our past performance, there are good grounds for being skeptical. For, might it be the case that increasing the practice of enhancement actually cedes more power to human structures that either at best prove no better than "nature" itself or at worse do damage?

The claim I want to advance is not that "nature" always knows better, but that humans too frequently attempt knowledge that is potentially destructive. I agree with Buchanan that the claim that "changing human nature itself is wrong" is not a necessary truth that can be established a priori.[32] But we cannot conclude that all seemingly beneficial changes will be that in the end. Having some sense of equilibrium is also a way to acknowledge the dangers Ingmar Persson and Julian Savulescu warn of: "It is easier to damage a functioning system than to improve upon it."[33] And later they reflect: "Since it is easier to harm than to benefit, more efficient technology will bring in its wake a greater risk of Ultimate Harm."[34] Persson and Savulescu have developed some of the most cogent defenses of certain enhancements and yet they remain wary about the possible detriments. Bringing in the criterion of equilibrium is a way to deepen their reflections by remembering, as Gadamer bids us do, that "from both perspectives we are partners in a life-world which supports us all. And the task which falls to us all as human beings is to find our own way in the life-world and to learn to accept our real limits."[35] Gadamer does not advocate fixing limits in a "premature" and "obscurantist" way but that does not mean that there are not limits that must be "respected."[36] In other words, there is no context transcendent criterion that will guarantee equilibrium. Equilibrium can only be assessed from within the present community. In concluding, I will suggest what such a process-based assessment may look like.

PANELS OF EXPERTS VERSUS A DIALOGUE OF PEERS

In reflecting on the ethics of biomedical enhancements, the working assumption of this chapter has been that before we are able to defend any concrete answers to the questions, we must attend to the prejudices driving much of the debate. I thus now want to propose one practical implication of this hermeneutic approach in terms of what providing answers might look like. In one of his recent articles, from which the epitaph at the beginning of this paper comes, Savulescu laments the lack of knowledge of philosophy and ethics by those sitting on ethics panels. While this paper has been an effort to attend to the general sentiment of this complaint, I want to close by examining one more assumption underlying the ethics of enhancement: namely, thinking that "experts" are the ones who can and should solve our problems.

One danger of our scientific age, Gadamer warns, is the belief that experts have answers that non-experts do not.[37] While experts indeed may be summoned for their technical know-how in order to suggest the best means for a particular end, Gadamer is wary of the way in which this endeavor affirms only the instrumental value of reason. Relying on experts to apply their knowledge to an isolated procedure neglects the multiple social interests and perspectives at play. Furthermore, given Gadamer's emphasis on the dialogic nature of all understanding, there is reason to believe that no armchair reflection by an autonomous mind will suffice for practical problems. While deepening our philosophical reflections is certainly necessary for achieving a more adequate perspective on enhancement, it is by no means a sufficient response if it is deemed to apply only to experts in medical ethics. Rather, as we move forward in broaching these ethical challenges, we must invite a genuine dialogue amongst a variety of players inhabiting a variety of social positions. Such a procedure reflects Gadamer's insistence that all understanding must remain open to an ongoing dialogue with the Thou (whether a person or text) in a process that entails refusing to objectify the other and listening in such a way that results in change. Neither an individual physician, nor philosopher, nor patient, alone is adequate to the task of weighing the pros and cons of a given enhancement. Indeed, dialogue about enhancement needs to be incorporated into a wider communal life in a way that fosters reflection on what counts as the good life for a human. Another way of describing the limitations of experts is that their knowledge pertains more to particular means than to ends more generally construed, like the good life. The way forward is not to proffer theory alone that is then narrowly applied by experts, but to establish avenues of praxis that invite communities to take part in transformative dialogues about the good life, which includes clarifying both limits to and dreams for transcendence. A hermeneutic approach to biomedical enhancement reminds us that particular interventions can only be adequately assessed in light of our overarching ends, ends which can never be set by armchair ethicists or hospital ethics panels. Hence the call is for dialogic circles of inquiry that can be established in communities that draw on multiple individuals from a variety of backgrounds and experiences in order to keep the question of ends in view.

Such a call for a more dialogical approach to bioethics makes sense not only theoretically but also practically. It could help resolve some of the difficulties in figuring out how to apply the results of biomedical enhancement research to actual situations. For instance, in their 2012 monograph, Persson and Savulescu defend the move to consider using pharmaceuticals to improve the moral behavior of humans. They detail the results of research that shows how the administration of oxytocin and serotonin can produce "moral effects." While they admit that such research is in its nascent stages and is not yet able to be applied to our human situation, they do hold out hope that with enough time and effort research will point to direct and specific moral changes in humans. They cautiously reflect: "Even if such means were discovered, the daunting task of applying them to a sufficient number of people ... would remain. In any event, we are not envisaging that moral bioenhancement will ever reach a point at which traditional methods of moral education – or other social strategies like institutional redesign using incentives – will be redundant."[38] In other words, even the most forceful proponents of certain biomedical enhancement therapies admit that some degree of human judgment will be required to apply these technologies in order to maintain human free-choice, not to mention to produce positive results and sustain human flourishing. Here is where a dialogue of peers would help by fostering enhanced judgment about the best use of biomedical technologies in order to promote equilibrium. Aiding the individuals involved in making the best decisions they can, rather than expecting a panel of experts to apply the data, encourages a more holistic and less instrumental approach. Inviting a dialogue encourages a plethora of questions and interpretations directed at the data and its application for certain individuals within a certain context. Such an approach might include not only taking into account an individual's desires, beliefs, and limitations, but also it might entail assembling a broader, more diverse group of people with whom the individual may dialogue. This process is different than a panel of experts charged with coming up with the best option for an individual relying on isolated facts abstracted from the context.

Any proposed answers to questions of enhancement must be committed to exposing the prejudices that underlie our current practices and language and understanding the questions driving the project. Gadamer's emphasis on equilibrium can be utilized as a criterion that aids us in reconciling the potential benefits of a particular enhancement with their implications for the good life over all. Such a process must be carried out amidst full recognition that all understanding requires a dialogical openness that accords with human finitude. In debating instances of biomedical enhancement, we must remain mindful of the hermeneutic task to engage the on-going and circular process of forging a definition of a good life that is itself constitutive of every flourishing human life.[39]

NOTES

1. David DeGrazia "Enhancement Technologies and Human Identity." *Journal of Medicine and Philosophy*. 30 (2005): 261–83 at pp. 262–3. Also see the discussion in Erik Parens "Is Better Always Good?" Parens (ed.), *Enhancing Human Traits: Ethical and Social Implications* (Washington, DC: Georgetown University Press, 2007), and John Harris, "Enhancements are a moral obligation," Savulescu and Bostrom (eds.), *Human Enhancement* (Oxford: Oxford University Press, 2009), pp. 141–3, who iterate some problems with this distinction.
2. DeGrazia, "Enhancement Technologies and Human Identity," p. 264.
3. I believe this distinction stands up even in cases where the debate is over whether the best "treatment" may be medical intervention or not. For example, we could think of the case of young boys diagnosed with ADHD – for some the best treatment may be behavioral and social rather than pharmacological. Similarly, some instances of mild depression may require a treatment of talk therapy or a change of diet/lifestyle rather than drugs. What these examples show is that treatment, while not necessarily requiring medical intervention, does aim to improve a condition that has been diagnosed as an illness.
4. Allen Buchanan, *Better than Human: The Problems and Perils of Enhancing Ourselves* (New York: Oxford, 2011), p. 5.
5. Ibid. p. 23.
6. Interestingly, he goes on to argue that there is no significant moral difference between biomedical and non-biomedical enhancements. I would agree with him and for this reason I believe we need to pay more critical attention to the wider implications of all alleged enhancements. Demonizing biomedical enhancements only serves to undercut inquiry about the effects of a variety of interventions-as-(alleged)-enhancements.

7. Harris, "Enhancements are a moral obligation," p. 131.
8. Ibid. p. 132.
9. Habermas encourages a similar set of questions directed at articulating the morality of human life, yet he relies on the dubious notion of "human nature" (Jürgen Habermas, *The Future of Human Nature*, trans. Hella Beister and William Rehg (Cambridge: Polity Press, 2003)), which I shall take issue with below.
10. Allen Buchanan, *Beyond Humanity? The Ethics of Biomedical Enhancement* (New York: Oxford University Press, 2011), p. 138.
11. Hans-Georg Gadamer, *The Enigma of Health*, translated by Jason Gaiger and Nicholas Walker (Stanford: Stanford University Press, 1996), p. 56.
12. I cannot think of an instance of a philosopher who would not concur, although a Kantian qualification would add that we must be worthy of our happiness.
13. Even Habermas would seem to agree with this basic analysis when he decries the reductionism of language as wholly private: "As historical and social beings we find ourselves always already in a linguistically structured lifeworld. In the forms of communication through which we reach an understanding with one another about something in the world and about ourselves, we encounter a transcending power" (*The Future of Human Nature*, 10, emphasis added). In other words, Habermas affirms the hermeneutic assumption of the transcendent nature of language, what he goes on to refer to as a "transubjective power" rather than "an absolute one" (11).
14. Michael Sandel, "The Case Against Perfection," in Savulescu and Bostrom, *Human Enhancement*, p. 72.
15. Jean Bethke Elshtain, "The Body and the Quest for Control," *Is Human Nature Obsolete?* Harold W. Baillie and Timothy K. Casey (eds.) (Cambridge, MA: MIT Press, 2005), pp. 168–70.
16. Habermas, *The Future of Human Nature*.
17. Elshtain, "The Body and the Quest for Control," p. 157.
18. Habermas, *The Future of Human Nature*, p. 23.
19. I also want to point out that the anti-enhancement camp is not the only side guilty of highfalutin verbiage. Titles like Harris's "Enhancements Are a Moral Obligation" and Savulescu's "Procreative Beneficence: Why We should Select the Best Children" (in *Bioethics* 5–6 (October 2001) pp. 413–26) feed into the "for or against" mentality. Hermeneutics calls us to attend to the prejudices and assumptions driving our arguments in order to tighten up vague language. The hermeneutic insight offered here is to pay more heed to the operative assumptions one is making about the good life when one refers to an intervention as enhancement. We must scrutinize: what exactly are we claiming is being enhanced and are we warranted in making such a claim? In other words, reflecting on our implicit beliefs about the human condition helps avoid overly generalized debates that promote a false dichotomy between pro- and anti-enhancement positions.

20. Buchanan, *Beyond Humanity*, pp. 115–42.
21. Gadamer, *The Enigma of Health*, p. 97.
22. DeGrazia, "Enhancement Technologies and Human Identity," p. 272.
23. See Savulescu and Bostrom (eds.), *Human Enhancement*.
24. Gadamer, *The Enigma of Health*, p. 113.
25. For example, Gadamer maintains: "We all need to learn once again that every disturbance in health, every complaint, however minor, and even every infection is actually a sign telling us that we need to restore what is appropriate, that we must regain the balance of equilibrium" (see *The Enigma of Health*, p. 136).
26. Ibid. p. 114.
27. Ibid. p. 37.
28. Harris, "Enhancements are a moral obligation," p. 134.
29. Gadamer, *The Enigma of Health*, p. 101.
30. Ibid. p. 139.
31. Ibid. p. 42.
32. Buchanan (2012: 132). *Beyond Humanity?* p. 137.
33. Ingmar Persson and Julian Savulescu, *Unfit for the Future: The Need for Moral Enhancement* (Oxford: Oxford University Press 2014), p. 132.
34. Ibid. p. 133.
35. Gadamer, *The Enigma of Health*, p. 101.
36. Ibid. p. 101.
37. See Hans-Georg Gadamer, *Reason in the Age of Science*, trans. Frederick G. Lawrence (Cambridge, MA: MIT Press, 1992).
38. Persson and Savulescu, *Unfit for the Future*, p. 121.
39. I am extremely appreciative for the comments made by Pablo Muchnik and Monica Vilhauer on earlier drafts of this paper.

Contributors

Lauren Swayne Barthold is Associate Professor of Philosophy and Director of Gender Studies at Gordon College in Wenham, MA. In addition to several journal articles on Gadamer's hermeneutics she is the author of *Gadamer's Dialectical Hermeneutics* (Lexington 2010). More recently she has focused on the relevance of hermeneutics for broader social issues. She has a forthcoming book chapter on a hermeneutic approach to religion, is completing a manuscript that applies Gadamer's hermeneutics to a feminist theory of social identities, and is working on an article that brings together Gadamer, political theory, and dialogic praxis to defend a critical, fallibilistic approach to dialogue.

Steven Paul Cauchon is a Ph.D. candidate in the Department of Political Science at University of California Riverside, with a focus on non-violent protest, environmental justice, and transnational activism. His current project examines the ways in which transnational environmental justice coalitions empower domestic activists to bring about long-term structural change.

Peter Fristedt is currently a Senior Program Officer at the National Endowment for the Humanities and has taught previously at George Washington, Towson and Hofstra universities. His articles on Gadamer and hermeneutics have appeared in *Philosophy and Social Criticism*, *International Journal of Philosophical Studies* and *Southwest Philosophy Review*.

Jeff Malpas is Distinguished Professor at the University of Tasmania and Visiting Distinguished Professor in the Department of Philosophy at Latrobe University. He is the co-editor of the *Routledge Companion to Hermeneutics* (Routledge, 2015) and the author, among other works, of *Heidegger and the Thinking of Place* (MIT Press, 2012). The project of philosophical topography around which his work is focused encompasses a wide range of issues across architecture, the arts, geography, and philosophy.

Whitney Mannies is a doctoral candidate in political science at the University of California, Riverside. She has published in *Philosophy and Literature* and her research interests include the intersection of philosophy and literature, modern political thought and feminist theory. Her dissertation considers the implications of writing style and form for philosophical and political knowledge.

Leah McClimans is Associate Professor of Philosophy at the University of South Carolina. In her research she is interested in the entanglement of ethics and epistemology in medicine and healthcare. She frequently borrows from Gadamerian hermeneutics to understand the limits of standardized approaches to health outcomes and physician–patient communication. Her articles in this vein include "Choosing a Patient-Reported Outcome Measure" (*Theoretical Medicine and Bioethics*, 2010), "The Art of Asking Questions" (*International Journal of Philosophical Studies*, 2011) and "Quality of Life is a Process Not an Outcome" (*Theoretical Medicine and Bioethics*, 2012).

Isaac Ariail Reed is Associate Professor of Sociology at the University of Colorado. He works in social theory, historical sociology, and philosophy of social science. He is the author of *Interpretation and Social Knowledge: On the Use of Theory in the Human Sciences* (University of Chicago Press, 2011). His current work concerns power and performance in early modern states and empires.

Lorenzo C. Simpson is Professor of Philosophy at Stony Brook University. He has published articles on hermeneutics, Critical Theory, philosophy of science, African American philosophy and musical aesthetics. In addition, he is the author of *The Unfinished Project: Toward a Postmetaphysical Humanism* (Routledge, 2001) and *Technology, Time and the Conversations of Modernity* (Routledge, 1995). He is currently completing a book manuscript tentatively titled "Towards a Critical Hermeneutics: Interpretive Interventions in Science, Politics, Race and Culture."

Monica Vilhauer is Associate Professor of Philosophy at Roanoke College. Her research interests are in hermeneutics, ethics, feminist philosophy and ancient philosophy. She is the author of *Gadamer's Ethics of Play: Hermeneutics and the Other* (Lexington Books, 2010). Currently she is currently working on a book that focuses on the character of Socrates and investigates the role of desire in philosophy

Georgia Warnke is Distinguished Professor of Political Science and Director of the Center for Ideas and Society at the University of California, Riverside. She is the author of five books including *Gadamer: Hermeneutics, Tradition and Reason* (Stanford University Press, 1987) and *After Identity: Rethinking Race, Sex and Gender* (Cambridge University Press, 2007) as well as numerous articles on Gadamer's hermeneutics. Her research interests include feminist theory, philosophical hermeneutics and critical theory.

Santiago Zabala is ICREA Research Professor at the Pompeu Fabra University in Barcelona. He is the author and editor of, among other books, *The Future of Religion* (2005), *The Hermeneutic Nature of Analytic Philosophy* (2008), *Art's Claim to Truth* (2008), *The Remains of Being* (2009) and with Gianni Vattimo, *Hermeneutic Communism* (2011), all published by Columbia University Press and translated into several languages. His forthcoming book is *Emergency Aesthetics: Only Art Can Save Us*. He has written for *The Guardian, The New York Times, Boston Review,* and *The Los Angeles Review of Books*.

Index

Abel, Theodore, 2–3
anarchy, 68
Aristotle, 88–9
   on causation, 42–3, 45–7; see also Levine, Donald
   phronesis, 106
art
   and the body, 167, 168–9, 177
   as tradition, 174
   and understanding, 161–2, 165, 168–9, 175, 177

Baker, Keith, 50–2
Benn Michaels, Walter, 4–5
body, the
   and art, 167, 168–9
   as horizon, 172
   and knowledge, 171–2
Buchanan, Allen, 219, 221, 226
Butler, Judith, 170

causation, 45–7
   in the social sciences, 48–9
Charon, Rita, 206–8, 209, 210, 211, 213, 214, 215
Coates, Ta-Nehisi, 124–5
critical theory, 7–9
cultural identity, 23, 29–30, 30–1

DeGrazia, David, 219, 227
Delbanco, Andrew, 132, 133
Denton, Nancy A., 123–4
Derrida, Jacques, 9, 93
dialogical critique, 23–4, 33, 34–5, 37–8n
   and autonomy, 33–4, 35
   of clitoridectomy, 32–3, 35–6
dialogue, 104–5, 107, 108, 116, 135, 165, 232–3

Dilthey, Wilhelm, 60, 73
disposition *see* openness

Ellison, Ralph, 126
Elshtain, Jean Bethke, 225
enhancement, 219
   biomedical, 219
   and the desire for transcendence, 226–7
   general, 219
   versus nature, 229–31
equilibrium, 227–31
event, 150, 151
everyday perspective *see* normative perspective
expertise, dangers of, 232

first-person perspective *see* normative perspective
forcing cause, 48, 54–5, 57–8; *see also* causation: in the social sciences
fore-meaning(s) *see* prejudice
forming cause, 48, 50–4, 56–60; *see also* causation: in the social sciences
Foucault, Michel, 90–1, 92
Frank, Arthur, 205–6, 208, 209, 210, 213, 214, 215
French Revolution, 49–59
Freud, Sigmund, 70–1
Fricker, Miranda, 81, 209, 210–11

Gandhi, 102–3
   on *ahimsa*, 102, 109–10, 112–13, 115–16, 117
   and religion, 112
   on *satyagraha*, 102, 110–11, 112–13, 116–17, 118
   on *tapas*, 109–10
   and truth, 108–9, 110, 114, 115

Index

Habermas, Jürgen, 7–9, 22, 32, 99n, 225
Hacking, Ian, 59–60
Harris, John, 220–1, 230
Heidegger, Martin, 131
   as topological, 146–8, 151
hermeneutic circle, 134
hermeneutical injustice, 210
hermeneutics, 21
   and ethnocentrism, 26
   and explanation, 42
   history of, 67–8
   and language, 174
   legal, 106–7
   radical potential of, 68, 73–5
Hirsch, E. D., 4–5
Hobbes, Thomas, 44
horizon of understanding, 83, 93, 102, 113–14
Hume, David, 89

illness narrative(s), 203
   as improving treatment, 206–9
   as pedagogy, 205–6
   subject to challenge, 215–16
intentionalism, literary, 4–5

Johnson, Mark, 143–4, 153–4

Kant, Immanuel, 103, 189
Katznelson, Ira, 124
Kennedy, Ashley Graham, 208–9, 211
Knapp, Steven, 4–5
Korsgaard, Christine, 186–7, 189, 190–1
Kuhn, Thomas, 71–2

Lakoff, George, 143–4, 153–4
language, 169, 176–7
   games, 153, 166–7, 171
   and hermeneutics, 174
   legal, 5–7
   non-verbal, 169–70
Levine, Donald, 43–5
lifeworld, 188
Lloyd, Genevieve, 89
Luther, Martin, 69–70
Lyotard, Jean-Francois, 95–6

MacArthur, David, 185–6
McCarthy, Thomas, 121–2, 125
MacIntyre, Alasdair, 46
Massey, Douglas S., 123–4
Melville, Herman, 132

Mills, Charles
   critique of hermeneutics, 133
   on standpoint theory, 128–30, 131
   on white ignorance, 122, 125–8, 131, 132, 136
Montaigne, Michel, 89
Montesquieu, 87, 89
music *see* art

narrative medicine *see* illness narrative(s)
natural science *see* scientific naturalism: scientific perspective
Nietzsche, Friedrich, 92–4, 184
non-violence *see* Gandhi
normative perspective, 189–90, 196
Nussbaum, Martha, 86, 87, 89–90, 92, 96–7, 211

objectification, of patients, 211
openness, 82–4, 104, 106, 114, 135, 212, 215
   and disposition, 85–6
   emotional, 87–8, 116
   and fallibility, 114, 117, 134–5, 137
   political importance of, 81–2
   reflective, 91–4
   social, 88–91
   and Socratic inquiry, 135
   and space, 149–50
   and style, 92–3, 95–7
   and suffering *see* Gandhi: on *satyagraha*
orientation, 151; *see also* place

paradigm shift, 71–2
Parsons, Talcott, 211
perception, as interpretive, 126, 128, 166, 171
Persson, Ingmar, 231, 233
place, 147, 149, 151, 154–5
placement problem, the, 185–6, 189
play, 149–50, 153, 161, 163–4, 227–8
   and topology, 143, 145, 147–8, 149, 154
   as verbal, 175–7
prejudice(s), 82–3, 103–5, 114, 131–2, 214, 215, 218–19

racism
   in America, 136
   toward African Americans, 121–2, 123–5, 126–8

reductionism, 44–5, 48, 199
   response to relativism, 27–9, 134
   in the social sciences, 48–9, 61
   of suspicion, 22–3, 31–2, 83–4
   and topology *see* topology;
     understanding
Rorty, Richard, 22–3, 29

Sache(n), 197
   determination of, 25–6
Sandel, Michael, 225
Savulescu, Julian, 224, 227, 231, 233
scientific naturalism, 185–6, 188
   hermeneutic integration of, 195–200
   normativity of, 192
   scientific perspective, 189–90, 193–5, 196
second-order rationality, 27
self-understanding
   in Continental philosophy, 184
   hermeneutic conception of, 189
   integrationist *see* scientific naturalism: scientific perspective
   naturalistic conception of, 183–4, 185, 189, 191
   as a project, 184, 186–7, 190
situatedness, 151
   and temporality, 150, 151, 153
   see also place; topology; understanding
social science, 3–4, 41, 186
social sciences
   causation in, 48–9
   distinction from natural sciences, 41, 47–8
   explanation in, 41–2
   hermeneutical approach to, 48, 60–1
sociohistorical analysis *see* social sciences

Socrates *see* openness
Spinoza, Baruch, 88
standpoint theory, 128
subjectivity *see* self-understanding
Symposium, 225

Tengelyi, Laszlo, 187
Thebaud, Jean-Loup, 95–6
third-person perspective *see* scientific naturalism: scientific perspective
topology, 152
   of linguistic structure, 153–4
   see also understanding
tradition, 1, 163, 169, 195
   authority of, 25, 103
   and language, 174–5
   and prejudice, 103, 214
   privileging of, 21, 25
   and understanding, 4
transcendentalism, 187, 188; *see also* normative perspective

understanding, 131–2, 161, 165–6, 193, 219
   art, 161–2, 165, 168–9
   and the body, 162, 165, 171–3, 177
   and explanation, 41–2
   intercultural, 24–7
   in the natural sciences, 183–4
   as play, 164, 165
   positivist critique of, 2
   practical, 171
   in the social sciences, 3–4, 41

Vattimo, Gianni, 69, 73–5
Verhesten see understanding

Warnke, Georgia, 105–6

EU representative:
Easy Access System Europe
Mustamäe tee 50, 10621 Tallinn, Estonia
Gpsr.requests@easproject.com

www.ingramcontent.com/pod-product-compliance
Lightning Source LLC
Chambersburg PA
CBHW051054230426
43667CB00013B/2294